Approaches to Teaching Conrad's "Heart of Darkness" and "The Secret Sharer"

Approaches to Teaching World Literature

Joseph Gibaldi, series editor

For a complete listing of titles,
see the last pages of this book.

Approaches to Teaching Conrad's "Heart of Darkness" and "The Secret Sharer"

Edited by

Hunt Hawkins

and

Brian W. Shaffer

The Modern Language Association of America
New York   2002

For information about obtaining permission to reprint material from
MLA book publications, send your request by mail (see address below),
e-mail (permissions@mla.org), or fax (646 458-0030).

Library of Congress Cataloging-in-Publication Data

Approaches to teaching Conrad's "Heart of darkness" and
"The secret sharer" / edited by Hunt Hawkins and Brian W. Shaffer.
p. cm.—(Approaches to teaching world literature, ISSN 1059-1133 ; 77)
Includes bibliographical references and index.
ISBN 0-87352-902-2 (cloth) — ISBN 0-87352-903-0 (pbk.)
1. Conrad, Joseph, 1857–1924. Heart of darkness. 2. Conrad, Joseph,
1857–1924—Study and teaching. 3. Psychological fiction, English—
History and criticism. 4. Psychological fiction, English—Study and teaching.
5. Conrad, Joseph, 1857–1924. Secret sharer. 6. Africa—In literature.
I. Hawkins, Hunt. II. Shaffer, Brian W., 1960– III. Series.
PR6005.O4 H4739 2002
823'.912—dc21   2002027874

Cover illustration for the paperback edition: the steamer *Roi des Belges* on
the upper Congo (1889), from Alexandre Delcommune, *Vingt années de vie
africaine: Récits de voyages, d'aventures et d'exploration au Congo Belge, 1874–93*,
vol. 1 (Brussels: Larcier, 1922). Photograph by permission of General Research Division,
Schomburg Center for Research in Black Culture, New York Public Library, Astor,
Lenox and Tilden Foundations. Conrad was on this boat from 4 August to 24 September 1890
between Kinshasa and Stanley Falls, to learn the river.

Printed on recycled, acid-free paper

Published by The Modern Language Association of America
26 Broadway, New York, New York 10004-1789
www.mla.org

CONTENTS

Teaching the Controversies

Specific Courses

PREFACE TO THE SERIES

In *The Art of Teaching* Gilbert Highet wrote, "Bad teaching wastes a great deal of effort, and spoils many lives which might have been full of energy and happiness." All too many teachers have failed in their work, Highet argued, simply "because they have not thought about it." We hope that the Approaches to Teaching World Literature series, sponsored by the Modern Language Association's Publications Committee, will not only improve the craft—as well as the art—of teaching but also encourage serious and continuing discussion of the aims and methods of teaching literature.

The principal objective of the series is to collect within each volume different points of view on teaching a specific literary work, a literary tradition, or a writer widely taught at the undergraduate level. The preparation of each volume begins with a wide-ranging survey of instructors, thus enabling us to include in the volume the philosophies and approaches, thoughts and methods of scores of experienced teachers. The result is a sourcebook of material, information, and ideas on teaching the subject of the volume to undergraduates.

The series is intended to serve nonspecialists as well as specialists, inexperienced as well as experienced teachers, graduate students who wish to learn effective ways of teaching as well as senior professors who wish to compare their own approaches with the approaches of colleagues in other schools. Of course, no volume in the series can ever substitute for erudition, intelligence, creativity, and sensitivity in teaching. We hope merely that each book will point readers in useful directions; at most each will offer only a first step in the long journey to successful teaching.

Joseph Gibaldi
Series Editor

PREFACE TO THE VOLUME

Conrad's "Heart of Darkness" and "The Secret Sharer" are among the most taught and studied works of twentieth-century British fiction. They are staple texts in various courses (literary history, theory, theme- and genre-based) at all undergraduate levels. Both are the subject of multiple, sometimes conflicting, interpretations; and both, but particularly "Heart of Darkness," remain at the center of various controversies over the nature of the modernist literary canon and the relation between politics and literature, issues that can be fruitfully explored in varying ways in high school, college, and graduate school classrooms.

"Heart of Darkness" is at the center of a number of debates—theoretical, canonical, and literary-political. Indeed, the current controversy surrounding the teaching of this novella is unparalleled in the British literature of the period. Witness, for example, David Denby's 1995 *New Yorker* exposé "Jungle Fever: Why Is Joseph Conrad under Suspicion?" Denby, reporting on an impassioned debate that surrounds "Heart of Darkness," explores this novella's appearance and the explosive responses it elicited in a core humanities course at Columbia University. Or observe the full-length *Envisioning Africa: Racism and Imperialism in Conrad's "Heart of Darkness"* (2000), in which Peter Edgerly Firchow examines the contention this enigmatic narrative has elicited over the past quarter century. The traditional view of the novella as a masterpiece of stylistic virtuosity, psychological depth, and modernist epistemological skepticism still holds sway in many classrooms, but increasingly, since the Nigerian novelist Chinua Achebe's now famous condemnation of this text, the ideological underpinnings and social ramifications of "Heart of Darkness" are being questioned by readers. While many defend the tale of Marlow's journey to Africa in search of Kurtz and adventure as the period's most sustained and subtle literary critique of European imperialism and the ideas of civilization and progress—the very grounds on which Achebe attacks it—others feel that Achebe's challenge did not go far enough: "Heart of Darkness" is for them not only racist but also sexist to the core, a literary modernist work that calls attention to its linguistic and ironic complexity in order to mask its subversive implications.

Conrad regarded "The Secret Sharer" as one of his two "calm-pieces" to balance his stormier sea fictions ("Author's Note" 4). But the story's subject matter is anything but calm; its tone, even when compared with that of the electrifying, entrancing "Heart of Darkness," is anything but serene. The story's working titles, "The Second Self" and "The Other Self," anticipate the chief way in which this tale has been taught: as a psychological and epistemological meditation. But myriad other productive readings of this tale, ranging from formalist to biblical to homoerotic, have been proposed. Indeed, the story of an untried young ship captain, the tale's first-person narrator, and Leggatt, the captain's mysterious double, is something of a Rorschach blot; the work seems Kafkaesque in its ability to point in numerous interpretive directions simultaneously without settling on any single one conclusively. Anyone who has taught "The Secret Sharer" can attest both to its deceptively simple appearance and to the disparate responses it generates in students. As Albert Guerard put it in his still influential introduction to the New American Library edition of "Heart of Darkness" and "The Secret Sharer," "Many critics and readers have liked 'The Secret Sharer,' but few of them have cared to say what the story is 'about.' And they may have been wise to be so cautious" (9).

The present volume aims to equip high school, college, and graduate school instructors with the materials, approaches, and insights necessary to help students come to grips with "Heart of Darkness" and "The Secret Sharer" and with their responses to both texts. Our volume also seeks to make available concrete interpretive and pedagogical strategies to enable teachers of Conrad's works—whether in humanities, literature, theory, or even creative writing courses—to explore the many relevant issues opened up by the two texts: the significance of point of view, narrator reliability, and narrative technique; the significance of the author's world and of his life experience to the works; and the significance of various contexts—political, social, philosophical, psychological, anthropological, and artistic-literary—to Conrad's fiction.

More than three dozen teacher-scholars contributed their expertise and experience to this volume, either by writing an essay or by completing a questionnaire on teaching Conrad. The first part offers descriptions of available editions, reference works, secondary sources, and aids to teaching (including audiovisual ones). The second part contains twenty essays on teaching various aspects of "Heart of Darkness" and "The Secret Sharer." These essays demonstrate the vitality and diversity of current work on teaching Conrad and have something to offer both beginning and experienced instructors of Conrad. *Approaches to Teaching Conrad's "Heart of Darkness" and "The Secret Sharer"* hopes to illuminate the teaching of two works that have been—and remain a century after their emergence—at the center of pedagogical interest and controversy.

Acknowledgments

I would like to thank three great scholars who nourished my early interest in Conrad at Stanford: Tom Moser, Ian Watt, and Albert Guerard; my fellow graduate students there who shared that interest: John McClure, Roger Harm, Sandra Drake, Paul Armstrong, and Marianne DeKoven; the former president of the Joseph Conrad Society Bruce Harkness, who encouraged me to follow him; my current colleagues and friends Rip Lhamon and Janet Burroway; my graduate student assistant Hyunsue Kim, who helped with the index and works-cited list; and my family—Elaine, Sam, Molly, Hermione, Bob, Pam, Daniel, and James—for their support and good cheer.

HH

I would like to thank three inspirational Conrad scholars with whom I worked or corresponded over the past decade: Eloise Hay, Daniel Schwarz, and Avrom Fleishman; my colleagues at Rhodes, particularly Jennifer Brady, Robert Entzminger, Michael Leslie, Cynthia Marshall, and Lynn Zastoupil, for their encouragement and example; the dean of the college, Robert R. Llewellyn, for his support of this project and faculty development at Rhodes; and members of my family—Rachel, Hannah, Ruth, and mother Dorothy—for their love and patience.

BWS

Both editors wish to thank Sonia Kane and Michael Kandel of the MLA for their invaluable editorial guidance and advice.

Part One

MATERIALS

Editions

Joseph Conrad's stories and novels exist in several forms, because he usually published them first serially, then revised for book publication, and slightly revised yet again for publication in a collected edition. Further differences may sometimes be noted, between British and American book publications and among the four collected editions that appeared in his lifetime. Finally, manuscript and corrected typescript versions, where they exist, offer other variations.

The manuscript for "Heart of Darkness," currently housed at Yale University, was written between December 1898 and February 1899. Conrad's wife, Jessie, typed fifty-seven of its ninety pages but stopped because of illness; this thirty-five-page typescript is currently at the New York Public Library. The story first appeared in three parts in 1899 in the February, March, and April issues of *Blackwood's Edinburgh Magazine*. It next appeared in book form, *"Youth" and Two Other Stories* published by Blackwood in 1902. The first limited collected edition of Conrad's work was published in 1921 by Doubleday in New York and William Heinemann in London. The first general editions were brought out in 1923 by Doubleday in New York and in 1924 by J. M. Dent in London. Since the 1921 Heinemann edition was mistakenly thought to be the last Conrad personally supervised before he died in 1924, it has usually been regarded as the authoritative text. The most authoritative text to date is that edited by Robert Kimbrough for the third Norton edition in 1988. It is based on the 1921 Heinemann edition but, in accordance with today's editing principles, goes back to the manuscript and typescript to remove accidental and a few substantive changes introduced by *Blackwood's* when the story was first published. When it is published, the *"Youth"* volume edited by Owen Knowles and Marion Michael in the new Cambridge University Press collected edition will become the authoritative text.

Conrad wrote the manuscript of "The Secret Sharer," now at the New York Public Library, in early December 1909. It was published in *Harper's Magazine* in August and September 1910. In 1912 it first appeared in book form in *'Twixt Land and Sea*, published by Dent in London. The 1921 Doubleday edition, which in fact was the last Conrad personally supervised, is currently the most authoritative. It will be superseded by the forthcoming *'Twixt Land and Sea* volume edited by Jacques Berthoud, Laura Davis, and Sid Reid in the Cambridge collected edition. Because of easy availability, the 1997 paperback Bedford edition, which Daniel Schwarz based on the 1924 Doubleday edition, is used for all textual references in this volume.

"Heart of Darkness"

"Heart of Darkness" is available in a great many paperback editions priced to student budgets. Currently there are editions from Dover, St. Martin's, Green

Integer, and Wordsworth; from Bedford edited by Ross Murfin, Broadview edited by D. C. R. A. Goonetilleke, Everyman edited by Cedric Watts, Modern Library introduced by Caryl Phillips, Norton edited by Kimbrough, Oxford edited by Watts, and Penguin edited by Robert Hampson. The most popular edition among our survey respondents purely for price was the Dover. The editions put out by Broadview and Norton are more expensive but valuable because they include background information on Conrad and the Congo. The Norton also has a selection of critical essays. The Bedford edition, part of a series, has five critical essays from different theoretical perspectives and is therefore especially useful in an introductory theory course. Our respondents noted, though, that the essays are uneven. A CD-ROM version put out by Quiet Vision might be helpful to those doing extensive work with the text.

"Heart of Darkness" is also available in several paperback editions combining it with other works. These might be good choices for courses covering several Conrad texts or treating Conrad with other writers. In the only edition to replicate Conrad's original book publication, "Heart of Darkness" is combined with his "Youth" and "End of the Tether" in a paperback from Penguin edited by John Lyon. It is paired with "The Secret Sharer" in an edition from New American Library introduced by Joyce Carol Oates, in a Bantam edition edited by Franklin Walker, and in a Dorset Press edition. "Heart of Darkness" is also combined with Conrad's "Falk" in an edition from Blue Unicorn and with his "Youth," "Karain," and "An Outpost of Progress" in an edition from Oxford edited by Watts. It is combined with Jane Austen's *Pride and Prejudice*, James Joyce's *Portrait of the Artist*, and Oscar Wilde's *Portrait of Dorian Gray* in an edition from Dover. Finally, many respondents to our questionnaire reported assigning "Heart of Darkness" in a large anthology such as *The Norton Anthology of English Literature*, volume 2; St. Martin's *Western Literature in World Context*, volume 2; *The Oxford Anthology of English Literature*, volume 2; St. Martin's *The Story and Its Writer*; *The Norton Anthology of Short Fiction*; and *The Longman Anthology of British Literature*, volume 2.

"The Secret Sharer"

"The Secret Sharer" is available in the editions from New American Library, Bantam, and Dorset mentioned above that combine it with "Heart of Darkness." These editions ultimately derive from Albert Guerard's pairing of the two texts in his Signet edition of 1950. This pairing emphasizes the psychological theme in both works and their use of the double. "The Secret Sharer" is also available combined with Conrad's "Tomorrow" and "Youth" in an edition from Blue Unicorn. Finally, it is available on its own in a paperback edition from Bedford edited by Schwarz and in a CD-ROM version from Quiet Vision. The most popular editions among our respondents are the New American Library and Bantam (both for price) and the Bedford. This last, like the Bedford for "Heart of Darkness," has critical essays from five different approaches and is thus especially useful (though the essays are again uneven) in an introductory theory course.

Note: All textual references in this volume, unless otherwise indicated, are, for "Heart of Darkness," from the Kimbrough edition; for "The Secret Sharer," from the Schwarz edition.

Reference Works

Bibliographies

Bibliographies of Conrad's work include Thomas J. Wise, *A Bibliography of the Writings of Joseph Conrad* (1921); Wise, *A Conrad Library* (1928); George T. Keating, *A Conrad Memorial Library* (1929); and Walter E. Smith, *Joseph Conrad: A Bibliographical Catalogue* (1978). Printed bibliographies of Conrad studies are quickly outdated but still of help in gathering references. They include Kenneth A. Lohf and Eugene P. Sheehy, *Joseph Conrad at Mid-Century: Editions and Studies, 1895–1955* (1957); Theodore G. Ehrsam, *A Bibliography of Joseph Conrad* (1969); Bruce E. Teets and Helmut E. Gerber, *Joseph Conrad: An Annotated Bibliography of Writings about Him* (1971); Teets, *Joseph Conrad: An Annotated Bibliography* (1990); and Owen Knowles, *An Annotated Critical Bibliography of Joseph Conrad* (1992). Bibliographic information may also be found in the five journals devoted to Conrad: *Conradiana* and *Joseph Conrad Today* in the United States, *The Conradian* in the United Kingdom, *L'époque conradienne* in France, and *CON-texts* in Poland. The annual *MLA International Bibliography*, searchable by computer, is also very useful. Further reference material is available in J. H. Stape, editor, *The Cambridge Companion to Joseph Conrad* (1996); Leonard Orr and Ted Billy, editors, *A Joseph Conrad Companion* (1999); and Knowles and Gene Moore, editors, *The Oxford Reader's Companion to Conrad* (2000).

Biographical Sources

A starting point for study of Conrad's life might be his own very partial and not entirely reliable autobiographical books, *The Mirror of the Sea* (1906) and *A Personal Record* (1912), together with relevant essays in his *Notes on Life and Letters* (1921) and *Last Essays* (1926). Biographies by his family and friends include his wife Jessie Conrad's *Joseph Conrad As I Knew Him* (1926) and *Joseph Conrad and His Circle* (1935); his son Borys Conrad's *My Father: Joseph Conrad* (1970); his son John Conrad's *Joseph Conrad, Times Remembered* (1981); Ford Madox Ford's *Joseph Conrad: A Personal Remembrance* (1924); Richard Curle's *The Last Twelve Years of Joseph Conrad* (1928); and J. H. Retinger's

Conrad and His Contemporaries (1941). Brief personal remembrances are collected in Martin Ray's *Joseph Conrad: Interviews and Recollections* (1990).

The major biographies are Frederick R. Karl's psychologically oriented *Joseph Conrad: The Three Lives* (1979) and Zdzislaw Najder's culturally oriented *Joseph Conrad: A Chronicle* (1983). Other significant biographies are G. Jean-Aubry, *Joseph Conrad: Life and Letters* (1927) and *The Sea Dreamer: A Definitive Biography of Joseph Conrad* (1957); Jocelyn Baines, *Joseph Conrad* (1960); John Batchelor, *The Life of Joseph Conrad* (1994); Bernard C. Meyer, *Joseph Conrad: A Psychoanalytic Biography* (1967); Jerry Allen, *The Sea Years of Joseph Conrad* (1967); Cedric Watts, *Joseph Conrad: A Literary Life* (1989); and Owen Knowles, *A Conrad Chronology* (1989). A readable, brief biography with many interesting photographs is Norman Sherry, *Conrad and His World* (1972).

Several partial collections of Conrad's letters have been published, notably Arthur Symons, *Notes on Joseph Conrad; with Some Unpublished Letters* (1925); Jean-Aubry, *Joseph Conrad: Life and Letters*, mentioned above; Curle, *Conrad to a Friend: 150 Selected Letters from Joseph Conrad to Richard Curle* (1928); Edward Garnett, *Letters from Joseph Conrad, 1895–1924* (1928); Jean-Aubry, *Lettres françaises* (1930) (Conrad, *Lettres*); John A. Gee and Paul J. Sturm, *Letters of Joseph Conrad to Marguerite Poradowska, 1890–1920* (1940); William Blackburn, *Letters to William Blackwood and David S. Meldrum* (1958); Najder, *Conrad's Polish Background: Letters to and from Polish Friends* (1964); and Watts, *Joseph Conrad's Letters to Cunninghame Graham* (1969). Five volumes of the projected nine-volume *The Collected Letters of Joseph Conrad*, edited by Frederick R. Karl and Laurence Davies, have now been published by Cambridge University Press.

Readings for Students and Teachers

Background Studies

Although "Heart of Darkness" gives no dates and very few place-names, it was based closely on Conrad's journey to the Congo in 1890. In his author's note, Conrad said the story was "experience pushed a little (and only very little) beyond the actual facts of the case" (*Heart* [Kimbrough] 4). His very fragmentary record of his trip is contained in his *"Congo Diary" and Other Uncollected Pieces* edited by Najder (1978). The trip, Conrad's contacts in the Congo, and possible sources for the story have been studied in Jean-Aubry's *Joseph Conrad in the Congo* (1926) and more extensively in Sherry's *Conrad's Western World* (1971).

There are many histories of the Congo Free State, which King Leopold II of Belgium owned as his personal colony between 1885 and 1908. The best in English are Ruth Slade, *King Leopold's Congo* (1962); Neal Ascherson, *The King Incorporated* (1963); Barbara Emerson, *Leopold II of the Belgians* (1979); L. H. Gann and Peter Duignan, *The Rulers of Belgian Africa, 1884–1914* (1979); William J. Samarin, *The Black Man's Burden* (1989); Samuel H. Nelson, *Colonialism in the Congo Basin, 1880–1940* (1994); and Adam Hochschild, *King Leopold's Ghost* (1998), which includes a chapter on Conrad. Hochschild's book is both the most recent and most thorough. It is based in part on the little-known archival research Jules Marchal published in *L'état libre du Congo: Paradis perdu: L'histoire du Congo, 1876–1900* (1996) and *E. D. Morel contre Leopold II: L'histoire du Congo, 1900–1910* (1996), but it adds much research of its own.

More general histories of Africa in Conrad's period are Ronald Robinson and John Gallagher, *Africa and the Victorians* (1961); David Levering Lewis, *The Race to Fashoda* (1987); Thomas Packenham, *The Scramble for Africa* (1991); and Frank McLynn, *Hearts of Darkness: The European Exploration of Africa* (1992). Studies of late-nineteenth-century imperialism worldwide and the protests against it include Bernard Semmel, *Imperialism and Social Reform* (1960) and *The Liberal Ideal and the Demons of Empire: Theories of Imperialism from Adam Smith to Lenin* (1993); Bernard Porter, *Critics of Empire* (1968); V. G. Kiernan, *The Lords of Human Kind* (1972) and *From Conquest to Collapse: European Empires, 1815–1960* (1982); D. K. Fieldhouse, *The Colonial Empires* (1965) and *Economics and Empire* (1973); Hannah Arendt, *The Origins of Totalitarianism* (1973); Michael B. Brown, *The Economics of Imperialism* (1974); Daniel R. Headrick, *The Tools of Empire* (1981); Jan Morris, *The Spectacle of Empire* (1982); A. J. P. Thornton, *The Imperial Idea and Its Enemies* (1985); Eric Hobsbawm, *The Age of Empire* (1989); Jan Berman, editor, *Imperial Monkey Business: Racial Supremacy in Social Darwinist Theory and Colonial Practice* (1990); and Jared Diamond, *Guns, Germs, and Steel* (1997).

Conrad's story "The Secret Sharer" was based partly on his trip as captain of the *Otago* from Bangkok to Singapore in 1888. This trip also formed the basis for his later novella *The Shadow-Line* (1917). "The Secret Sharer" was further based on an incident on the clipper *Cutty Sark* in 1880, when Captain Wallace helped his prisoner, the murderer Sydney Smith, to escape. Sherry's *Conrad's Eastern World* (1966) studies both Conrad's trip and the *Cutty Sark* incident as sources. Basil Lubbock's *The Log of the Cutty Sark* (1924) also gives information on that incident. Books on the world of sail in the nineteenth century include David R. MacGregor, *Fast Sailing Ships: Their Design and Construction, 1775–1875* (1973) and *Merchant Sailing Ships, 1850–1875* (1984); Rosemary Mudie, *The History of the Sailing Ship* (1975); Philip McCutchan, *Tall Ships: The Golden Age of Sail* (1976); Robert Gardiner, editor, *Sail's Last Century: The Merchant Sailing Ship, 1830–1930* (1993); Veres Laszlo, *The Story of Sail* (1999); and Stephen Howarth, *Historic Sail* (2000). Conrad's attitudes on ships and seamen have been studied in C. F. Burgess, *The Fellowship of the Craft: Conrad on Ships and Seamen and the Sea* (1976).

Critical Commentary

The criticism on Conrad is immense and growing. He has been fortunate in attracting the attention of the most notable critics of each generation. As Conrad's books came out, they were reviewed by H. G. Wells, Arnold Bennett, Arthur Symons, Harold Frederic, Edward Garnett, George Gissing, John Masefield, John Galsworthy, Edward Thomas, Henry James, Walter de la Mare, E. M. Forster, and Virginia Woolf. These reviews have been gathered in Sherry's *Conrad: The Critical Heritage* (1973). Following his death, Conrad's reputation declined, but it revived in the 1940s, and F. R. Leavis's *The Great Tradition: George Eliot, Henry James, Joseph Conrad* (1948) secured his place in the canon.

A good beginning point for reading Conrad criticism focused on these stories would be the essays in the easily available casebooks: the Norton *Heart of Darkness* edited by Robert Kimbrough, especially the essays by Michael Levenson ("Value") and by Garrett Stewart; the Bedford *Heart of Darkness* edited by Ross Murfin, especially the essays by Patrick Brantlinger ("*Heart*"), J. Hillis Miller ("*Heart*"), Johanna M. Smith, and Brook Thomas; and the Bedford *The Secret Sharer* edited by Daniel Schwarz, especially the essays by J. Hillis Miller ("Sharing"), James Phelan, and Schwarz himself ("Secret Sharer"). The best general critical books to start with are Albert J. Guerard's *Conrad the Novelist* (1958) for its psychological and stylistic insights and Ian Watt's *Conrad in the Nineteenth Century* (1979) for placing Conrad in intellectual and social history. Both have stood the test of time. An excellent poststructuralist account published more recently is Daphna Erdinast-Vulcan's *Joseph Conrad and the Modern Temper* (1991).

Other significant general studies of Conrad follow in chronological order. These roughly reflect trends in literary criticism from the biographical studies of the 1930s and 1940s to the formalist New Critical and the psychoanalytic studies of the 1950s and 1960s, the structuralism of the 1970s, the deconstruction of the 1980s, and the new-historicist and cultural studies thereafter. Not every book, of course, follows the trends of its era, and each has its own strengths. These studies are Gustav Morf, *The Polish Heritage of Joseph Conrad* (1930); Edward Crankshaw, *Joseph Conrad* (1936); John D. Gordan, *Joseph Conrad: The Making of a Novelist* (1940); M. C. Bradbrook, *Joseph Conrad: England's Polish Genius* (1941); Douglass Hewitt, *Conrad: A Reassessment* (1952); Paul Wiley, *Conrad's Measure of Man* (1954); Thomas C. Moser, *Joseph Conrad: Achievement and Decline* (1957); Adam Gillon, *The Eternal Solitary* (1960); Frederick Karl, *A Reader's Guide to Joseph Conrad* (1960); Leo Gurko, *Joseph Conrad: Giant in Exile* (1962); Edward Said, *Joseph Conrad and the Fiction of Autobiography* (1966); James Guetti, *The Limits of Metaphor* (1967); Claire Rosenfield, *Paradise of Snakes: An Archetypal Analysis of Conrad's Political Novels* (1967); Paul Kirschener, *Conrad: The Psychologist as Artist* (1968); John A. Palmer, *Joseph Conrad's Fiction* (1968); J. I. M. Stewart, *Joseph Conrad* (1968); Robert Ryf, *Joseph Conrad* (1970); Bruce

Johnson, *Conrad's Models of Mind* (1971); Royal Roussel, *The Metaphysics of Darkness* (1971); John Saveson, *Joseph Conrad: The Making of a Moralist* (1972); C. B. Cox, *Joseph Conrad: The Modern Imagination* (1974); David Thorburn, *Conrad's Romanticism* (1974); H. M. Daleski, *Joseph Conrad: The Way of Dispossession* (1977); Jacques Berthoud, *Joseph Conrad: The Major Phase* (1978); R. A. Gekoski, *Conrad: The Moral World of the Novelist* (1978); Jeremy Hawthorn, *Joseph Conrad: Language and Fictional Self-Consciousness* (1979); William Bonney, *Thorns and Arabesques* (1980); Daniel Schwarz, *Conrad:* Almayer's Folly *to* Under Western Eyes (1980) and *Conrad: The Later Fiction* (1982); Werner Senn, *Conrad's Narrative Voice* (1980); Aaron Fogel, *Coercion to Speak: Conrad's Poetics of Dialogue* (1985); Ross Murfin, editor, *Conrad Revisited: Essays for the Eighties* (1985); Suresh Raval, *The Art of Failure: Conrad's Fiction* (1986); Jakob Lothe, *Conrad's Narrative Method* (1989); Mark Wollaeger, *Joseph Conrad and the Fiction of Skepticism* (1990); Richard Ambrosini, *Conrad's Fiction as Critical Discourse* (1991); D. C. R. A. Goonetilleke, *Joseph Conrad: Beyond Culture and Background* (1991); Robert Hampson, *Joseph Conrad: Betrayal and Identity* (1992) and *Cross-Cultural Encounters in Joseph Conrad's Fiction* (2000); Bruce Henricksen, *Nomadic Voices: Conrad and the Subject of Narrative* (1992); Brian Spittles, *Joseph Conrad: Text and Context* (1992); John W. Griffith, *Joseph Conrad and the Anthropological Dilemma* (1995); Robert Wilson, *Joseph Conrad: Sources and Traditions* (1995); Geoffrey Galt Harpham, *One of Us: The Mastery of Joseph Conrad* (1996); Zdzislaw Najder, *Conrad in Perspective* (1997); Beth Sharon Ash, *Writing In Between: Modernity and the Psychosocial Dilemma in the Novels of Joseph Conrad* (1999); and Ian Watt, *Essays on Conrad* (2000).

Books about various aspects of modernism that relate Joseph Conrad to that movement are Stephen Spender, *The Struggle of the Modern* (1963); J. Hillis Miller, *Poets of Reality* (1966); Lionel Trilling, *Beyond Culture* (1966) and *Sincerity and Authenticity* (1972); Robert Langbaum, *The Modern Spirit* (1970); Raymond Williams, *The English Novel from Dickens to Lawrence* (1970); Peter Faulkner, *Modernism* (1977); Robert Caserio, *Plot, Story, and the Novel* (1979); John B. Foster, Jr., *Heirs to Dionysus* (1981); Peter Brooks, *Reading for the Plot* (1984); Michael Levenson, *A Genealogy of Modernism* (1984); Mark Conroy, *Modernism and Authority* (1985); Paul Armstrong, *The Challenge of Bewilderment* (1987); Sandra Gilbert and Susan Gubar, *No Man's Land* (1989); Perry Meisel, *The Myth of the Modern* (1987); Kenneth Graham, *Indirections of the Novel* (1988); Vincent Pecora, *Self and Form in Modern Narrative* (1989); Bette London, *The Appropriated Voice* (1990); Marianna Torgovnick, *Gone Primitive* (1990); Elaine Showalter, *Sexual Anarchy* (1991); Brian Shaffer, *The Blinding Torch: Modern British Fiction and the Discourse of Civilization* (1993); Tony Jackson, *The Subject of Modernism* (1994); Michael North, *The Dialect of Modernism* (1994); Michael Moses, *The Novel and the Globalization of Culture* (1995); Joyce Wexler, *Who Paid for Modernism?* (1997); and Jonathan Quick, *Modern Fiction and the Art of Subversion* (1999).

Books that discuss specific aspects of Conrad (as indicated by their titles) are Lawrence Graver, *Conrad's Short Fiction* (1969); Adam Gillon, *Conrad and Shakespeare* (1976); Elsa Nettles, *James and Conrad* (1977); Alan Hunter, *Joseph Conrad and the Ethics of Darwinism* (1983); Redmond O'Hanlon, *Joseph Conrad and Charles Darwin* (1984); Dwight Purdy, *Conrad's Bible* (1984); Robert Secor, *Joseph Conrad and American Writers* (1985); Robert Wilson, *Conrad's Mythology* (1987); John Lester, *Conrad's Religion* (1988); David Tutein, *Joseph Conrad's Reading* (1990); Yves Hervouet, *The French Face of Joseph Conrad* (1991); Mary Morzinski, *The Linguistic Influence of Polish on Joseph Conrad's Style* (1994); Theodore Billy, *A Wilderness of Words: Closure and Disclosure in Conrad's Short Fiction* (1997); Nic Panagupoulos, *The Fiction of Joseph Conrad: The Influence of Schopenhauer and Nietzsche* (1998); and Daphna Erdinast-Vulcan, *The Strange Short Fiction of Joseph Conrad* (1999).

The criticism on "Heart of Darkness" alone is huge. Robert Burden's *"Heart of Darkness": An Introduction to the Variety of Criticism* (1991) and Nicolas Tredell's *Joseph Conrad: "Heart of Darkness"* (1998) provide surveys of this criticism. Casebooks that collect critical essays on the work are Leonard F. Dean's *Joseph Conrad's "Heart of Darkness": Backgrounds and Criticisms* (1960) and Bruce Harkness's *Conrad's "Heart of Darkness" and the Critics* (1960) as well as the Kimbrough and Murfin editions mentioned above. Seven entire books have focused on the story: Henryk Zins, *Joseph Conrad and Africa* (1982); Gary Adelman, *"Heart of Darkness": Search for the Unconscious* (1987); Harold Bloom, editor, *Joseph Conrad's "Heart of Darkness"* (1987); Anthony Fothergill, *Heart of Darkness* (1989); Sven Lindquist, *Exterminate All the Brutes* (1996); Cedric Watts, *Conrad's "Heart of Darkness": A Critical and Contextual Discussion* (1997); and Peter Firchow, *Envisioning Africa: Racism and Imperialism in Conrad's "Heart of Darkness"* (2000).

Studies of Conrad's attitudes toward race and empire in Africa and world-wide may be found in Susanne Howe, *Novels of Empire* (1949); Eloise Knapp Hay, *The Political Novels of Joseph Conrad* (1963); Avrom Fleishman, *Conrad's Politics* (1967); Alan Sandison, *The Wheel of Empire* (1967); Robert F. Lee, *Conrad's Colonialism* (1969); Jonah Raskin, *The Mythology of Imperialism* (1971); Terry Eagleton, *Criticism and Ideology* (1976); D. C. R. A. Goonetilleke, *Developing Countries in British Fiction* (1977); Molly Mahood, *The Colonial Encounter* (1977); Martin Green, *Dreams of Adventure, Deeds of Empire* (1979); Fredric Jameson, *The Political Unconscious* (1981); John Mc-Clure, *Kipling and Conrad: The Colonial Fiction* (1981) and *Late Imperial Romance* (1994); Jacques Darras, *Joseph Conrad and the West: Signs of Empire* (1982); Benita Parry, *Conrad and Imperialism* (1983); Hugh Ridley, *Images of Imperial Rule* (1983); Christopher Miller, *Blank Darkness* (1985); Patrick Brantlinger, *Rule of Darkness* (1988); Edward Said, *Culture and Imperialism* (1993); Andrea White, *Joseph Conrad and the Adventure Tradition* (1993); Christopher GoGwilt, *The Invention of the West* (1995); David Denby, *Great*

Books (1996), which contains his essay "Jungle Fever"; Gail Fincham and Myrtle Hooper, editors, *Under Postcolonial Eyes: Joseph Conrad after Empire*
(1996); and Linda Dryden, *Joseph Conrad and the Imperial Romance* (1999).

African reactions to Conrad may be found in Robert Hamner, editor, *Joseph
Conrad: Third World Perspectives* (1990). Chinua Achebe's well-known essay
"An Image of Africa" is available in Hamner's volume, in Achebe's own *Hopes
and Impediments* (1988), and in Kimbrough's edition of "Heart of Darkness"
(1988).

Conrad's attitudes toward women in "Heart of Darkness" and generally are
discussed in Marianne DeKoven's *Rich and Strange: Gender, History, Modernism* (1991); Ruth Nadelhaft's *Joseph Conrad* (1991); Andrew M. Roberts's
Conrad and Gender (1993) and *Conrad and Masculinity* (2000); and Susan
Jones's *Conrad and Women* (1999).

"The Secret Sharer," while not quite attaining the book-length criticism of
"Heart of Darkness," has nonetheless been the subject of innumerable articles.
Two collections of such articles are Bruce Harkness's *"The Secret Sharer" and
the Critics* (1962) and Daniel Schwarz's Bedford edition of the story (1997).
Notable articles are Louise K. Barnett, "'The Whole Circle of the Horizon': The
Circumscribed Universe of 'The Secret Sharer'"; Carl Benson, "Conrad's Two
Stories of Initiation"; Anthony B. Dawson, "In the Pink: Self and Empire in
'The Secret Sharer'"; Mary Ann Dazey, "Shared Secret or Secret Sharing in
Joseph Conrad's 'The Secret Sharer'"; Mark A. R. Facknitz, "Cryptic Allusions
and the Moral of the Story"; Robert Hodges, "Deep Fellowship: Homosexual-
ity and Male Bonding in the Life and Fiction of Joseph Conrad"; Barbara John-
son and Marjorie Garber, "Secret Sharing: Reading Conrad Psychoanalytically";
Michael Murphy, "'The Secret Sharer': Conrad's Turn of the Winch"; J. D.
O'Hara, "Unlearned Lessons in 'The Secret Sharer'"; Josiane Paccaud, "Under
the Other's Eyes: Conrad's 'The Secret Sharer'"; Robert W. Stallman, "Conrad
and 'The Secret Sharer'"; Joyce Wexler, "Conrad's Dream of a Common Language: Lacan and 'The Secret Sharer'"; James F. White, "The Third Theme in
'The Secret Sharer'"; and Robert D. Wyatt, "Joseph Conrad's 'The Secret
Sharer.'" Discussion of "The Secret Sharer" is also included in most of the general critical books on Conrad mentioned above.

Audiovisual Aids

The Stories (Film Adaptations)

Two books describe the more than eighty film versions of Conrad's work: Gene
D. Phillips's *Conrad and Cinema* (1995) and Gene M. Moore's *Conrad on Film*
(1997). In all, nine films have been based on "Heart of Darkness," but only

three are available on videotape. Of these, the closest to the original is the 1994 Turner Network Television *Heart of Darkness*, directed by Nicolas Roeg with John Malkovich as Kurtz and Tim Roth as Marlow. The most famous is surely the 1979 Omni Zoetrope *Apocalypse Now*, directed by Francis Ford Coppola, which adapts Conrad's story to the Vietnam War. Marlon Brando plays Colonel Kurtz, and Martin Sheen is the very un-Marlow-like Captain Willard. A documentary describing the difficult genesis of this film is the 1991 ZM/Zoetrope *Hearts of Darkness: A Filmmaker's Apocalypse*, made by Fax Bahr, George Hickenlooper, and Eleanor Coppola. The third version of Conrad's story available on videotape is the 1988 reverse-gender spoof *Cannibal Women in the Avocado Jungle of Death*, directed by Jonathan Lawton and released by Amer-Guacamole Films. The other films of "Heart of Darkness" are a 1955 Camera Three WCBS-TV production, a 1958 CBS-TV Playhouse 90 show with Boris Karloff as Kurtz, a 1968 Italian Documento Film adaptation, the 1977 French *Le Crabe-Tambour* based on Pierre Schoendoerffer's novel inspired by Conrad, a 1978 Spanish-Arando Films version, and a 1995 BBC-TV reading of the story with background footage. Finally, it should be mentioned that in 1939 Orson Welles and John Houseman wrote a screenplay of "Heart of Darkness" that was never produced (but undoubtedly colored Welles's subsequent movie *Citizen Kane*). The script summaries of this unmade film are now at the University of Indiana.

In addition to these films, there are many recordings of "Heart of Darkness" available on audiocassette or CD with readings by David Threlfall, Richard Thomas, Anthony Quayle, Ralph Cosham, Norman Barrs, Rubin Ship, Brian Cox, and Alistair Maydon. John Powell's 1917 *Rhapsodie Negre for Piano and Orchestra*, a musical rendering of Conrad's story, is available from New World Records.

Several educational films give background and analysis of "Heart of Darkness." These include the 1983 *"Heart of Darkness" and Modernism*, a twenty-five-minute segment of the BBC Open University series The Nineteenth-Century Novel and Its Legacy, with presenter Dennis Walder. It includes an interview with Conrad's son John. Bride Media International has released the thirty-minute *Joseph Conrad: "Heart of Darkness"* with host James H. Bride and critics Bruce Harkness, Frederick Karl, Jerome Meckier, and Dwight Purdy. It is available from Films for the Humanities and Sciences, which also has a CD-ROM *Joseph Conrad: "Heart of Darkness"* with the text of the story, excerpts from other Conrad works, critical essays, bibliography, hyperlinks, and a map. An audio *Study Guide to Joseph Conrad's "Heart of Darkness"* by John F. Jones has been put out by Time Warner Audio Books.

Six films have been based on "The Secret Sharer," none currently available on videotape. They are a 1950 BBC version, the 1952 RKO *Face to Face* directed by John Brahm with James Mason as the captain, the 1967 Italian TV *L'ospite segreto*, a 1967 Polish Teatr TV production, the 1972 Encyclopedia Britannica *The Secret Sharer* directed by Larry Yust with David Soul as the captain, and the 1988 French Telefilm *Le compagnon secret*. The thirty-minute Encyclopedia Britannica version is accompanied by an eleven-minute discussion by Carl Van Doren.

The Author

Films on Conrad's life and work include the six-part 1990 French-Polish *Joseph Conrad* coproduced by FR3-Doridis-Vamp-RTVE-Poltel. Available on videotape is the 1993 French *Berau, sur les traces de Conrad* directed by Frederic Compain and produced by Io Studios. No films or recordings of Conrad himself are known to exist.

Part Two

APPROACHES

Introduction

Survey participants seemed eager to share the joys—and the frustrations—they experienced when teaching Conrad's "Heart of Darkness" and "The Secret Sharer." Most respondents spent one or two class sessions on "The Secret Sharer" and five or six sessions on "Heart of Darkness." Although no consistent pattern of literary pairings with "The Secret Sharer" emerged, numerous survey respondents taught one or more of the following texts in conjunction with "Heart of Darkness": Chinua Achebe's *Things Fall Apart*; Conrad's *Lord Jim*, "An Outpost of Progress," *Nostromo*, and the preface to *The Nigger of the "Narcissus"*; Francis Ford Coppola's film *Apocalypse Now*; Henry James's *The Turn of the Screw*; and Mary Shelley's *Frankenstein*.

Survey respondents were in surprising agreement on what they took to be the stories' most engaging and challenging features for students. Respondents cited the motif of the double in "The Secret Sharer" and the story's unsettled (and unsettling) question of narrator reliability as absorbing their students most. Students of "Heart of Darkness" tended to find the text's treatment of racism and colonialism; its representation (and the conspicuous dearth) of female characters; its depiction of Kurtz's horrific conversion; and, in the words of one instructor, the text's portrayal of the "brutality and stupidity of the company's enterprise" to be of most interest.

The vast majority of participants located the novella's most challenging feature for students in its notorious "narrative indirection." The comment of one respondent is typical: "The style presents difficulties for my students because it is so dense—so full of imagery, seemingly repetitious qualifications, endless paragraphs, obscure allusions, and an apparent concern by Marlow with everything *but* the actual narrative action of locating and retrieving Kurtz from the Inner Station." Taking time in class to determine why Conrad employs this style, according to this and many other respondents, helped students penetrate the tale's "deliberate" narrative complexity.

Indeed, many surveyists were adept at turning just such a pedagogical challenge into an opportunity. As one respondent noted, "Most of my beginning students claim to find 'Heart of Darkness' to be a difficult text; at the same time, some of the very things they find most challenging often end up being the most engaging and stimulating to them." As another put it, "Students are mostly challenged by the density of the text. They expect action and dialogue. One usual complaint is that they wait so long to reach Kurtz and then they only see him for a few pages. This complaint is a good way to begin discussion. I simply turn the question back on them—why does this happen? By answering this, they eventually realize much about both Kurtz and Marlow." Yet another respondent wrote of the novella's complex narrative structure, "I think Conrad's narrative frames confuse students a bit at first, but later come to delight them when they understand, for instance, why Marlow's audience are the quintessentially appropriate auditors for his narrative."

"The Secret Sharer" is regarded by students as difficult reading, but for different reasons, according to the surveys. Stylistically, this story provides few problems; superficially, it is far easier to grasp. At a deeper level, however, it may be the more difficult of the two texts for students, as the relationship between the two major characters of "The Secret Sharer" is perhaps even hazier, and the homosocial bonding more enigmatic, than that between Kurtz and Marlow. Most respondents who teach "Heart of Darkness" and "The Secret Sharer" together emphasize the doubling, the context of late-Victorian adventure writing, and the modernist narrative techniques of the two tales.

The twenty essays that follow are divided into three groups. The first group concerns the social contexts and literary issues that inform Conrad's works as well as the teaching of these works. Ray Stevens examines the impact of slavery and the African ivory trade of the 1890s on "Heart of Darkness." In particular, he explores the ways in which Conrad's experience of the ivory trade can be presented to students. Andrea White examines a literary context for both "Heart of Darkness" and "The Secret Sharer" that has a significant ideological undertone: late-nineteenth-century adventure and travel writings. She argues both that this popular literature was an informing cultural context for Conrad's works and that this literature can help demystify his works, which are initially experienced as difficult and canonical, to students who traditionally have felt most excluded by them. John A. McClure considers the various ways in which the colonial and postcolonial contexts for "Heart of Darkness" may be approached in class. He demonstrates, using the criticisms leveled against the novella by Edward Said and Achebe and the discourse theories of Mikhail Bakhtin and Raymond Williams, that Conrad's novella is in fact dialogic: an ideological battleground and site of conflicting discourses that can be exposed and examined in class.

Jeffrey J. Williams explores a fresh context for "Heart of Darkness" and "The Secret Sharer" that nicely complements the stories' imperial context: the issue of professionalism. He argues that the ideology of modern professionalism helps explain the motivations, actions, comportment, judgments, and loyalties of Conrad's primary characters in these works—Marlow and his unnamed auditors on the *Nellie* in the earlier tale; the narrator and his double in the later one—as well as how these characters set themselves apart from those who are outside their professional cohort: the natives, ordinary deckhands, company owners, and rogue imperialists, for example. Mark A. Eaton focuses on an important theoretical development with pedagogical implications: the teaching of "Heart of Darkness" after new historicism. He observes that both new historicism and Conrad (in his essays and fiction) provocatively problematize the distinctions between history and fiction, with significant ramifications for our students' understanding of the novella. Avrom Fleishman focuses on the currently neglected aspect of characterization in "Heart of Darkness." He argues that ignoring the novella's rich variety of characterizations—whether of the colonists and natives in the Congo, the Englishmen in the frame narrative, or the Belgians in the early phase of the story—leads students to misapprehend the novella's structure and meaning.

Brian W. Shaffer considers the role of Marlow's *Nellie* audience in "Heart of Darkness." He argues that this audience is central to the text's meaning, despite its apparently peripheral nature, and that, in coming to grips with the multidimensional significance of this audience—particularly its function as a mirror of and commentary on Conrad's initial readers—students can begin to determine their own angle of vision on and ideological relation to Conrad's narrative. Brian Richardson also explores narrator and audience issues, but this time in "The Secret Sharer." He concludes that the story is much more ironic and the narrator vastly more unreliable than has previously been proposed and that exploring this issue provides both an exemplary instance for the discussion of larger issues of narrative interpretation and a good introduction to modernist literary strategies. Daniel Schwarz rounds out this section with a psychological approach to teaching "The Secret Sharer" that complements the preceding essay. Schwarz demonstrates, using R. D. Laing's *The Divided Self* among other texts, how the captain's reading of Leggatt is revealed in the text to have less to do with "objective fact" than with his own emotional and moral needs.

The second group of essays explores the controversies—largely pertaining to gender, race, and imperial politics—that surround the teaching of "Heart of Darkness" and "The Secret Sharer." As do the essays in the first group, the essays here enact their own implicit conversation. Marianne DeKoven explores "Heart of Darkness" as a dialogue with various feminist and modernist currents of its day. Specifically, her juxtaposition of "Heart of Darkness" with Virginia Woolf's first novel, *The Voyage Out*, reveals surprising structural, stylistic, and thematic parallels between the two works and exposes meanings in Conrad's text, particularly its dialectic of masculinist misogyny and empowered femininity, that would not be otherwise apparent. Carola M. Kaplan also considers Conrad's treatment of gender and sexuality, this time in both "Heart of Darkness" and "The Secret Sharer." Invoking the work of DeKoven, Judith Butler, Freud, Lacan, and others, she moves from a consideration of two questions her students typically ask her of these texts—"Where are the women?" and "Why does the male protagonist risk his life for such a questionable friend (i.e., Kurtz and Leggatt, respectively)?"—to arrive at a number of pedagogically useful connections between the marginalization of women and the intensity of homosocial bonding among men in the two tales.

The next two essays concern matters of race and politics in "Heart of Darkness." In one way or another, both respond to the political challenge to this novella's canonical status advanced by Achebe—what might be called the politics of teaching "Heart of Darkness"—and take a more personal tack. Padmini Mongia explores the how and why of teaching a novel that many, following

Achebe, regard as racist and imperialist; she uses her experience as an Indian teacher-scholar of Conrad and Achebe. Joseph F. Militello describes his experience teaching "Heart of Darkness," with its overtly racist terminology, at a historically black university in the Mississippi Delta. Both Mongia and Militello make interesting connections between the recent "Heart of Darkness" and *Huckleberry Finn* controversies; and both seek to use Achebe's indictment of Conrad not to condemn "Heart of Darkness" and close down debate but, echoing a phrase of Gerald Graff's, to "teach the conflicts" and encourage students to evaluate the novella from numerous—indeed even competing—perspectives.

The final essay in this group concerns the politicomilitary context for Conrad's stories. Margot Norris reads "Heart of Darkness" through Coppola's 1979 film *Apocalypse Now*. She argues that juxtaposing these two texts allows students to see that Conrad's exposé of turn-of-the-century Belgian and British imperialism is relevant to United States military intervention in Southeast Asia six decades later. As Norris reminds us, such a displacement of one historical context onto another is inscribed in the novella's frame narrative itself, with its twice-told structure, and in the analogy Marlow constructs between the Roman and British empires.

The final group of essays is devoted to the specific enterprise of teaching Conrad in six different courses—and in a wide range of institutions, both public and private, denominational and nonsectarian, large and small. Mark D. Larabee shares his experience teaching "The Secret Sharer"—a nautical coming-of-age tale that treats identity, community, ethics, classmate loyalty, and leadership—at the United States Naval Academy. He describes the ways in which the story's physical and psychological settings are related, reveals how a British sea captain's experience in a distant ocean a century ago might be relevant to American naval students today, and argues that the ability to read highly nuanced texts—like the ability to read obscure topographic features—is a crucial skill for his students. William M. Hagen describes how he integrates "Heart of Darkness" into the Western Civilization / Core Humanities program at Oklahoma Baptist University; and Philip M. Weinstein describes the role that the novella plays in his Modernism/Postmodernism Seminar at Swarthmore College. Both authors share recommended pairings of "Heart of Darkness" with other texts. Barry Stampfl of San Diego State University describes his strategy for teaching the novella across numerous disciplinary boundary lines—history, psychology, autobiography, and journalism, for example—as a means of facilitating his students' responses to the text without dictating their conclusions. The novelist Janet Burroway describes her use of "Heart of Darkness" in a fiction writing workshop at Florida State University. Looking at the text from the standpoint of Conrad's narrative strategy—less "What does the story do or say?" than "What problem did the writer face here?" and "Why does the author choose this technique?"—she shows how Conrad's novella offers students an immensely varied repertoire of techniques from which to choose, particularly when it comes to the manipulation of point of view. The section concludes with a discussion by Mark Osteen of Loyola College, Maryland, of the ways in which "Heart of Darkness" can be taught through film. He draws on an array of film scripts and completed movies to illustrate his approach. The final three essays all conclude with recommended writing exercises for students.

It is our hope that this volume will give instructors of "Heart of Darkness" and "The Secret Sharer" a clear sense of the state of the art of teaching Conrad today and will suggest productive pedagogical routes, from high school through graduate school, that they might elect to take in the future.

Conrad, Slavery, and the African Ivory Trade in the 1890s

Ray Stevens

> You are a slave-dealer. I am a slave-dealer. There's
> nothing but slave-dealers in this cursed country.
> —Conrad, "An Outpost of Progress"

I approach any undergraduate class with the following assumptions. (1) A work of literary art is created because the author has something to communicate; and readers—all of whom are individuals with varying perspectives—grow in understanding of literature to the extent that they continue to expand aesthetic and intellectual contexts. (2) The literary artist communicates for all time—but from a particular time and place—ideas based on experience transformed through creative vision. (3) The role of the instructor is to assist in opening minds to various possibilities for critical interpretation, not to close them by trying to superimpose a critical or philosophical schema. As a humanist who "just happens"—as Conrad might say—to teach literature rather than philosophy, history, or the fine arts, I incorporate other disciplines into class presentations.[1]

My approach is eclectic, encouraging discussion. Class begins with a question such as "What is the heart of darkness?" or "What is the Intended's problem?" or "Why brass wire and ivory rather than conch shells and copper crosses?"[2] Discussion, which includes references to critical schools based on textual evidence, leads to context—biographical, historical, aesthetic—with emphasis on "An Outpost of Progress," the companion piece to "Heart of Darkness." I distribute eight short passages from "Heart of Darkness" and other texts to illustrate how Conrad's experience with the ivory trade helped shape his aesthetic development.

The biographical context is given by three passages. The first, from Conrad's "Author's Note" to *Tales of Unrest* (1898), places "Heart" and "Outpost" in the context of European spoils carried out of Africa. The second, from "The Congo Diary" (1890), refers to Conrad's hands-on experience with the ivory trade. The third, from "Geography and Some Explorers" (1924), reminisces about his knowledge of Congo Arab slave traders in 1890.

The historical context is shown by two contemporary passages confirming European knowledge and tolerance of the ivory and slave trades and by one passage from Conrad. The first is from the *Encyclopaedia Britannica* (1890), the second from Henry M. Stanley's *In Darkest Africa* (1890). The third, from "Outpost," is Conrad's assertion, through Carlier, of the reality of European involvement in the ivory and slave trade. I also refer to at least two of Conrad's letters written after he left the Congo and to the diary of a British missionary in the Congo.

The aesthetic context, given by two passages from "Heart," illustrates the growing sophistication of Conrad's art, suggesting how the ivory and slave trade evolves from relatively mechanistic objects of "Outpost" into the very being of Kurtz and the Intended.

The Biographical Context

> "An Outpost of Progress" is the lightest part of the loot I carried off from Central Africa, the main portion being of course "The Heart of Darkness" [. . .]. As for the story itself it is true enough in its essentials. The sustained invention of a really telling lie demands a talent which I do not possess. (Conrad, *Tales* ix)

> Gosse and R[oger]. C[asement]. gone with a large lot of ivory down to Boma. On G.['s] return intend to start up the river. Have been myself busy packing ivory in casks. Idiotic employment.
> (Conrad, "Congo Diary" 161; Matadi, 24 June 1890)

> The subdued thundering mutter of the Stanley Falls hung in the heavy night air [. . .] while no more than ten miles away, in Reshid's Camp just above the Falls, the yet unbroken power of the Congo Arabs slumbered uneasily. [. . .] I said to myself with awe, "This is the very spot of my boyish boast."
>
> A great melancholy descended on me . . . . the unholy recollection of a prosaic newspaper "stunt" and the distasteful knowledge of the vilest scramble for loot that ever disfigured the history of human conscience and geographical exploration. What an end to the idealised realities of a boy's daydreams! (Conrad, "Geography" [*Last Essays*] 17)

These texts and that of "Heart" suggest that Conrad, however reluctantly or inadvertently, was a part of the exploitation of the Congo. He was employed by Albert Thys, l'Administrateur-Délégué of the Société Anonyme Belge pour le Commerce du Haut-Congo and aide-de-camp to King Leopold, ostensibly to command a steamboat. The real purpose was to create profit for the investors in the great civilizing enterprise. Conrad had literally a hands-on experience with ivory, a major export to Europe in 1890. As Makola, Kayerts, and Carlier realize in "Outpost" and as contemporary records confirm, one could barter Africans for large tusks to enhance profit, because the enslavement of natives did not need to be recorded in the company's cooked books.

Significantly, the introductory paragraphs of both "Outpost" and "Heart" refer to accountants and to accountancy. The accountant on the *Nellie* "brought out [. . .] dominoes, and was toying architecturally with the bones" (*Heart* 7), anticipating a game. The Europeanized Makola, in turn, labors with account books, occasionally referring to ivory as bone.[3]

At this point I refer to the biographical passages, and, through discussion, observe that the dreams and romantic illusions of youth often founder on the realities of adult life. The first impression many have of Conrad's river journey, forgetting for a moment "Heart," is mentioned in "Geography and Some Explorers" and elsewhere—the day he put his "finger on a spot in the very middle of the then white heart of Africa," and "declared that some day [he . . .] would go there" (*Last Essays* 16). Romance remained with Conrad only until he packed ivory at Matadi.

He comments in the "Author's Notes" to *Tales of Unrest* (ix) that among the "very small amount of plunder" that he carried out of Africa with him were "Outpost" and "Heart." Further, in the first and last essays of *Last Essays,* he refers to his involvement with the ivory trade, first at Matadi in 1890 and, eight months before his death in 1924, in a reminiscence about the Congo Arab slave trader Reshid[4] at Stanley Falls.

The Historical Context

> But since [1880 . . .] the [slave] traffic seems to have received a fresh impetus from an increased demand for ivory, the slave and ivory trades being "hand and glove."   (*Encyclopaedia* 22: 144)

> It is simply incredible that, because ivory is required for ornaments or billiard games, the rich heart of Africa should be laid waste at this late year of the nineteenth century, signalized as it has been by so much advance, that populations, tribes, and nations should be utterly destroyed.   (Stanley 1: 240)

> You are a slave-dealer. I am a slave-dealer. There's nothing but slave-dealers in this cursed country.   (Conrad, *Tales* 110)

Discussion of the biographical and historical quotations leads students to speculate that Conrad could have framed his writing career in the context of comments about the ivory trade, especially when it is pointed out that he carried seven chapters of *Almayer's Folly*, his first novel, into the Congo with him. Conrad, like Europe, knew that ivory and slavery were almost inseparable, as specific incidents in "Outpost" confirm, as the invidious presence of ivory in "Heart" reiterates, and as records of the 1880s and 1890s chronicle.

If one had read the article on slavery in the ninth edition of the *Encyclopaedia Britannica* in 1890 or had followed, as most literate people in Europe and the United States did, the exploits of Henry M. Stanley in Africa, the association would have been obvious. Stanley and the owner of the *New York Herald* created the "newspaper stunt," as Conrad refers to it in *Last Essays*, to increase readership: Stanley's search for Dr. Livingstone. Conrad read about Stanley's later expeditions initially in the London *Daily Telegraph*. Stanley's search for Emin Pasha led Stanley up the Congo in 1887 along the route that Conrad followed three years later. Stanley would go much farther into the interior of Africa; Conrad's excursion ended at Stanley Falls. Stanley and his expedition traveled through Matadi and arrived at Bangala on 30 May (1: 107), where Conrad stopped charting the vagaries of the Congo River in "Up-river Book" in 1890,[5] the year Stanley's newspaper accounts were collected in *In Darkest Africa*.

In addition to linking the slavery and ivory trades, the *Britannica* article on slavery also commented on the Berlin conference of November 1884, which regulated the boundaries of the new Congo Free State and affirmed that "those regions shall not be used as markets or routes of transit for the trade in slaves. [. . . E]ach of these powers [signed by plenipotentiaries of most European states] binds itself to use all the means [. . .] to put an end to this trade and to punish those engaged in it" (22: 144).

Next, I supply additional information about ivory and slavery from Stanley and other sources. Stanley records the exploits of the ivory hunters of Ipoto, who, having arrived from their base on the Lualaba River,

> sent on about 200 guns and 200 slave carriers to strike further in a north-easterly direction, to discover some [. . .] prosperous settlement [. . .] whence they could sally out in bands to destroy, burn and enslave natives in exchange for ivory. Through continual fighting, and the *carelessness which the unbalanced mind is so apt to fall into after one or more happy successes*, [the hunters] *had decreased in number* [. . .] *into a force of about ninety guns.*   (1: 236; emphasis mine)

The parallels to Kurtz are striking. Conrad's diary records his passage through the area where the Lualaba becomes one with the Congo. In that vicinity the owners of the ivory caravans[6] remained at their bases living profligately while "every tusk, piece and scrap in the possession of an Arab trader has been steeped and dyed in blood. [. . .] For every two tusks a whole village has been destroyed" (Stanley 1: 240). Stanley does not mention the European tolerance of the slave trade, but Conrad does in his letter of 21 December 1903 to Roger Casement (*Collected Letters* 3: 96).[7]

If time permits, I cite other examples to emphasize the importance of thorough research to substantiate conclusions about literature based on historical records. Among the sources that might be used are the diaries of the British missionary George Grenfell (available in excerpts in works such as Kimbrough's Norton edition of *Heart* and Sherry's *Conrad's Western World*); the African American George Washington Williams, who was in the Congo reporting for President Benjamin Harrison (Franklin, *Williams*); Casement (Hawkins, "Joseph Conrad, Roger Casement"); and Mark Twain (Hawkins, "Joseph Conrad and Mark Twain").

Discussion returns to Conrad's personal record. Conrad confirms the preceding accounts in a letter to T. Fisher Unwin of 22 July 1896 referring to "Outpost," locating the outpost on the Kassai River, a tributary of the Congo. He comments on his bitterness in Africa and on his "indignation at masquerading philanthropy," as he divested himself "of everything but pity—and some scorn—while putting down the insignificant events that bring on the catastrophe" (*Collected Letters* 1: 294). Enslavement, of course, is not insignificant. The Kassai River, not mentioned in "Outpost," where Carlier and Kayerts worked their ill will, is deep in African forests. Slaves and ivory returned to the banks of the Lualaba and Congo Rivers, where Conrad packed casks of ivory to be shipped to Europe to create bibelots, dominoes, cutlery, piano keys, and billiard balls. In "Heart" the Congo river men sport their brass wire; for the most part, however, the company's trading goods remain in the fetish at Kayerts's outpost because quality ivory requires slaves in return. Live Africans are substituted for dead elephants—flesh and blood for bones.

Next I discuss two pages from the manuscript of the "Congo Diary," to introduce Conrad's aesthetic development. These pages return to Conrad sorting ivory at Matadi, where the Congo River has passed through the thirty-two cataracts of the Livingstone Falls, which prevent a water route from the coast to the interior of Africa. The cataracts required a rail link, which was being built with the slave labor that Conrad witnessed and that Marlow recorded.

I point out that this incomplete record, buried in an unpublished part of the diary manuscript, confirms Conrad's hands-on experience with ivory. The page records Conrad's initials "J. C. K." (Joseph Conrad Korzeniowski) and the date: "Matadi. 23d. 6th. 90." Figures on the first page record weights of casks packed with ivory, while the second page records some of Conrad's enumerations jotted down when packing the casks. Also recorded are three references to the letters "SAB," which stand for Société Anonyme Belge, Conrad's employer, and two references to "GK," Georges Antoine Klein, the agent who died on board the *Roi des Belges* on Conrad's return from Stanley Falls and who some critics believe was a source for Kurtz. Conrad's penciled comments remind one of Kayerts's comments when the large ivory tusks were being weighed: he "[put] his hand in his pocket found there a dirty bit of paper and the stump of a pencil. He [. . .] noted stealthily the weights" ("Outpost" 106).

This fragmentary record at Matadi introduces similar information in "Outpost." Just as Conrad refers to the varying weights of the casks of ivory, "Outpost" records that the ivory-slave traders invade the interior of Africa from the coast and elsewhere (97), that ivory must be kept out of the sun, and that Makola cheapens tusks by calling them "bone." Carlier and Kayerts destroy themselves through overexposure, but they protect the ivory, which is more important than human beings in the Congo.

Statistics clarify contexts. Conrad knew about slaughtering elephants. England imported about 550 tons of ivory annually. Single tusks vary from one pound to 165 pounds: a pair of tusks averages 28 pounds. Large tusks are bought with slaves: Makola's scale is inadequate to weigh the slave dealers' six tusks. Approximately 40,000 elephants had to be killed annually for English imports. Sheffield cutlers required 170 tons, which means that more than 12,000 elephants would be slaughtered so that the British could adorn their tables with ivory (*Stanley and Africa* 381–82), and many tons went into the making of billiard balls or piano keys like those entombed in the sarcophagus of the grand piano in the Intended's mausoleum-like household, where her pale complexion, like Kurtz's ivory complexion in death, signifies Conrad's concluding metaphor for the ivory trade.

The ivory-slave trade knew no boundaries. Much of Europe went into the making of the Sierra Leonean Henry Price (Makola)—"taciturn and impenetrable," speaking English and French, writing a beautiful hand, understanding bookkeeping, and justified in trading Africans for ivory. Further, devastation caused by Kurtz's looting led to the manager's complaint that Kurtz's method is unsound because the area around the inner station will be temporarily unproductive. Similarly the director in "Outpost" knows that lack of productivity is more significant than Kayerts's cross-assisted suicide.

The Aesthetic Context

> I saw on that ivory face the expression of sombre pride, of ruthless power, of craven terror—of an intense and hopeless despair. Did he live his life again in every detail of desire, temptation, and surrender during that supreme moment of complete knowledge? He cried in a whisper at some image, at some vision—he cried out twice, a cry that was no more than a breath:
> "The horror! The horror!"   (Conrad, *Heart* 68)

> A grand piano stood massively in a corner with dark gleams on the flat surfaces like a sombre and polished sarcophagus. [. . .] She came forward

all in black with a pale head [substitute "ivory complexioned"], floating towards me in the dusk. [. . .] I saw her and him in the same instant of time—his death and her sorrow—I saw her sorrow in the very moment of his death.   (72–73)

At this point, I turn to the aesthetic, irony first. Carlier and Kayerts, representatives of colonialism, demonstrate its futility. First, the ex-military Carlier, interpreting the worth of African natives only in the context of their unfitness for European military cavalry units, nevertheless conveys with more wisdom than he is aware of the truth of their enterprise in a fight over a dwindling supply of sugar: "You are a slave-dealer. I am a slave-dealer. There's nothing but slave-dealers in this cursed country." In fact, Kayerts prefigures Kurtz's "The horror! The horror!": "If I give way now to that brute of a soldier [Carlier] he will begin this *horror* again tomorrow [. . .] every day—raise other pretensions, trample on me, torture me, make me his slave—and I will be *lost! Lost!*" (*Tales* 112; emphasis mine). Carlier foresees the future of colonialism a century later in a peculiarly circular and ironic vision of military barracks and billiard balls: kill elephants and sever tusks; sell ivory to Europeans for slaves—no matter if they are station hands and nearby villagers drunk on malafu (palm wine)—and shoot the sober ones (101–02); have someone like Conrad pack the ivory; ship it to Europe; make billiard balls, cutlery, bibelots, and piano keys; and send ivory back to Africa as billiard balls so that soldiers have something to amuse themselves with while civilizing Africa. Colonial glory is ironically reduced to billiards at military bases, and dinner tables and after-dinner piano music are made resplendent by slaughtered elephants and enslaved Africans.

To emphasize Conrad's evolving aesthetic treatment of ivory, I ask whether or not references to ivory in "Outpost" contrast with those in "Heart." "Outpost" emphasizes negotiating, weighing ivory on scales, numbering tusks and bartering station hands, cataloging goods stored in the fetish, and affirming the link between ivory and slavery, concluding with Kayerts hanging from a cross. The focus in "Heart" differs, because ivory becomes increasingly allusive and metaphoric as Marlow leaves the heart of darkness.

Prophetic is a comment early in "Heart," when the narrator refers to the "august light of abiding memories," linking the Thames, through Roman colonialism, to the Congo (8). Later Marlow comments ironically, in the presence of the deathlike indifference of unhappy savages chained and with iron collars: "I also was a part of the great cause of these high and just proceedings" (19), where "rubbishy cottons, beads, and brass-wire" return "a precious trickle of ivory" (21). The exception is people like Makola and Kurtz, who garner "as much ivory as all the others put together" (22).[8] As Marlow travels upstream, white men rush out of the wilderness near their small stations, where they "had the appearance of being held there captive by a spell. The word 'ivory' would ring in the air for a while—and on we went again into the silence" (36). Ivory becomes so controlling and haunting that Marlow finally sees Kurtz "grubbing for ivory in the wretched bush" (44), like Thomas Hardy's vision-impaired Clym Yeobright seeking furze on Egdon Heath.

It is not so much the ivory acquired as how it affects the Europeans, how it becomes integral to the health and well-being first of Carlier and Kayerts and later of Kurtz and the Intended. The piano keys—about the same size but unlike the Accountant's dominoes at the beginning of "Heart"—are not visible at the Intended's residence: the ivories are entombed in the piano-sarcophagus.[9] The Intended's pale complexion reflects Kurtz's ivory complexion in her ivoryless mausoleum, where the "tall marble fireplace had a cold and monumental white-ness" that contrasts strikingly to the black piano-sarcophagus (72-73). The dark-ivory imagery of "Heart" is complete: Kurtz dies; the Intended will lead a Coleridgean death in life; the African woman left behind is vibrantly if sorrow-fully alive, bedecked with the baubles and brass wire of colonialism: "She must have had the value of several elephant tusks upon her" (60). Conrad's irony is also complete, because Marlow evaluates the African woman in the context of ivory accountancy.

I conclude with a question: How often after Conrad left Africa might he have reminisced about the Congo when he heard the click of billiard balls or dined with ivory-handled cutlery? Marlow said of the Romans: "The fascination of the abomination—you know. Imagine the growing regrets, the longing to escape, the powerless disgust, the surrender, the hate" (10). And Conrad records the "end to [. . .] a boy's daydreams" in "the unholy recollection of a prosaic news-paper 'stunt' and the distasteful knowledge of the vilest scramble for loot that ever disfigured the history of human conscience and geographical exploration."

NOTES

[1]Typical writing assignments for "Heart of Darkness" are: first-year writing students react to some aspect of the work—brass wire, ivory, the Intended's situation, colonial-ism; survey-course students write a ten-to-fifteen-page paper demonstrating some knowledge of secondary sources; upper-division-course students write an extensively researched thirty-to-forty-page paper, focusing on one school of criticism.

[2]I point out that seven commodities were used for currency at various locations in the Congo in 1890: brass wire, conch shells, copper crosses, palm-fiber tissues, blue beads, cotton handkerchiefs, and iron arrowheads ("La monnaie"; see Hawkins, "Joseph Con-rad and Mark Twain" 131).

[3]Dominoes was a popular game in the 1890s. Such pieces, usually made of flat pieces of ivory or bone, were among the gimcracks for which elephants were slaughtered and Africans made slaves. Ivory is often called "bone." British slang "black ivory" once referred to "African negro slaves as an object of commerce."

[4]Reshid's uncle was Tippu Tib, the notorious slave trader.

[5]"Up-river Book" records the navigational notes Conrad made on the *Roi des Belges*, the river steamer that carried him to Stanley Falls.

[6]Emin Pasha, whose rescue Stanley recorded in *In Darkest Africa*, possessed about seventy-five tons of ivory (Conrad, *"Heart"* [Hampson] xxi).

[7]For a discussion of Conrad's letter to Casement, see Hawkins, "Joseph Conrad, Roger Casement." The state bought slaves ostensibly to free them but actually forced them to work at minimal pay to earn their release (see Hawkins, "Joseph Conrad and Mark Twain"). Hunt Hawkins has been especially helpful in discussions with me as I prepared this essay. Among other things, he suggested the identities of SAB and GK, below.

[8]References in "Heart" become redundant: "Ivory [. . .] lots of it—prime sort" (33); Kurtz had "collected, bartered, swindled, or stolen more ivory than all the other agents together" (48); "You should have heard him say 'My ivory. [. . .] My Intended, my ivory, my station, my river'" (49).

[9]I introduce the importance of using authoritative texts, pointing out that Conrad is consistent throughout the prepublication texts of "Heart" in not mentioning the piano keys, as Robert Trogdon of the Center for Conrad Studies at Kent State University has confirmed. Frederick R. Karl ("Introduction" 128) mentions piano keys when discussing the role that art can play in the exploitation of Africans for ivory. Karl's discussion complements my reading that the absence of a reference to piano keys (see the British colloquial expression "tickle the ivories") in a work filled with references to ivory is a conscious and aesthetic omission.

Conrad and the Adventure Tradition

Andrea White

The MLA's Approaches to Teaching World Literature series attests to the rather recent but long overdue concern with the actual teaching, not simply professing, of literature. Three years after the series began, in 1983, Terry Eagleton enjoined us to direct our textual analysis at a "whole field of practices rather than just those sometimes rather obscurely labeled 'literature'" (*Literary Theory* 205). To look at texts not only as aesthetic artifacts but also as cultural productions can help involve students in the very real ways in which values are produced in the here and now of our multiethnic classrooms as well as in turn-of-the-century British literary texts. That the popular literature of nineteenth-century adventure writing in particular was an informing cultural context for many Conradian texts can help demystify those texts that students first experience as eminently difficult and canonical. Revealing the connections to popular fiction can serve to open up "literature" to those who have traditionally felt most excluded by it. Whether we are to honor adventure writing with the name of "literature" or not is arguable, but that it influenced generations of readers and writers alike and that Conrad's fictions are an often subversive reworking of adventure motifs have already been thoroughly demonstrated.

A rich tradition of adventure and travel writing existed in the nineteenth century (see esp. Brantlinger, *Rule*; Green; White, *Joseph Conrad*; Eby; MacKenzie). The texts were varied: *Boy's Own Paper, The Youth's Magazine, Young England,* and *Boy's Own Volume* were only the most popular of dozens of boys' magazines in which both firsthand narratives and fictional stories told of adventures and action at home and in colonial outposts. Novels of adventure were written about and for plucky British lads by Frederick Marryat, G. A. Henty, R. M. Ballantyne, W. H. G. Kingston, Mayne Reid, George Manville Fenn, and Jules Verne, among others, most of whom wrote also for the boys' magazines. Henty's more than eighty novels, either in book form or serialized in magazines, told of the dangerous exploits of boy heroes usually in service to empire and often in the company of historical heroes, as his titles indicate: *With Clive in India, Under Drake's Flag, With Moore at Corunna.* Ballantyne also wrote of brave British heroes on adventures in the service of the Hudson's Bay Company (*Ungava: A Tale of Esquimau Land* [1857]), in the South Seas (*The Coral Island* [1857]), or in Africa (*Black Ivory: A Tale of Adventure among the Slavers of East Africa* [1873]). Rudyard Kipling's popular verses and stories of regimental life in India and Rider Haggard's imperial romances *King Solomon's Mines* (1885), *Allan Quatermain* (1887), and *She* (1887) appealed widely to all ages, as did the very popular travel writing and memoirs of the day that appeared in books, magazines, and illustrated newspapers by missionaries, explorers, and various colonial officers. In fact, magazines in which much of

Conrad's fiction first appeared—*Blackwood's, The Illustrated London News, Cosmopolis,* for example—regularly featured items about life in colonial outposts. Many scholars have looked at the ways in which Conrad's texts bear the traces of that adventure tradition, but little attention has been paid to ways in which that influence might be dealt with in the classroom.

The understanding that texts of all sorts are situated in particular contexts—social, historical, economic, political—is axiomatic not only to cultural studies but to most areas of literary study now. We are more willing to grant a work its intertextuality, its inevitable borrowings, inheritances, echoes. The "belief that literature is linguistically autonomous, that is, possessed of intrinsic linguistic properties which distinguish it from all other kinds of discourse," is false, Mary Louise Pratt wrote in 1977 (xii). And in his *Crusoe's Footprints,* Patrick Brantlinger agrees that "literature is a leaky category [. . .] not a separate, transcendent discourse" (15) and cites Raymond Williams's contention that "intellectual work cannot and should not stop at the borders of single texts [. . .] the connections of texts and histories with our own lives and experience must be recognized and become part of what we analyze" (ix). Certainly knowing something about the adventure tradition can help students grasp Conrad's work as earlier readers did. Most of those initial readers came to "Youth," "Outpost of Progress," "Heart of Darkness," *Lord Jim,* and "The Secret Sharer"—among the most anthologized and taught Conradian texts—through an abundant reading of Victorian adventure writing, a literature that usually promoted imperial attitudes and assumptions either implicitly or quite directly. Characteristic of much of this writing is Charles Kingsley's exuberant celebration in *Westward Ho!* (1855) of those heroes "who sailed out to colonize another and a vaster England, to the heaven-prospered cry of Westward Ho!" (568). Without this background, the various allusions, motifs, plot movements, and points of reference in Conrad's fiction lose their force. Such a grounding is necessary to help students better appreciate the complexities of Conrad's positioning vis-à-vis adventure, empire, and the possibilities of ethical action in the modern world.

Something of Conrad's biography, then, can leak most profitably into a study of any of these texts. That Conrad lived in exile with his parents in Siberia as a young boy, a consequence of his father's role in the abortive Polish revolution of 1863, and that he grew up in Poland in the presence of arguments about and resistance against imperial Russia's autocracy would help students understand Conrad's complicated personal involvement in an imperial history. That he evaded service in the Russian army by going off to sea at seventeen, sailing on French imperial business to the West Indies in the French Mercantile Service out of Marseilles, where he also engaged in conspiratorial talk—and perhaps deeds—in support of the Carlists in Spain, and that he then served in the British Merchant Service on British imperial business for twenty years might give students the sense that this author knew something firsthand about adventure.

His thoughts were shaped not only by a life of felt and lived historic incident and action but by his youthful reading as well, some of which he recalled in 1898 in an article for the *Outlook* entitled "Tales of the Sea." Here he wrote of the profound pleasures of reading Frederick Marryat and James Fenimore Cooper's sea stories, of their widely felt influence, and of their shaping power in particular on "the life of the writer of this appreciation" (*Notes* 56). Though this article needs to be read as part of Conrad's growing commitment to his identity as an English writer in 1898, it also expresses an early enthusiasm for adventure writing, an enthusiasm also expressed in the later essay "Geography and Some Explorers" for Captain James Cook, Sir John Franklin, Sir Francis Leopold McClintock, and David Livingstone, imperial adventurers all whose writings were not just the "fine words" of many earlier explorers, for they told of disinterested deeds inspired by service, not greed (*Last Essays* 10).

Although these were shaping discourses for the young Conrad, as they were for his contemporaries, his trip up the Congo in 1890 provided yet another firsthand encounter with imperial tyranny and radically affected those easy enthusiasms. "I was a perfect animal," Conrad told Edward Garnett. "[. . .] meaning, of course, that he had reasoned and reflected hardly at all over all the varieties of life he had encountered," Garnett concluded. "The sinister voice of the Congo with its murmuring undertone of human fatuity, baseness and greed had swept away the generous illusions of his youth, and had left him gazing into the heart of an immense darkness" ("Art" 195). While Conrad's admiration for the ideal of disinterested adventure remained undimmed, there was now a more pronounced skepticism about the actions those often imperial dreams in fact led to. Leopold's Congo was a brutal case in point. In a late essay, "Well Done," Conrad makes a telling distinction:

> The mere love of adventure is no saving grace. It lays a man under no obligation of faithfulness to an idea and even to his own self. [. . . C]ourage in itself is not an ideal. A successful highwayman showed courage of a sort, and pirate crews have been known to fight with courage [. . .] but there is no sort of loyalty to bind him in honour to consistent conduct.

In fact, Marlow's fear for Jim, that eager consumer of adventure stories, is that his fate will be that of many adventurers, who end "in mysterious nooks of islands and continents, mostly red-nosed and watery-eyed. [. . .] Yes, there is nothing more futile than an adventurer" (*Notes* 189, 190).

The distinction, read against a tradition that argues forcefully and with such confidence for the attractiveness of adventure, helps students make more sense of those most unattractive adventurers in "Heart of Darkness," the Eldorado Exploring Expedition. These "sordid buccaneers" are so clearly not the pluckish heroes of story and sketch or emissaries of light, and that they fancy themselves great adventurers points to adventure's potential for self-interested rapaciousness, for it is they who are described as tearing "treasure out of the bowels of the land [. . .] with no more moral purpose at the back of it than there is in burglars breaking into a safe" (32, 33). Similarly, Chester and Robinson's sobriquet, "the Argonauts," becomes more ironic and we hear more clearly the critique of mere reckless, self-interested adventure. The distinction, finally, helps Conrad tell the Livingstones from the Stanleys as well. While Henry Morton Stanley's fame seemed to eclipse David Livingstone's—Stanley's *In Darkest Africa* (1890) sold over 150,000 copies, while Livingstone's *Missionary Travels* (1857) had sold only 70,000, though both were best-sellers in their day— for Conrad, Livingstone was the hero and Stanley the mere opportunistic adventurer sensationalizing a profound experience. That Conrad's Eldorado Exploring Expedition resembled Stanley's various journeys and became part of an exposé of Leopold's Congo was soon clear to many readers. Conrad wrote later of his own 1890 trip to Africa and of his great disappointment, for all that remained of his boyhood dreams of coming to Africa was "the unholy recollection of a prosaic newspaper 'stunt' and the distasteful knowledge of the vilest scramble for loot that ever disfigured the history of human conscience and geographical exploration. What an end to the idealised realities of a boy's daydreams!" (*Last Essays* 25). Such insights were generally not the stuff of adventure writing.

"To reveal the hollowness of many of the values of the romance," Linda Dryden argues, is central to Conrad's use of the adventure tradition (*"Outcast"* 139). While Dryden focuses on the earlier novels of the Malay trilogy, less often taught, the same scrutiny provides an informing reading of Conrad's most anthologized works. A classroom reading of "Youth," for example, could well be accompanied by the *Outlook* article, for it appeared the day after Conrad finished that early story, and both concern the naval services, the midshipmen and the sailors of the merchant service. A comparison of story and article would reveal that the opening of "Youth" echoes the language of "Tales of the Sea": "This could have occurred nowhere but in England, where men and sea interpenetrate, so to speak–the sea entering into the life of most men" (*"Youth"* 3). The narrator goes on to remember his younger self in exclamations that characterize the enthusiastic language of a Henty or Ballantyne or Marryat lad: "There was on [the *Judea*'s stern], below her name in big letters, a lot of scrollwork, with the gilt off, and some sort of a coat of arms, with the motto 'Do or Die' underneath. I remember it took my fancy immensely. There was a touch of romance in it, something that made me love the old thing—something that appealed to my youth!" (5).

To teach "Youth," then, along with the *Outlook* article, some information about Marryat and perhaps some illustrative excerpts from Marryat's fictions would help substantiate the influence of the adventure tradition on Conrad. He had admitted as much to his publisher, William Blackwood, explaining that he had written "Youth" "out of the material of a boys' story" (*Collected Letters* 2: 417). But what can this mean to our students? They would be served by Brantlinger's insight that Marryat's eponymous heroes Jacob Faithful, Peter Simple, Mr. Midshipman Easy, and Masterman Ready are, like the boy heroes of Ballantyne or the brawny British tars of Henty's and others' stories, full of resourcefulness and honor. As their names imply, they are ready young men of action, loyal and true and full of pluck. Since Marryat's adventures characteristically take place during the Napoleonic Wars, they look back

> nostalgically to an age of youthful adventure when heroic action was almost routine, or certainly represented as such [. . .] they imply that the peace and national prestige enjoyed by their first readers in the 1830's and 1840's are founded upon valiant deeds that comprise the glory of British history. [. . . T]he themes of patriotism and martial valor are deeply ingrained in his fiction.   (Brantlinger, *Rule* 49)

But a comparison between the narrator of "Youth" and a Marryat hero would also reveal significant differences and provide a way of measuring the seemingly easily congratulatory mood in this early story against the more complex views of empire and history in Conrad's subsequent writing. Marlow's somewhat bemused, sympathetic but distanced account of his younger self might be less obvious to readers who know nothing of the tradition Conrad writes out of and makes conscious use of, because "Youth," for all its outward resemblance to those celebratory sea stories of Marryat, is of a most unheroic, even comic, fiasco at sea. That youth and "the romance of [its] illusions," particularly about adventure in "exotic" climes, is being gently mocked here would not be as apparent without this context ("*Youth*" 42).

Not to know something of this history and the conscious use of the late-nineteenth-century romance and adventure tradition is to miss not only Conrad's complex attitudes toward heroic adventure but also the challenges his fiction presents to adventure writing's generally uncritical attitudes toward England's past. Martin Green argues that "the adventure tales that formed the light reading of Englishmen for two hundred years and more after *Robinson Crusoe* were, in fact, the energizing myth of English imperialism" (3). As Green goes on to note, the first stirrings of the imperial idea occur in the Elizabethan age as England became a mercantile state and a world power and colonies were seen as essential. Contemporary readers of "Heart of Darkness" would have needed no footnotes to recognize the references by the frame narrator to Raleigh and Drake and *The Golden Hind*; these were familiar, cherished subjects, and readers would have shared that narrator's sympathetic views. Raised on magazine stories and annuals and books of exploration that heroized these national figures, they would have responded sympathetically to "the great spirit of the past upon the lower reaches of the Thames" (*Heart* 8) as a reference to a specifically Elizabethan past when England's mercantile power was growing.[1] And references to Sir Leopold McClintock, whose *Voyage of the Fox* (1860) was known as far as Poland—where a young Korzeniowski read it and was enchanted by it, a quest romance that recounted the attempted rescue of Sir John Franklin, whose ships *Erebus* and *Terror* set out to discover the Northwest Passage—would also have been familiar to contemporary readers of

"Heart of Darkness." In fact, contemporaries would have read without a hitch until Marlow's abrupt "and this also [. . .] has been one of the dark places of the earth" (9). That line would have delivered the jolt Conrad intended, but too often our students don't distinguish between those two voices and miss the questioning of imperialistic adventure that the book engages.

Early readers would also have known that Drake's *Golden Hind* reached the Pacific coasts of North and South America and established the beginnings of a very successful trade in the Spice Islands. In *Lord Jim*, Marlow's recollections of the pepper trade in connection with Patusan's early history could only have jarred the sensibilities of readers accustomed to those evocations as part of a noble history that sang of England as a prosperous sea power and of the sanctified civilizing mission of English heroes. Knowing the context makes Marlow's observations more darkly ironic; slitting throats wasn't the usual characterization of the activity of imperial trade:

> The seventeenth-century traders went [to Patusan] for pepper, because the passion for pepper seemed to burn like a flame of love in the breast of Dutch and English adventurers about the time of James the First. Where wouldn't they go for pepper! For a bag of pepper they would cut each other's throats without hesitation, and would forswear their souls, of which they were so careful otherwise [. . .].   (Conrad, *Lord Jim* 137)

The incursion of European explorers and traders, imaged in "Heart of Darkness" as "a fantastic invasion" (26, 35, 57), and finally of Jim himself, belies the promise of so much of the adventure writing Conrad's texts initially resembled. Those representatives of progress—Kurtz, Kayerts, Carlier, and Jim—bring only darkness to the colonial world, not the promised enlightenment imaged in the fictions of Marryat, Ballantyne, Henty, and others.[2]

Conrad's relation to the adventure tradition was a pronounced but complex one. As was noted in the *Outlook* article as well as in "Geography and Some Explorers," Conrad admits his admiration for the ideal of heroic adventure and romance. To the editor of the conservative *Blackwood's Magazine* he readily connected "Youth" to "the material of a boys' story." But earlier he admitted to Blackwood that "the paraphernalia of [*The Rescue*] are hackneyed. The yacht, the shipwreck, the pirates, the coast—all this has been used times out of number; whether it has been done, that's another question" (*Collected Letters* 1: 381). The disclaimer here is advanced on artistic grounds and should be heard as a refutation of those early reviewers who read his fiction as adventure writing and, measuring him against it, faulted his fiction for its paucity of action and overabundance of description. A reviewer of *An Outcast of the Islands* compared Conrad unfavorably with Kipling, who was "a master of rapid delineation of character, of vivid directness of style. [. . .] Mr. Conrad, on the contrary, is diffuse [. . .] a serious charge to make against a book of adventure" (Sherry, *Conrad: The Critical Heritage* 69–70). While in its themes and settings Conrad's work might have resembled that of Ballantyne, Stevenson, and Kipling, especially to a generation raised on adventure writing, it differed from that tradition in its treatment, and such was Conrad's frequent defense.

He distances himself from adventure writing not only on artistic grounds but on ideological grounds as well. He seeks to distance himself from opportunistic adventurers on the one hand—the Eldorado Exploration Expedition et alia, as we have seen—but on the other from a kind of facile romanticism of boy's adventure fiction that could be equally disastrous. It is Jim's "light holiday literature," after all, that fatally shapes his dreams of himself: "saving people from sinking ships, cutting away masts in a hurricane, swimming through a surf with a line." Becoming a hero in one of those seductive fictions, he imagines that he too "confronted savages on tropical shores, quelled mutinies on the high seas, and in a small boat upon the ocean kept up the hearts of despairing men—always an example of devotion to duty, and as unflinching as a hero in a book" (*Lord Jim* 9). But Jim's confusion here between the actual events of his life as they unfold and "something you read of in books" (141) leads to tragic consequences for himself and others. Repeatedly, Conrad objects to the reading of "boy's stories" as truth; as his fiction makes clear, such a conflation reduces and oversimplifies the complexities his protagonists encounter.

In both *Lord Jim* and "The Secret Sharer," evoking adventure writing itself serves to disrupt the privileging it traditionally conferred on imperial heroes of British tradition. Foregrounding stories and storytelling in this way, as Bruce Henricksen notes, serves to reveal "the connections between adventure stories [as] culturally naturalized forms of narrative, and a failing imperial project" (83). We find the familiar disclaimer again in "The Secret Sharer": "We aren't living in a boy's adventure tale," the young captain tells his secret sharer when asked by Leggatt to maroon him on a nearby island (52). The word "maroon" seems to have set him off. In it he perhaps has recognized the language of a Henty tale of pirates or of Robert Louis Stevenson's criminally abandoned Ben Gunn.

The word evokes a dangerous romanticizing that makes the young captain uneasy, as though Leggett were reducing this affair to a simplistic, easily resolved adventure tale and ignoring the situation's complex moral dimensions. His ready complicity in Leggatt's escape has carried him far from the tenets of a heroic code upheld by a Marryat midshipman, and both Leggatt and the young captain, viewed in the tradition of adventure writing, have committed those breaches of faith that are, as Marlow noted, "the real significance of crime" (*Lord Jim* 96). Here Conrad refers to and complicates the tenets of heroic adventure to suggest the distance between the ideal and the actual. "The Secret Sharer" is usually read from an archetypal or psychological point of view as a rite of passage, in which the captain is viewed more or less sympathetically as having successfully realized the ideal conception of himself he set out to achieve. But reading the story in the context of the adventure tradition suggests a more complex view of the narrator and a more skeptical view of the situation. That the captain's apparent success is at the same time, and perhaps unavoidably, a kind of failure is more evident with some awareness of this influential cultural context.

How students are made familiar with this adventure tradition—from summary lectures to assigned in-depth readings—depends on the context of their Conradian encounter: lower-division surveys that might include only "The Secret Sharer," upper-division courses in modern British fiction that could deal with several texts, or graduate seminars devoted exclusively to Conrad. Lectures could be prepared using handouts containing information about several important writers in the tradition and some representative passages. At any level, such background knowledge would serve our students' understanding of the cultural context of "literature."

Students could be asked to examine a periodical issue in which a Conrad text first appeared and to consider the piece in the light of the accompanying articles, fictions, and poems and their attitudes toward heroic adventure and England's colonial responsibilites: the June-July 1897 *Cosmopolis*, in which "Outpost of Progress" appeared; the thousandth number of *Blackwood's*, in which "Heart of Darkness" first appeared; or the *Illustrated London News* for 30 November 1901, which featured the second installment of "Amy Foster."[3] Students, alone or in pairs or small groups, could read and report back to the class on Haggard's *King Solomon's Mines* or Ballantyne's *The Coral Island*, both easily available in World Classics paperbacks (Oxford). Other works, a bit more difficult to find, could be placed on reserve in the college library, and different groups of students could be made responsible for various bits of the material: copies of juvenile periodicals, works of nineteenth-century travel writing, or excerpts from the fiction. In this way, a fair amount of ground could be covered in a small amount of time.

Reading or referring to these examples of adventure writing should also involve students in an examination of style to notice that the infamous Conradian achronicity and multiple viewpoints that often bewilder them in fact work to challenge the historical truth claims of adventure writing. His fiction can thus be better appreciated as a counter telling to colonialist adventure writing's false historicism and to its straightforward linear development, which suggests the naturalness of the European incursion. Conrad uses but complicates the adventure tradition to reveal imperialistic adventure as anything but inevitable and "heaven-prospered" (Kingsley 568). The initial resemblance serves to mark the distance from a tradition that valued the kernel at the center of the yarn; frustrated readers seeking that kernel had to learn to look for the real adventure in the enveloping narrative, in the multifaceted and inconclusive telling itself.

NOTES

My thanks to colleagues Joanne Zitelli, Lois Feuer, Lyle Smith, Ephriam Sando, and Roger Bowen for their pedagogical insights and suggestions.

[1]One wonders about the article Conrad proposed to write but apparently failed to produce, in which he would compare "the spirit of Elisabethan [sic] times with ours as expressed in the respective literatures" (*Collected Letters* 2: 369).

[2]In Henty's *In Times of Peril*, for example, which tells of the Indian Mutiny of 1857, the narrative represents the inhabitants of the area around Delhi as doubting the advisability of overthrowing the Raj: "[. . .] the mutineers took what they wanted without paying, and were already behaving as masters of the country, and even thus early the country people were beginning to doubt whether the fall of the English Raj, and the substitution of the old native rule, with its war, its bloodshed, and its exactions, was by any means a benefit so far as the tillers of the soil were concerned" (88).

[3]In this issue, for example, a reviewer recommends Christmas books for children and singles out "the indefatigable Mr. Henty [who] has so skillfully blended fact with fiction in *With Roberts to Pretoria*" as timely Boer War reading ("Christmas Books"). Also in this issue is the first installment of "Amy Foster," a story in which the patriotism of heroic adventure becomes a destructive xenophobia.

Colonial and Postcolonial Contexts
for Teaching "Heart of Darkness"

John A. McClure

An instructor presenting "Heart of Darkness" as a work of colonial fiction can draw on a rich fund of archival and critical material. The history of central Africa in the late nineteenth century has been mapped in considerable detail, and Conrad has left a record of his experiences and responses not only in his fiction but also in "The Congo Diary," essays such as "Geography and Some Explorers," and any number of letters.[1] Critical discussions of colonial fiction in general and "Heart of Darkness" in particular abound.[2] When it comes to course building, one can choose from a range of models. "Heart of Darkness" is required reading in surveys of colonial fiction, courses that begin with *Robinson Crusoe* or *Jane Eyre* and continue across the range of Victorian and modernist texts—Charles Kingsley's *Westward Ho!*, Rudyard Kipling's *Kim*, Mary H. Kingsley's *Travels in West Africa*, Virginia Woolf's *The Voyage Out*, E. M. Forster's *A Passage to India*. It fits well in courses that pair colonial novels with postcolonial, *Crusoe* with *Foe* (Coetzee), *Jane Eyre* with *Wide Sargasso Sea* (Rhys), *Kim* with *The English Patient* (Ondaatje), and "Heart of Darkness" with *Season of Migration to the North* (Salih). I have also taught "Heart of Darkness" as a crucial prototype for American novels of empire by Robert Stone, Joan Didion, Don DeLillo, and Thomas Pynchon. And I have taught it as a text in the tradition of the oriental renaissance, that movement of transcultural appropriation through which two centuries of Western philosophers and writers have drawn on Hindic and Buddhist ideas to challenge the hegemony of Western values. Each of these approaches turns the text in certain ways, highlights certain of its powers, preoccupations, and problems. But in every case, one comes face to face with aspects of the text that have led two postcolonial critics, Chinua Achebe and Edward Said, to condemn it as racist, Eurocentric, and imperialistic.

Said's and Achebe's criticisms must be taken into account in any reading of "Heart of Darkness" as a colonial novel. Said's theory of colonial discourse founds and informs virtually all contemporary critical work on colonial literature, and to ignore Achebe's powerful denunciation would be to repeat the crime of cultural silencing coincident with colonialism. But there is another reason to address Said's and Achebe's arguments. I teach colonial fiction at the graduate level as well as the undergraduate, and many of the students I encounter have already taken a course in the subject by the time they reach me. What strikes me about a significant number of these students is their unqualified antipathy to "Heart of Darkness." They have read Said; they have read Achebe; they have studied "Heart of Darkness." And the experience has taught them to deploy what Aijaz Ahmad calls a "rhetoric of dismissal" (224), a way of speaking that reduces a complex and deeply ambivalent text to a mere instance of colonial propaganda. Because I think that Conrad's novel is deeply critical of colonialism and because I think that recognizing this has important political as well as aesthetic consequences, I approach the novel in a way that both attends to and interrogates Said's and Achebe's judgments.

I assign "The Scope of Orientalism" from Said's *Orientalism* early on in any course I teach on colonial fiction, and when we get to "Heart of Darkness," I assign both Achebe's "An Image of Africa: Racism in Conrad's *Heart of Darkness*" and the apposite sections of Said's *Culture and Imperialism*. My students are moved by Achebe's lucid anger and dazzled by Said's erudite argument. Studying Said challenges their sense of the innocence, individuality, and originality of verbal practices and enables them to begin thinking about all sorts of texts as permeated with politically significant structures and effects. Reading Achebe helps them understand what is at stake in "Heart of Darkness," and in its canonization, for a postcolonial reader.

I want my students to understand Said's vision of colonial discourse, but I also want them to think critically about his claim that in the colonial era all Western representations of non-Western peoples are of necessity othering and inferiorizing. Said insists, in *Orientalism*, that the discursive codes of the West imposed a "set of constraints" upon "[e]ven the most imaginative writers" of the nineteenth century and compelled them to affirm "the ineradicable distinction between Western superiority and Oriental inferiority" (42, 43, 42). This assertion is repeated in *Culture and Imperialism*. In the England of the 1890s, Said contends, "imperialism [. . .] *monopolized* the entire system of representation" (25). Indeed, when exploring the texts of this time, "there is *no use looking* for other, non-imperialist alternatives; the system has simply eliminated them and made them *unthinkable*. The circularity, *the perfect closure* of the whole thing is [. . .] mentally unassailable" (24; emphasis mine). It is this insistence on absolute discursive closure, I believe, that sponsors the posture of contemptuous dismissal assumed by many of my students. After all, if every Western text that addresses the subject of colonialism is condemned to rehearse Western claims to superiority and legitimacy, then all such texts are equally complicit, equally unsavory.

I challenge the argument that late-nineteenth-century English thought was inescapably imperialistic first by asking my students to note that Said himself sometimes backs away from the claim. "We must not forget," he remarks in *Culture and Imperialism*, "that there was *very little* domestic resistance to these empires" (10; emphasis mine). This qualification is not trivial, for it means that we cannot determine in advance the political valence of any metropolitan text, including "Heart of Darkness." Said qualifies his claims for discursive closure again in his discussion of Conrad, when he declares that the writer "was both anti-imperialist and imperialist, progressive when it came to rendering fearlessly and pessimistically the self-confirming, self-deluding corruption of overseas domination, deeply reactionary when it came to conceding that Africa or South America could ever have had an independent history or

culture" (xviii). The very existence of this "anti-imperialist" Conrad, a naturalized Englishman publishing in England, testifies to the rivenness of a discursive terrain that Said describes, elsewhere, as imperialist through and through.[3]
And it calls into question the fundamentally monologic model of discourse,
borrowed from the early Foucault, that Said deploys in *Orientalism*.

To help students struggle free of this model, I introduce pluralistic alternatives such as those elaborated in Mikhail Bakhtin's *The Dialogic Imagination*
and Raymond Williams's *Marxism and Literature*. In the light of these alternatives, colonial discourse takes its place in the larger discursive field as an
"authoritative" (Bakhtin 341) or a "dominant" (Williams 122) discourse: a strong
but unstable code undermined by its own contradictions and challenged by
Western and non-Western antagonists alike. Similarly, texts such as "Heart of
Darkness" can be seen not as cannons loaded with the murderous clichés of
colonial discourse but as battlefields that display the power of the dominant discourse, the weakening effect of the contradictions that emerge as it is deployed,
and the presence of important counterdiscourses.

To show that alternatives to the categories and politics of colonial discourse
were in fact thinkable in Conrad's day, I draw on historical studies that record the
discursive heterogeneity of the period. The final decades of the nineteenth century were indeed, Eric Hobsbawm writes, "the age of empire." But the eminent
British historian insists that anti-imperial agitation and "strong anti-imperial
[and] anti-colonial" traditions (70) could be found in the heart of the European
empires even at the moment of their greatest ascendency. Chapter 3 of his *Age
of Empire* traces both the climax of imperial expansion in the last decades of the
century and the domestic opposition the expansion provoked. A fuller picture of
the challenges to empire has yet to be pieced together from a range of sources.
When one goes to these sources, it becomes clear that in the India of the Mutiny
and the nascent Congress Party; in the Ireland of Home Rule agitation; in the
Africa of the Madhists, Arabi Bey, and Mwanga's rebellion; and in the innumerable small-scale wars of resistance chronicled by David Levering Lewis in *The
Race to Fashoda*, local peoples were already protesting with words and deeds
against imperial incursions and assumptions of superiority. These protests were
unevenly but emphatically audible in England, and while the majority of English
people were ready to back or passively assent to continued imperial rule, a vocal
minority challenged imperial motives, rhetoric, and practices. In many cases
these challenges took the form of calls for reform of colonial policy and for limited local autonomy, yet the challengers usually supported some form of imperialism or thought it was inevitable, given the terrific imbalance of power between
Western and non-Western communities and the ambitions of European govern-
ments and capitalists. But not always: we have published evidence that some
people were thinking the unthinkable.

Indeed, the debate over the "new imperialism" that raged through the
1890s led to an interrogation of virtually every aspect of the imperial project
and every element of the pro-imperialist argument, including the arguments

for racial or civilizational superiority. A record of this debate can be found in Bernard Porter's *Critics of Empire: British Radical Attitudes to Colonialism in Africa, 1895–1914*. Here we find voices protesting, in a manner very close to Conrad's, the capitalist imperialism of the chartered companies and the concessions, the waste and cruelty of the Scramble for Africa, and the whole vainglorious idea of the "civilizing mission." We are introduced as well to Englishmen and other Europeans who are quite capable of questioning the rhetoric of inferiority and imagining the independence of colonized peoples. The influence of anti-imperialist Little Englanders such as Richard Cobden ("Hindoostan must be ruled by those who live on that side of the globe" [qtd. in Porter 26]) is still being felt in the final decades of the nineteenth century. When Arab nationalists rebel in Egypt in 1881, Wilfred Blunt, an Englishman assigned to evaluating public opinion in Egypt, declares that the movement is "a patriotic movement, a movement of 'national regeneration,' aiming to achieve by a peaceful revolution what natural justice demands: 'Egypt for the Egyptians'" (Packenham 124). In 1899, the year "Heart of Darkness" is published, a Liberal MP responds to a Ugandan rebellion by proclaiming, in the House of Commons, that "the Ugandese have patriotism which we think is confined to Englishmen. They like their independence, they have a Government—it may be a bad Government, but they want it. They want to be Ugandese" (Porter 85). If such voices were being heard in Parliament, I suggest to my students, then surely Conrad was not confined, "as a creature of his time" (Said, *Culture* 30), in the "perfect closure" of an imperialistic discourse and horizon. Nor was it only his "exilic marginality" (24) as a Pole that made his criticism of imperialism (in an English novel published at the turn of the century first in an English journal and then by an English press) possible.

Having framed discussion of "Heart of Darkness" in this manner, I turn to the text itself. At what points in the novel, I ask my students, do we find the discourse of imperialism, with its proclamations of cultural and racial superiority, its exoticizing of colonial others, and its celebration of European expansion as a civilizing mission, most dramatically deployed? How, in these moments of its clearest deployment, do we find this discourse evaluated: is it corroborated or contested by other fictional events, images, or articulations? This question takes us to several crucial passages in the text: to the frame narrator's rhapsodic rehearsal of English imperial heroism, Kurtz's equally intoxicated depiction of the civilizing mission in his report to "the International Society for the Suppression of Savage Customs" (50), and Marlow's celebration of the accountant's efficiency. I direct attention as well to briefer eruptions of starkly orientalist representation and to the routine deployment of racist categories ("savage," "cannibals," "simple") and tropes (the African fireman who is like "a dog in a parody of breeches" [38]). Studying these passages gives students a sharper sense of what Said means by colonial discourse and of why Achebe finds "Heart of Darkness" so profoundly objectionable.

Studying them in context produces other effects. For in almost every case, one finds that the constructions of reality proposed in these passages are sharply criticized, or at least called into question, in the passages that follow. The frame narrator's imperial rhapsody is interrupted by Marlow's portentous rejoinder, "And this [England] also [. . .] has been one of the dark places of the earth" (9); and in the two narratives that follow, the first a reconstruction of Roman imperialism in England, the second the story of European imperialism in the Congo, the imperial venture is re-presented as violent, selfishly motivated, and culturally catastrophic. In a like manner, Kurtz's report, with its vision of European power and "Benevolence" (50), is undercut by its infamous postscript, "Exterminate all the brutes!"(51), a clear signal of European savagery, frustration, and unreadiness to rule. Marlow's celebration of the chief accountant's efficiency closes in a more muted fashion, with an implicit comment on the ethical unsavoriness of that virtue. The Accountant, it turns out, reacts with "gentle annoyance" when asked to share his shady space with a sick European colleague. And he goes on "making correct entries of perfectly correct transactions" while scores of Africans starve in the "grove of death" (22) some fifty feet from his door.

The flow of imperial discourse is checked and challenged even in individual sentences. Thus for instance the following sentence begins on a familiar exoticizing note but then pauses and rewrites its representation of African culture in a manner profoundly subversive to European projects of othering and inferiorizing. "Perhaps on some quiet night," Marlow begins, "the tremor of far-off drums, sinking, swelling, a tremor vast, faint; a sound weird, appealing, suggestive, and wild—and perhaps with as profound a meaning as the sound of bells in a Christian country" (23). Without reducing the sound of drums to the sound of bells or claiming to know what the drums signify, Marlow draws a blasphemous parallel: instilling the heathen drums with the pacific, domestic, and sacred connotations of church bells, he invests African culture with a profundity equal to that of European. Such a sentence models the fundamental syntax of "Heart of Darkness": its relentless interrogation of the tropes of colonial discourse.

It models as well the narrative and geographic trajectories of the novel. Said argues that "Heart of Darkness" communicates "the imperial attitude" through its "sheer historical momentum," the unrelenting "temporal forward movement" both of Marlow's journey and of his account. Conrad "wants us to see how Kurtz's great looting adventure, Marlow's journey up the river, and the narrative itself all share a common theme: Europeans performing acts of imperial mastery and will in (or about) Africa" (*Culture* 22, 23). It dramatizes and exemplifies "the assertive authority" (24) of these Europeans. But both Marlow's narrative and the journeys he relates are dramatically unsuccessful in the conventional imperial sense. Marlow asserts again and again the impossibility of mastering his African experiences and delivering them in consumable form to his English audience. He checks the forward momentum of his narrative repeatedly, sometimes in mid sentence. Furthermore, his account is a story of failure: he fails to rescue Kurtz, and Kurtz fails to establish a sustainable empire in the heart of Africa. "The district is closed to us for a time," the Manager concedes, reflecting on the chaos at the Inner Station (61). In this regard, the title of Conrad's first novel, *Almayer's Folly*, may be said to articulate the central theme and in its plot the trajectory of all his major colonial fiction. If Almayer's attempt at imperial assertion and mastery fails, so does Jim's (in "Lord Jim's Folly"), Kurtz's (in "Kurtz's Folly"), and Gould's (in "Gould's Folly").

We find this checking of imperial momentum even in a passage frequently interpreted as an attempt to exempt British imperialism from the general condemnation, a passage that serves as the epigraph to Said's *Culture and Imperialism*. "The conquest of the earth," Marlow declares,

> which mostly means the taking it away from those who have a different complexion or slightly flatter noses than ourselves, is not a pretty thing when you look into it too much. What redeems it is the idea only. An idea at the back of it, not a sentimental pretence but an idea; and an unselfish belief in the idea—something you can set up, and bow down before, and offer a sacrifice to. . . . (10)

This passage opens on a note of general condemnation, which, it should be observed, mocks the very idea that racial differences are more than skin deep. Then comes the apparent effort to draw a distinction between different sorts of imperialism, an evil, self-interested version and a purer, more idealistic, and therefore authentically civilized form. We should be prepared by now, however, for what happens next. Having drawn this distinction, Marlow pauses (the dash is a crucial diacritical mark in "Heart of Darkness") and proceeds to deconstruct it. Idealism, which is first offered as the marker of English imperialism's difference and superiority, both with regard to uglier forms of imperialism and to less civilized peoples, is now represented as a form of idol worship, a practice repeatedly identified in the novel with savagery and "unspeakable rites" (50). Imperial idealists, Conrad suggests, are not so different from the peoples they would "civilize"; indeed, in their insatiable appetite for conquest (Kurtz seems determined "to swallow all the air, all the earth, all the men before him" [59]) they are arguably less civilized than the cannibal crewmen of Marlow's steamboat, who at least possess a capacity for "restraint" (43).

I emphasize the anti-imperial arguments of "Heart of Darkness" not to clear the text of all the charges laid against it by Said and Achebe but to check the rush to dismissal that a cursory study of colonial theory seems to inspire in many students. To recall students to the cogency of Said's and Achebe's arguments, I turn discussion finally to the scene in which Kurtz attempts to rejoin the Africans "deep within the forest" (63). An all too familiar set of equations runs across this episode: the Africans are figures of "intense blackness," "monstrous," "fiend-like." Their leader, a "black figure [. . .] on long black legs, [with] long black arms," is an "it," not a "he" (63, 64). These particular locutions stand unchallenged in the pages that follow, bearing out Achebe's charge that "Heart of Darkness" is "a story in which the very humanity of black people is called into question" (259).[4]

Here as in other works, Conrad's argument against colonialism is based on both anticolonial and colonial premises. Sometimes the argument asserts Europeans' inadequacy for rule, sometimes the rights of non-Europeans to their space and culture. Sometimes it develops a kind of disenchanted argument from equality, in which colonizers and colonized alike are depicted as deeply flawed beings. But in scenes such as the one discussed above, Conrad figures colonial others as savages or worse and bases his opposition to colonialism on the claim that Europeans can only be contaminated by contact with those they seek to conquer.

This argument from contamination surfaces most dramatically when the novel takes on a Christian cast: first in Kurtz's report with its messianic enthusiasm and chillingly apocalyptic postscript and then in the forest scene where Marlow prevents Kurtz's potentially soul-destroying surrender to satanic forces. But the novel's evaluation of Christianity is characteristically complex. Perhaps it is to protest Christianity's imperial modes of thinking, I suggest to my students, that the novel makes what is perhaps its most audacious assault on Western assumptions of righteousness and superiority. What are we to make of the fact that Marlow is represented, at certain moments in the novel, as "a Buddha preaching in European clothes" (10)? And what are we to make of Marlow's recollection of the effects of his Eastern travels: "I had just returned to London after [. . .] a regular dose of the East [. . .] and I was [. . .] invading your homes, just as though I had got a heavenly mission to civilise you" (11)? One recognizes here a wry reversal of the trope of the civilizing mission: Marlow not only depicts that mission as intrinsically uncivilized—an act of uncouth invasion—but suggests as well that Europe might be more in need of civilizing than the East. The invocation of Buddhism may have a deeper purpose, for that tradition (familiar to Conrad not only through his journeys but also through the work of Schopenhauer and Alfred Russell Wallace) rejects at once the dualistic thinking that sponsors demonization and the traditions of militant, world-saving expansion that underwrote imperialism. Perhaps, in other words, the text's audacious representation of Marlow as a particular sort of cultural hybrid challenges colonial discourse and especially the religious discourse that infused and underwrote it.

In approaching "Heart of Darkness" in the manner sketched out above, I seek at once to honor postcolonial readings of the text and to revise these readings in a manner consistent with the values of postcolonial criticism. My argument is that the novel contributes, powerfully if imperfectly, to the anticolonial, antiracist positions Said and Achebe champion and testifies eloquently to the weakness of colonial discourse at the height of its power. Colonialism had, when Conrad wrote, little more than half a century yet to live. During this period, the counterdiscourses of its opponents grew ever more audible both in the colonies and in England, and the will to preserve the empire was undermined by metropolitan voices and movements as well as by colonial rebels. To emphasize the audibility of dissent and amplify metropolitan challenges to colonial legitimacy is especially important when teaching "Heart of Darkness" to Western students. It serves to remind them that the dissent of peoples beyond the borders but not the power of the West is audible (if only one will listen) and that domestic resistance to the formulas and forces that render life wretched for people elsewhere in the world is possible (if only one will make the effort).

NOTES

[1]While the "Criticism" section of the Norton Critical Edition of "Heart of Darkness" is badly in need of updating, the "Backgrounds and Sources" section provides an invaluable archive of such materials, including "Geography and Some Explorers," "The Congo Diary," and a number of letters. David Levering Lewis's *The Race to Fashoda* and Thomas Packenham's *The Scramble for Africa* provide detailed and harrowing accounts of European campaigns in central Africa at the end of the nineteenth century.

[2]See, for instance, Parry; Brantlinger, *Rule*; Fincham and Hooper; Hawkins, "Conrad's Critique." In the opening chapter of my book *Late Imperial Romance*, I argue that Conrad's novel sponsors a tradition of mid-century, North American novels of empire.

[3]See Geoffrey Galt Harpham's concise and cogent analysis of Said's argument in *One of Us: The Mastery of Joseph Conrad*. Harpham cites Said, from *Culture and Imperialism*, to the effect that Conrad's "*Western* view of the non-Western world [. . .] blind[s] him to other histories, other cultures, other aspirations." Noting that Said contradicts himself on this point, Harpham argues that in "Heart of Darkness," "two Europeans, Marlow and Kurtz, come to realize [. . .] that other people [have] lives and cultures not totally controlled by Europeans" (51).

[4]For qualified and carefully argued challenges to Achebe's reading of "Heart of Darkness," see Hawkins, "Issue"; Armstrong, *"Heart."*

Conrad and Professionalism

Jeffrey J. Williams

Regardless of the critical perspective one espouses, one would be hard pressed not to see Conrad's "yarns of the sea" as representations of imperialism. The adventurous seafaring life that Conrad is most famous for depicting is predicated on the seeming ubiquity of the European merchant navy, which was literally the vehicle of the great colonial empires of the late nineteenth century, particularly the British Empire. And, as Conrad declares with a sometimes jaded irony, the European colonial venture is driven not by humanistic impulses but by the profit-seeking search for exotic products, in *Lord Jim* for pepper and in "Heart of Darkness" for ivory. While the earlier criticism of Conrad focused more on literary issues, such as Conrad's impressionism or the journeys of his flawed heroes, contemporary criticism largely devolves on this historical context, debating whether Conrad is critical or supportive of imperialism and whether he resists or reproduces the racial biases implicit in it.

While the general historical context of imperialism is essential to understanding and teaching "Heart of Darkness" and "The Secret Sharer," there is a more specific context that decisively informs them and that has rarely been commented on: professionalism. The ideology of modern professionalism helps explain the motivations, actions, comportment, judgments, and loyalties of Conrad's primary characters. The characters that Conrad most privileges—Marlow and those with whom Marlow identifies, such as the unnamed auditors on the deck of the *Nellie* and some of the agents that he meets along his journey in "Heart of Darkness," and the narrator's double in "The Secret Sharer"—are crucially figured as professionals. They mutually recognize one another in their adherence to a professional code of conduct and sense of duty; in their common training; in their managerial roles; and also, somewhat surprisingly, in their distance from the profit of empire. And they set themselves apart from characters who do not belong in their professional cohort—not only the "natives" but ordinary deckhands and ships' mates, company owners, and rogue imperialists.

In broad strokes, these characters stand as representative figures of an intermediary, "professional" class, one that arose in the late nineteenth century, positioned between the owner class and ordinary workers in modern capitalist societies. This class encompasses not only lawyers and doctors but also military officers, sea captains, company agents, and educative personnel, who, in various ways, adopt the mantle of professional distinction. This view of Conrad's sea tales does not dispel or replace the larger context of imperialist capitalism but shows its internal class structure; imperialist capitalism requires such a class to manage the day-to-day operations of its far-flung enterprises—in the large military and civilian administrative staffs in India, Asia, and Africa as well as in those at home. In other words, Conrad's tales, though rarely set in England, reveal something of British class structure and its ideology. This view of Conrad is especially relevant in teaching; it adds a class dimension to the focus on imperialism that largely concentrates on racial divisions. It is also relevant in foregrounding issues of professionalism that still have bearing on us, particularly those of us involved in university education, which is the most prominent institutional channel inculcating professional behavior and granting professional credentials in contemporary society.

Let me provide some historical background. The late nineteenth century witnessed the rise and formalization of modern professions in England, much of Europe, and the United States. At the beginning of the century, professions were loosely defined, encompassing disparate groups of practitioners under the provenance of varying aristocratic and guild models without any overarching organizational structure. For instance, in England there were several different kinds of practitioners that we would now group under the auspices of professional medicine, including apothecaries, midwives, surgeons, and physicians. The British Medical Association (BMA) was founded in 1832 and solidified through the middle part of the century, particularly after the Medical Registration Act of 1858, which unified surgeons, apothecaries, and physicians into a single professional cohort (Parry and Parry 115; see also Macdonald 77–79). (Before this, and ironically in the light of present-day expectation, surgeons were considered hacks and physicians had the highest status.) Similarly, other professions, such as law, engineering, or education, established organizations, formalized education and training, and codified their credentializing processes by the end of the century.

Professions arose to fulfill a need of the bureaucratic organization of modern capitalist societies, creating a new middle class positioned between the traditional division of the proletarian or working class and the ruling class. As the sociologist Terence Johnson defines them, professions are "part of a class which carries out the global functions of capital without owning the means of production (therefore distinct in relation to a capitalist class), while at the same time and in various ratios carrying out the functions of the collective labourer—they are then both labourer and non-labourer, exploited and exploiters" (104). Barbara Ehrenreich and John Ehrenreich have called this class professional-managerial to correct the vague attribution of a middle class and to denote its role in managing bureaucratic institutions that organize and control contemporary capitalist societies. The professional-managerial class typically attains its status through education and professional training, culminating in the award of professional credentials, which distinguish it from the ordinary working classes, although it does not own the means of capital.

In the standard sociological view, professions work by attributing a social need, by establishing a body of knowledge and lore, by claiming a disinterested or altruistic purpose (a calling), and by credentialing those who can fulfill that need (see Larson 40–47). They thus garner a monopolistic control on the service of that need. In one account, professionalism

> is a strategy for controlling an occupation in which colleagues, who are in a formal sense equal, set up a system of self-government. This involves restriction of entry to the occupation through the control of education, training and the process of qualification. Another aspect is the exercise of formal and informal management of members' conduct in respects which are defined as relevant to the collective interests of the occupation. [. . .] Professionalism developed as an ideology of the middle class and was associated with the high-status ethic of the gentleman. It has been an ideology of groups concerned to achieve upward assimilation by a process of collective mobility and by exercising closure against any parvenu groups attempting to follow in their footsteps.   (Parry and Parry 118)

To show how this process works, let us take again the example of medicine. MDs answer a public need: health. They go through medical school to attain a formal body of knowledge that can be attained only there. Their training is also informal, in codes of conduct emblematized by the Hippocratic oath. Further, doctors claim an altruistic purpose and disinterest in simple profit; they claim to be motivated by the higher calling of improving health, beyond worldly goals like money. They receive credentials from a professional organization—the BMA in England or the AMA in the United States—after passing through sanctioned training. And their control is enforced by law—for instance, neither a clerk at Osco nor you, however capable, can prescribe medicine, and barbers may not perform surgery. The professional organization of medicine controls all the disparate tasks a doctor might perform, from dispensing birth control to performing brain surgery, from checking your tonsils to talking about your oedipal complex. The organization therefore has a monopoly on the service of health, staving off other groups, such as midwives. This monopoly confers not only material rewards but also status—a quasi gentility attained not through birth, the traditional aristocratic channel, but through credentials, the more democratic channels of education and professional training.

How does this background bear on "Heart of Darkness"? It helps explain Marlow's sense of duty; his concern for a code of conduct; and, despite his dutiful service to imperialism, his separateness from the imperial project. Oddly enough, in avowing professional standards, he disavows material gain. It also helps explain his relation to and judgment of those he encounters, his identification with other agents and sea captains and his contempt for white Europeans who do not adhere to professional codes.

Marlow defines his work as a calling—as he puts it in the frame on the deck of the *Nellie*, he has "followed the sea"—which he proudly shares with many of the other characters (8, 9). He is adamant that he does not do his job for venal motives—money—disdaining those who do, such as the "rather too fleshy" Englishman he comes across on the caravan inland (23) and those in the Eldorado Exploring Expedition. However, neither does he do his job for some grand missionary motive, for the sake of Christianity or Western civilization, "weaning those ignorant millions from their horrid ways," as his aunt assumes. He declares this view naively "out of touch" (16). Rather, he does it for his dedication to a craft (sailing) and a guild (of seamen), driven particularly by his position of responsibility as a captain, overseeing the practice of his profession. He is so committed that he is restless while awaiting a command at the start of his tale. This impatience is remarkable, since one would normally expect an ordinary sailor to enjoy some R and R; however, Marlow seems to live for his profession, at points risking life and health for it.

Although Marlow serves the imperial project, his ironic detachment from it is apparent in many places, notably in the scene where he travels inland with the fleshy Englishman, who, when Marlow asks him why he is in Africa, responds, "To make money, of course" (23). Marlow is contemptuous of him, describing him harshly as obese and fainting and so unable to behave with appropriate professional pride that he has to be carried, which impedes their travel. Marlow's attitude is especially strange, because, as he himself disabuses his aunt, imperialism operates not for humanitarian reasons but for profit, so we would expect someone coming to Africa to endure such hardship with the express promise of making a fortune. But, again, Marlow's loyalty is single-mindedly to his profession and cohort; he explicitly rejects ordinary worldly interests like money.

Marlow privileges the characters who share his professional bearing, such as his auditors in the frame, on the deck of the *Nellie*, who mutually heed the calling of the sea and who are named only by their professional positions—the Lawyer, the Director, the Captain. Though they have risen to different positions, they all share a similar class identification and origin (the Director might seem to present a different case, but, a seaman in his youth, he affirms the promise of upward mobility of the professional class). Similarly, many of the characters whom Marlow encounters over the course of the journey are also unnamed except by their professional roles—the Doctor, the first agent, the Accountant, and so on. Like Marlow, they seem uninterested in gross profit or in any blatantly ideological or religious aspect of imperialism, but they share a tacit code of duty and calling. In a striking portrait during his journey downriver, Marlow admires how the Accountant has retained his professional comportment and demeanor: even while living in the jungle, he wears pressed clothes and carries on his work efficiently and, in a word, professionally (21). In this, they show what the sociologist Magali Sarfatti Larson, in her classic work on professions, *The Rise of Professionalism*, calls the subculture of professions, which regulates conduct through informal as well as formal control. "Heart of Darkness" portrays and privileges this subculture.

That these characters are unnamed except by their professional functions invokes the terrain of allegory, and "Heart of Darkness" indeed has striking allegorical resonances. Among other details, places are unnamed, and Marlow descends to a mysteriously dark, unknown spot on the map. Criticism has, reasonably enough, taken these tags to signal the novel's allegorical status, as a descent into the unknown or evil or as a psychic journey of discovery. However, in the continual coding by professional position—captain, agent, accountant, doctor, and so on—the novel might be seen instead as an allegory of professionalism, of the testing and behavior of professional men. (In "Narrative Calling," I call the novel an allegory of narrative, focusing on Marlow's compulsion to gather stories of Kurtz along the journey and to tell his spellbinding tale on the *Nellie*, but I also argue that narrative functions as the currency of the shared professional bond of these men of the sea.)

Marlow and his cohort obviously set themselves apart from the natives, who, as Chinua Achebe ("Image") and other have pointed out, are dehumanized. But Marlow also sets himself apart from ship hands and other workers, who are barely represented, shown scuttling about doing quotidian work. He also distinguishes himself from the company executive in the "whited sepulchre" (13), for whom he has contempt as a stuffed shirt insulated from the hands-on, concrete operation of the imperial venture. In other words, the novel adjudges its characters not according to a simple dichotomy between white colonialists and those of color who are colonized; the dichotomy is inflected by their class as well as racial position. A central line of distinction is predicated on professionalism.

Further, in his own cohort of imperial agents, Marlow judges negatively those who do not live up to professional standards of conduct, such as those in the Eldorado Exploring Expedition or the fleshy Englishman. Thus "Heart of Darkness" turns on the depiction of good and bad professionals. The problem presented by Kurtz—which haunts Marlow and which draws the enthralled interest of his auditors (such that they miss the tide)—is Kurtz's transgressing professional detachment and remove, by going native and garnering excessive profit. His problem, in other words, is not his failing the interests of empire, for he is an extraordinarily productive agent; rather, it is his failing the code of professionalism. His methods are incorrect.

The tale Marlow tells, then, is a cautionary moral tale of professional temptation and what professionals shouldn't do. While the bearing of the good professionals might take part in the "Victorian ethic" that Ian Watt foregrounds in *Conrad in the Nineteenth Century* (148–51), their sense of duty is not a religious or humanitarian one but a professional one—responsible to those in their cohort, not to those outside it. It is thus not simply a general Victorian ethic that governs their behavior but the specific ethic or ideology of their class. Marlow's tale is also a reaffirmation of the professional code and its detachment from worldly corruptions and the dirt of imperialism. This exemplifies a certain uneasiness if not contradiction in professionalism. As Bruce Robbins argues in *Secular Vocations*, professions have an ambivalent relation to their worldly role. On the one hand, they describe their interests as altruistic (a calling, for the sake of duty itself) and detached from worldly interests and profit, almost in the sense of a religious vocation. On the other hand, they claim an essential role in the efficient operation of modern capitalism—here, in cultivating the smooth running of trade and sea transport.

In "The Secret Sharer," the context of professionalism helps explain the narrator's otherwise strange action to hide the outlaw. The narrator identifies with him in part through their common training—that both are "Conway boys" stamps them as brothers in a fraternity—and sense of professional duty, which is the sharer's defense when he claims his action was to repair the captain's not fulfilling his duty ("I assure you he never gave the order" [47]). Paralleling Marlow's sympathy for Kurtz in "Heart of Darkness" and for Jim in *Lord Jim*, the narrator's professional identification with his sharer overrides a normal moral condemnation, or that moral framework is reconfigured according to professionalist codes: the sharer justly killed the deckhand for impeding the proper functioning and order of the ship. Like Kurtz or Jim, he is a fallen professional rather than a criminal. Also, the narrator explicitly disidentifies with the captain of the *Sephora*; though he violates what one would assume is a standard of professionalism, in a sense we could say that the narrator and his double both represent the rise of the new professionals, supplanting the lax, earlier model of professionalism of the *Sephora* captain. While this tale may reasonably be read as focusing on the question of narcissistic identity or homosociality, a significant facet of its sharing is the bond of professional training and identification, situated in the specific historical context I have described. In fact, male homosociality plays a large part in the professional subculture that Conrad depicts.

Given this historical evidence, why has the class reading of "Heart of Darkness" and "The Secret Sharer" been largely ignored? One simple explanation is that imperialism is indeed a major, explicit theme and has yet to be exhausted. One less benign explanation is that we avoid such a reading because it uncomfortably exposes our own class position, one that carries substantial ambivalence if not denial (we live in a classless society, all in the same middle class). Ian Glenn goes so far as to argue that, despite common views, "Heart of Darkness" "survives, not so much because of its early treatment of colonialism, nor on account of its dramatization of the clash between nineteenth-century virtue and twentieth-century decadence, but because of a presentation of the class ambivalence of many Western intellectuals in the twentieth century that has held an unanalyzed power and fascination" (253).

Modifying Glenn, I would speculate that part of our identification, as professors and university students who might strive to be professionals, is with Conrad's dwelling on the workings of professional culture. We take pride in our work and control who joins the professional circle. We claim an altruistic vista—literary knowledge—beyond the fetters of worldly gain, at the same time claiming a worldly relevance and therefore value for our credentials and services. As most of Conrad's professional characters eschew the stain of imperialism while doing its bidding, we eschew the material role of higher education as job training, espousing the higher and more edifying values of literature while in actuality doing personnel work for postmodern corporations—credentialing people for white-collar jobs, one hopes, rather than for positions at McDonald's. So, in teaching Conrad's tales, we might be teaching about our own class position and professional desires, codes, and controls.

Teaching "Heart of Darkness" after New Historicism

Mark A. Eaton

> Fiction is history, human history, or it is nothing. But it is also more than that; it stands on firmer ground, being based on the reality of forms and the observation of social phenomena, whereas history is based on documents, and the reading of print and handwriting— on second-hand impression. Thus fiction is nearer truth. But let that pass. A historian may be an artist too, and a novelist is a historian, the preserver, the keeper, the expounder, of human experience.
>
> —Conrad, *Notes on Life and Letters*

Drawing on a familiar distinction between fictional and historical narratives, Conrad inverts the usual hierarchy that associates history with facts, reality; truth and fiction with lies, fantasy, falsehood (17). My dictionary defines fiction as a "lie" or, alternatively, as a "literary work whose content is produced by the imagination and is not necessarily based on fact." For Conrad, though, fiction actually comes closer to the truth of human experience than history: history is based on secondhand impressions, on previous documents, whereas fiction relies on "the observation of social phenomena." Conrad attests to the idea that, as Fredric Jameson puts it, "history is inaccessible to us except in textual form, and that our approach to it and to the Real itself necessarily passes through its prior textualization, its narrativization in the political unconscious" (35). Conrad also acknowledges that fiction depends on what he calls "the reality of forms," which I take to mean that fiction is one of the textual forms that provides access to history as lived experience. Indeed, fiction is still historical even if it is not based on actual events, for it always derives from the author's experience. Jameson would add, however, that both fictional and historical narratives are in the same boat: they are textual representations of history. And just as historical narratives are not a transparent window on history, so too fiction does not provide direct, unmediated access to the real.

These are among the many issues explored by new-historicist scholars in literary studies. In their introduction to *New Literary Study*, Jeffrey N. Cox and Larry J. Reynolds have written that new historicism strives "to reconnect text and context, without either allowing the text to exist transhistorically apart from the world, or reducing the text to a mere falsification of a reality that precedes it: that is, the text must be conceived as a material *fact* but the power of fiction must not be reduced to the ability to lie about social realities" (13). Literary fiction, in this sense, exists as a material fact in the world but also represents the world. Far from falsifying or lying about social reality, fiction "reflects it in a mediated way such that aesthetic form is a sedimentation of content" (Adorno 6). New historicism thus supports Conrad's statement that fiction is a form of history, if not his assertion that fiction is nearer truth.

The term *new historicism* was first used by Stephen Greenblatt in the early 1980s and has since gained widespread currency as the name for, not a school of criticism exactly, but a certain set of assumptions shared by a wide variety of critics about the relations between authors and texts and the larger culture they inhabit (Veeser xi). At the most basic level, new historicism explores how myriad historical forces—social, economic, political, and aesthetic—affect the writing and reading of literary texts. It also challenges the traditional view that these historical forces are only so much background material, helpful but not essential to the task of interpreting the text itself. For new historicists, the text itself is intimately bound up with the complex dynamics of culture and history, instead of floating free in some autonomous aesthetic realm, as it was sometimes characterized by formalist critics. According to Greenblatt, "the work of art is the product of a negotiation between a creator or class of creators, equipped with a complex, communally shared repertoire of conventions, and the institutions and practices of a society" (*Learning* 158). He is careful not to downplay artists; he admits elsewhere that literary works are "intensely marked by the creative intelligence and private obsessions of individuals" (*Negotiations* vii).

New historicism can also be seen as part of a general turn to history that "now involves all areas of literary study," including pedagogical approaches to literature (Cox and Reynolds 3). While formalist approaches taught students to analyze the complexities of literary form, they tended to isolate literary texts from history and politics. Formalist approaches to "Heart of Darkness" now seem particularly egregious, especially if they exclude any mention of colonialism or ignore its many images of suffering and brutality. "High school teachers and college professors who have discussed this book in thousands of classrooms over the years," Adam Hochschild contends, have "cast *Heart of Darkness* loose from its historical moorings," perhaps in part because they did not fully realize the "genocidal scale of the killing in Africa at the turn of the century" (143). Another critic concurs that teachers at all levels "are going to have to approach Conrad's work with a renewed willingness to read historically" and ask tough questions about its vexed relation to imperialism (Murfin 232).

Teaching "Heart of Darkness" after new historicism means coming to terms with the ways in which Conrad mediates history in writing a fictionalized account of his experiences in Africa. "Heart of Darkness" is an exemplary text to teach historically because it allows students to see not only how Conrad's literary practice is grounded in the observation of social phenomena but also how such observation depends on a perspective or way of seeing that is itself historically contingent. Certainly the novella offers a critique of European imperialism in King Leopold's Congo, but this critique does not mean Conrad is immune to the presumptions and prejudices about Africa in his time. To go beyond merely affirming the obvious fact that he draws on his experiences in

Africa, students need to consider how those experiences were transmuted aesthetically. Conrad creates two persona-narrators to tell the story, for one thing, and he calls attention to the difficulty of interpreting such a tale when he suggests that in Marlow's case "the meaning of an episode was not inside like a kernel but outside, enveloping the tale" (9).

Conrad's notoriously difficult prose style presents problems for some of my students, so I spend five class sessions on "Heart of Darkness" and move very slowly through the text, starting with a careful examination of the frame: Where exactly is the *Nellie* anchored? Who is the first narrator and what does he think about imperialism? When does Marlow begin his tale, and when does he suddenly break off? These are elementary questions, to be sure, but the answers aren't necessarily obvious to everyone, and I suspect that even my best students benefit from a thorough review of plot details. Like all great works, "Heart of Darkness" repays careful, sustained attention over successive readings. By foregrounding the problems and possibilities of narration itself in my approach to the novella, I try to remind students that events from the past are accessible either through human memory or through various texts. The novella thus provides a pedagogical opportunity to practice the new-historicist maxim that we must consider both "the historicity of texts and the textuality of history" (Montrose 20).

Whereas many of Conrad's contemporaries regarded the project of empire building with, in Edward Said's words, "optimism, affirmation, and serene confidence" (*Culture* 187), Conrad himself cast doubt on the integrity of that project by revealing the underlying profit motive that drives it. In "Heart of Darkness," he undercuts the idealistic rhetoric of imperialism from the start of the novel by employing a subtle critical irony against his own narrators. In a long passage at the beginning of the book, for instance, the unnamed first narrator waxes eloquent about England's great explorers: "all the men of whom the nation is proud." With sword and torch in hand, these men carried "a spark of the sacred fire" of civilization to every corner of the earth, planting "the seed of Commonwealths, the germ of Empires" (8). Students may not detect the optimism, affirmation, and supreme confidence of this passage without prompting, so I ask them to contemplate whether the narrator is being overly nostalgic and hyperbolic in his praise. In order to understand Conrad's critique of imperialism, I think we must first discern the disparity between such puffed-up rhetoric and the actual practices of imperialism.

Marlow deflates that rhetoric by relativizing the concept of civilization itself. "And this also," he says, "has been one of the dark places of the world," explaining that "when the Romans came" to England, it must have seemed to them "the very end of the world" (9). Later he acknowledges that imperialism "is not a pretty thing when you look into it too much." Even though he clings to the possibility that the "idea at the back of it" is noble, he knows full well what the empire looks like close up: "just robbery with violence, aggravated murder on a great scale, and men going at it blind" (10). In a passage Conrad cut from the manuscript, he wrote disparagingly of the "pretty fictions" used to persuade people that imperialism had a "philanthropic basis" (10n). Marlow too exposes the "philanthropic pretence" of imperialism as a pretty fiction (20).

In discussions of Marlow's arrival in Africa and his subsequent journey to the Inner Station, I emphasize the historical dimensions of Conrad's extremely unsettling picture of the Congo under King Leopold's rule. The resources for placing "Heart of Darkness" in historical context are readily available. The Norton Critical Edition includes over 150 pages of information—twice as many as the novella itself—about the Congo and Conrad's involvement there in a section titled "Backgrounds and Sources." While the section title seems to subscribe to a notion that history is merely background rather than intricately woven into the text, the range of material included allows students to assess what aspects of the Congo are highlighted in (or left out of) "Heart of Darkness." Through a careful reading of contemporary documents about the Congo, students learn how the situation in Africa at the time was more than just context; it also clearly informs the content and even infuses the book's form, since retrospective narration is the norm in eyewitness accounts. I break students into several groups and ask them to report back on one of the historical documents, such as George Washington Williams's "Report upon the Congo-State" (1890) and King Leopold's "The Sacred Mission of Civilization" (1898). From these reports, students gain a better sense of how the rhetoric of civilizing the natives was propagated despite contradictory information about what was going on. To indicate how King Leopold's civilizing mission could have been perceived as anything other than pure propaganda, I put on an overhead projector a passage from Hegel's *The Philosophy of History* that expresses the prevailing nineteenth-century view that Africa possessed neither culture nor history because it remained stuck in an infantile state of primitivism, while Europe had undergone a slow, progressive march toward civilization.

The contrast Conrad stages in the novella between rhetoric and reality culminates, of course, in Kurtz's pamphlet. Commissioned by the International Society for the Suppression of Savage Customs, the pamphlet offers a long "peroration"—seventeen pages of "close writing," we're told—on the benevolence of European colonists. But these lofty sentiments are rendered moot by the scribbled afterthought, added apparently much later: "Exterminate all the brutes!" (50, 51). Hochschild claims that Kurtz is based on Leon Rom, who became station chief at Stanley Falls shortly after Conrad left Africa. Whether or not Conrad met Rom in the course of his travels in Africa (Hochschild argues persuasively that he did), the author may well have read an account of Rom published in the *Saturday Review*, a magazine Conrad read regularly. This article, which appeared just before Conrad resumed work on his novella, disclosed that Rom surrounded his hut with the severed heads of African rebels (Hochschild 145). Conrad's Kurtz, in any case, is a fictional portrait of a Rom-like station chief; he is an enigmatic figure who embodies Europe's noble ideals but at the same time reveals the horror at the "heart of darkness." As a kind of composite character for European colonizers, Kurtz is a compelling example of what Conrad could do with the information at his disposal, whether he observed it directly or picked it up from other sources. But if Kurtz demonstrates the depths of evil to which some colonizers sank, he obviously conveys an ambiguous truth, for as Brook Thomas astutely points out, Marlow ironically feels compelled to lie about him in the final pages: "In a world in which the truth that Marlow tells about civilized Europe is expressed through a lie, it is no wonder that Conrad claimed that fiction is nearer to truth than history. [. . .] Conrad's story proves to be truer than history, not in its explicit statements but in its forms" (242).

Depending on how much time I've spent analyzing the details of the text and placing it in historical context, I usually try to discuss, in fairly broad terms, the book's literary-critical history. Convinced that students benefit from knowing something about the interpretive frames through which "Heart of Darkness" has been read, I provide a brief overview of how recent historical and postcolonial approaches differ from formalist and psychological ones. I've also found Chinua Achebe's withering attack on the book's canonical status helpful in showing students what is at stake—what can be at stake, anyway—in literary studies. Students are often surprised and challenged by his scathing indictment of what he sees as Conrad's ethnocentric perspective on Africa. Achebe rightly points out that Africa appears as a kind of backdrop and that Africans are not individuated in the novella. Yet surely he overstates his case when he asserts that Conrad "celebrates this dehumanization" of Africans ("Image" 257). If Conrad's critical irony allows us to perceive the narrative point of view as ideological, then we cannot simply equate that view with his own, however imbricated the author may be in Marlow's perspective. While Marlow does indeed call into question "the very humanity of black people," as Achebe alleges, he does so in a passage where he is trying to affirm their humanity (259).

Literary criticism leads us back, as it should, to the text, in particular to a well-known passage that is crucial to my argument about Conrad's use of critical irony. In a moment that is at once highly self-conscious and fatally unaware, Marlow says, "We are accustomed to look upon the shackled form of a conquered monster, but there—there you could look at a thing monstrous and free. It was unearthly and the men were. . . . No they were not inhuman. Well, you know that was the worst of it—this suspicion of their not being inhuman. It would come slowly to one" (37). Slowly, indeed. Marlow is about to say that they are inhuman when it suddenly occurs to him that they are in fact human. But he does not—cannot—express this recognition in positive terms; instead, he uses a double negative. Now strictly speaking, a double negative implies a positive; Marlow means that they are human. Yet plainly that is not how he says it; he says rather that they are not inhuman, which doesn't necessarily imply that they are inhuman, only that the fact of their humanity is precisely what bothers him, what he feels necessary to acknowledge in a somewhat indirect, backhanded way. The passage reveals his latent racism even though he ostensibly questions the basis of racism (i.e., the repugnant view that blacks are not human). Marlow's double negative shows the strain of an incipient self-/ consciousness about race in someone whose views are still mostly inflected/ with a racist ideology.

Having read Achebe's essay and recognized Marlow's latent racism, students understandably want to know: What did Conrad himself think about Africa and Africans? Here again new historicism is helpful in training us to think about the force of ideology, particularly about whether authors, and by extension texts themselves, are potentially subversive or mostly contained by the dominant culture. As H. Aram Veeser remarks, "every act of unmasking, critique, and opposition uses the tools it condemns and risks falling prey to the practice it exposes" (xi). Recent critics have realized the mistake of insisting on a false choice between subversion and containment, since literature's relation to society is after all much more complex than these stark alternatives suggest. In reading "Heart of Darkness" through the lens of new historicism, one needs to stress the contingency of all accounts of the Congo, including Conrad's fictionalized account. In his book *Culture and Imperialism* (1993), Said provides an admirably balanced discussion of Conrad's views: "Conrad does not give us the sense that he could imagine a fully realized alternative to imperialism, [. . .] and because he seemed to imagine that European tutelage was a given, he could not foresee what would take place when it came to an end" (25). "As a creature of his time," he continues, "Conrad could not grant the natives their freedom, despite his severe critique of the imperialism that enslaved them" (30). Even bearing in mind the dominant view of Africa at the turn of the century, Said refuses to let Conrad off the hook for his illiberal notions about Africans. This judgment amounts to more than just a banal recognition that Conrad was a creature of his time. Students are often quick to excuse authors for almost any view, no matter how objectionable, on the grounds that they lived in a less enlightened time. "Heart of Darkness" can help direct students to a much more subtle understanding of how ideology works, not in the older false-consciousness sense of blinding Conrad to what he should see, but in the post-Althusserian sense of allowing him to see what he did.

Students appreciate Conrad's critique of colonialism better if they realize that cultural relativism was not the dominant view, although it was available in the emergent anthropological discourse of the period. "By the turn of the century," James Clifford has argued, the notion of culture as a single evolutionary process of progress began to lose credibility, and "a new ethnographic conception of culture became possible." Culture came to be seen "in the plural, suggesting a world of separate, distinctive, and equally meaningful ways of life" (*Predicament* 93). This conception was not likely the one that Conrad took with him to the Congo. For even among those who were highly critical of imperialism, European superiority remained largely unquestioned, as did the commonplace distinction between "their barbarism" and "our civilization" (A. White, "Conrad" 197). Perhaps Conrad's greatest achievement, Said avers, lies in demonstrating precisely the historicity of his culture's ideas and practices: "Since Conrad *dates* imperialism, shows its contingency, records its illusions and tremendous violence and waste, he permits his later readers to imagine something other than an Africa carved up into dozens of European colonies, even if, for his own part, he had little notion of what that Africa might be" (*Culture* 26). Because the horizon of possibilities has been enlarged, let us say, by living through the last half century of what we have come to call postcolonialism, our students may well be in a position to see, if not more, then at least in a different light, some of the things that Conrad shows us in his remarkable novel about colonial Africa.

Exploring Characterization in "Heart of Darkness"

Avrom Fleishman

Teachers of Conrad's "Heart of Darkness" may become so preoccupied with its political challenges that they are led to neglect more basic narrative issues like characterization. Yet attention to such basics can help frame if not dispel the work's intractability. Marlow's voyage into the dark continent is ostensibly a passage through geographic space, although it has also been interpreted as a journey into the interior of human nature and of his own consciousness. It is, as well, a trip through a populated landscape and takes the form of a series of encounters with men and women, as individuals and groups, climaxing in his meeting with Kurtz and culminating in an interview with Kurtz's Intended. These last two encounters have been fully commented on, and the characterization of both Kurtz and his fiancée has been well studied. But Conrad's methods of characterizing the colonists and natives in the Congo, the Englishmen in the frame narrative, and the Belgians in the early phase of the story require further attention, both because they display a mastery—almost a repertoire—of such methods and because neglecting them leads to misapprehensions about the novella's structure and even its themes.

The sequence of encounters begins at the company office with the old doctor who examines Marlow's physical and, perfunctorily, mental fitness for the job. The style is in the tradition of *satire* of opinionated doctors, but there are hints of hidden depths: the "unshaven little man in a threadbare coat like a gaberdine, with his feet in slippers," whom Marlow thinks a "harmless fool," is capable of remarks like "the changes take place inside, you know" and "What you say is rather profound, and probably erroneous" (15). Marlow asks if he's an "alienist" (in a time before the term *psychiatrist*), with overtones suggesting that the doctor's specialty is aliens and alienation. His scientific detachment—"interesting" is his repeated watchword—irritates Marlow, who anticipates that his counsel, "Avoid irritation," will prove hard to follow (15).

Another version of the ominous hints of and distant observers' indifference to the Congo's horrors is the *allegorical* portrayal of the office receptionists as avatars of the Fates (or at least two of that triad): "An eerie feeling came over me. She seemed uncanny and fateful. Often far away there I thought of these two, guarding the door of Darkness, knitting black wool as for a warm pall, one introducing, introducing continuously to the unknown, the other scrutinising the cheery and foolish faces with unconcerned old eyes" (14). This phase of the story also offers a flash-forward to a Congo encounter with another monitory personality, the former captain of Marlow's riverboat, in the grotesque mode: "nobody seemed to trouble much about Fresleven's remains, till I got out [there] and stepped into his shoes. [. . .] when an opportunity offered at last to meet my predecessor, the grass growing through his ribs was tall enough to hide his bones. They were all there" (13). Marlow keeps accurate accounts of his predecessors, those who've preceded him in the journey all must take.

Progress upriver halts first at the company's outer station, scene of apparently random blasting for a railroad and of the grove of death for exhausted laborers, and personalized in the figure of the company's chief accountant. He is rendered with a listing of details typical of *realist* narrative: "I saw a high starched collar, white cuffs, a light alpaca jacket, snowy trousers, a clean necktie, and varnished boots. No hat. Hair parted [. . .]." Neutral observation allows, however, for moral judgment: "His appearance was certainly that of a hairdresser's dummy; but in the great demoralisation of the land he kept up his appearance. That's backbone" (21). The accountant's guarded hints of Kurtz's achievements and prospects, while professing hatred of the "savages" whose nearby "babble" interrupts his labors, provide a sketch of the discoveries Marlow is to make (22).

After a two-hundred-mile safari, parallel to the unnavigable river, to the company's Central Station, the narrator's first impressions of the company manager are understandably—he's not even invited to sit down—couched in negatives: "He was a common trader, nothing more. He was obeyed, yet he inspired neither love nor fear, nor even respect. He inspired uneasiness. [. . .] Not a definite mistrust—just uneasiness—nothing more. [. . .] He had no genius for organising. [. . .] He had no learning, and no intelligence. His position had come to him—why? Perhaps because he was never ill" (24–25). *Description by negation* (as in medieval definitions of God) functions here to establish a character type that will include most of the colonists, culminating in Marlow's perception of Kurtz as "hollow at the core" (58). (This imagery was later magnified in T. S. Eliot's poem "The Hollow Men," on the negativity of modern culture, which employs "Mistah Kurtz—he dead" as its epigraph.)

Marking time at the station while awaiting repair materials for the riverboat, Marlow meets the good, bad, and ugly colonist varieties. The boilermaker repairman is approved as a "good worker"—a Conradian gnomon for moral worth—while displaying even more charming attributes in a *comic* account. Beyond perfect baldness combined with a waist-length beard, "He was a widower with six young children [. . .] and the passion of his life was pigeon-flying. [. . . At work] he would tie up that beard of his in a kind of white serviette he brought for the purpose. It had loops to go over his ears" (31–32). In anticipation of the repair rivets, he joins Marlow in a jig and caper on the deck, answered by jungle noises "as though an ichthyosaurus had been taking a bath of glitter in the great river" (32). The dismal nature of the scene and the disappointments of inadequate supplies don't deter these competent craftsmen for a whoop and a lark and a degree of mild absurdity, echoed by primeval reverberations. The comic scene can be thought of as acting out the cliché "whistling in the dark."

The bad is well represented in the person of the "brickmaker" (28; a clerk with that responsibility rather than a manual worker). His moral status is subtly manifested in personal attributes: "He was a first-class agent, young, gentlemanly, a bit reserved, with a forked little beard and a hooked nose" (26). The "young aristocrat" is outwardly debonair, but his attributes—forked beard, hooked nose—associate him with the diabolic (according to the formula "the devil is a gentleman"). His discourse, during a session of "pumping me," reveals him to be a "perfectly shameless prevaricator"—which his appearance further supports ("His little eyes glittered like mica discs" [27]). At last this peculiar mixture of allegory and *parody* becomes explicit: the brick maker is labeled a "papier-mâché Mephistopheles" (29) hostile to what he supposes Marlow represents, "the new gang—the gang of virtue" (28).

The ugly is equally well represented by the manager's uncle, leader of the Eldorado Exploring Expedition, whom Marlow one evening overhears plotting with his nephew against Kurtz. The uncle "resembled a butcher in a poor neighbourhood, and his eyes had a look of sleepy cunning. He carried his fat paunch with ostentation on his short legs, and during the time his gang infested the station he spoke to no one but his nephew" (33). The gross features are not merely ugly but, by time-honored convention, marks of depravity, as is revealed when he with satisfaction predicts Kurtz's demise: "'Ah! My boy, trust to this—I say, trust to this.' I saw him extend his short flipper of an arm for a gesture that took in the forest, the creek, the mud, the river [. . .]" (35). Conrad may be excused for mixing his or Marlow's metaphors: porcine, insect, reptilian, and piscine associations ("fat paunch," "infested," "flipper") maintain a consistent register of animality. The characterization mode here, *metaphoric abstraction*, is capable of pointing the features while broadly limning the subject's grossness.

Marlow's subsequent encounters at the Inner Station, with the harlequin-costumed Russian disciple of Kurtz, and on his return to Brussels, with a company representative and a family member, are sufficiently vivid and well known to require no further comment. More problematic are his relationships with a series of native individuals and groups. Those receiving extended commentary include the riverboat's cannibal crew. Their headman is first described: "a young broad-chested black, severely draped in dark-blue fringed cloths, with fierce nostrils and his hair all done up artfully in oily ringlets" (42). His request for any local natives captured in the coming fray (they themselves hail from a remote tribe) spurs the anthropologist in Marlow to cultural speculations: "Yes—I looked at them as you would on any human being with a curiosity of their impulses, motives, capacities, weaknesses, when brought to the test of an inexorable physical necessity. Restraint! What possible restraint? Was it superstition, disgust, patience, fear—or some kind of primitive honour?" (43).

This often cited passage on the crew's inexplicable failure to assuage its hunger with the white men they outnumber thirty to five has proved equally beguiling to readers and critics, but some clarity may be gained from attention to the characterization mode: "They were big powerful men with not much capacity to weigh the consequences, with courage, with strength, even yet, though their skins were no longer glossy and their muscles no longer hard"—

because of prolonged malnutrition (42–43). These physical characteristics, and the implied judgment of intellectual capacity, contrast with those of the white bosses: "just then I perceived—in a new light, as it were—how unwholesome the pilgrims [Marlow's tag for the colonists] looked" (43). Putting these data together—the tall physique, the courage, the once glossy muscles, and the impressive dark-blue costume—there's no difficulty in recognizing the time-honored *rhetorical topos* of the noble savage.

In the intellectual tradition known as primitivism, a doctrine appearing consistently in Western philosophy and literature from ancient times to the present, ostensibly uncivilized peoples are regarded as holding advantages over the products of sophisticated and corrupt civilizations. They are ruled by instinct, a surer guide than reflection to efficiency and morality. Hence the noble savage topos's insistence on "primitive honour": the adjective marks original and retained purity rather than conveying condescension. When Conrad's employment of the topos and its burden of primitivistic thought are recognized, it becomes impossible to regard the characterization of this native group as other than positive, even celebratory, however mystifying or mystified it may be.

The portrait of one crew member, the "savage who was fireman," is untouched by primitivistic rhetoric, since he has made a step toward participating in an advanced technology:

> He squinted at the steam-gauge and at the water-gauge with an evident effort of intrepidity—and he had filed teeth, too, the poor devil, and the wool of his pate shaved into queer patterns, and three ornamental scars on each of his cheeks. He ought to have been clapping his hands and stamping his feet on the bank, instead of which he was hard at work, a thrall to strange witchcraft, full of improving knowledge. He was useful because he had been instructed; and what he knew was this—that should the water in that transparent thing disappear the evil spirit inside the boiler would get angry through the greatness of his thirst and take a terrible vengeance. So he sweated and fired up and watched the glass fearfully (with an impromptu charm, made of rags, tied to his arm and a piece of polished bone as big as a watch stuck flatways through his lower lip) [. . .].   (38–39)

The deplorable condescension of this portrait cannot be overlooked, yet its concreteness may be appreciated as an effort at *anthropologically specific depiction*. The fireman's tribal characteristics are vividly presented though insufficient for identification: his marks are distinct from those ascribed to the cannibal crew, but Marlow's remark that "he ought to have been [. . .] on the bank" is a broad-brush rather than a localizing statement. Otherwise, Marlow, and Conrad with him, wants to get it right.

The fireman's mixture of tribal traits and Western commitments lends credence to Conrad's sociological accuracy. According to an enlightening study of the fireman and the helmsman (whom I shortly consider), the two stand among those known in social science as "detribalized natives," although other terms are sometimes employed (see Collins). Like the protagonists of most African writers' fiction—including that of Chinua Achebe, except for his uncharacteristic *Things Fall Apart*—these are men of two worlds, bereft of the normative security of their tribal cultures while only partially assimilated to the requirements and assumptions of an advanced technology. In their in-between state, they sometimes look foolish, hence the clownish aspect of Marlow's depiction. At the same time, they are often conscientious and even admirable: the fireman attends to his task with "intrepidity" although irrationally fearful of a mechanism in which he has been mythically and inadequately instructed. As with the boilermaker and helmsman, Marlow accords him the ultimate Conradian honors of the work ethic—"he sweated and fired up and watched the glass fearfully"—while acknowledging his merely instrumental use and abuse in the colonial enterprise.

The helmsman has achieved some celebrity for receiving the Conradian merit badge "He steered for me" (51), but with him, too, Marlow's condescension is flagrant. At least his regional provenance is specific—"an athletic black belonging to some coast tribe"—but his personality is hardly prepossessing: "He sported a pair of brass earings, wore a blue cloth wrapper from the waist to the ankles, and thought all the world of himself. He was the most unstable kind of fool I had ever seen. He steered with no end of swagger while you were by, but if he lost sight of you he became instantly the prey of an abject funk and would let that cripple of a steamboat get the upper hand of him in a minute" (45). In short, the helmsman's accolade is somewhat compromised by his job evaluation, yet Marlow's disdain is touched by sympathy. This tolerance may be due to a thread of psychological insight that he displays in passing observations: the helmsman is "unstable," "thought the world of himself," and is given to periods of "abject funk" or depression. What part of his subsequent hysteria during the natives' attack, leading to his bloody death, may be accounted to his detribalized and dislocated condition and what part to personal psychology, it is impossible to say. (His blue costume reinforces his membership in the cannibals' tribe, as the headman is similarly dressed, so the helmsman shares with them an eight-hundred-mile displacement from home.) But this vividly individualized black man is clearly accorded something of the *psychological characterization* employed for white folks.

Marlow's string of epithets for the man—"that fool-helmsman," and so on— may therefore be read not as scornful but as referring to a personality disorder: mental instability leading to self-destructive behavior. The string reveals a further modulation in the boss's attitudes toward his directly supervised underling. In narrating the attack, he passes from "the fool-nigger" through the "mad helmsman" (46) to "the man" (47) when describing his murder. Marlow seems to be taking successive steps toward humanistic vision, transcending his own tribal prejudice in acknowledging our common humanity in death.

The next paragraph provides the basis of this transcendence: "We two whites stood over him and his lustrous and inquiring glance enveloped us both. [. . .] Only in the very last moment as though in response to some sign we could not see, to some whisper we could not hear, he frowned heavily, and that frown gave to his black death-mask an inconceivably sombre, brooding, and menacing expression" (47). It may, of course, be troubling that the story's narrator and protagonist confronts the irrefragable fact of human equality only at "the very last moment," when staring at the black death mask. The novella invites its readers to follow him in his journey to the heart of darkness, human mortality, for which blackness, terrestrial and physiognomic, is the *archetypal symbol*.

The Role of Marlow's *Nellie* Audience in "Heart of Darkness"

> *Heart of Darkness* has been squandered upon the reader
> who still feels secure after reading it [. . .].
> —Patrick Reilly

Many students of Conrad's "Heart of Darkness" find its patina of epistemological ambiguity—in particular, the novella's overdetermined title, Kurtz's resonant deathbed cry "The horror! The horror!" (68), and Marlow's questionable reliability as a narrator—to be among the most vexing and provocative aspects of the text. Less scrutinized, but implicated in all these interpretive cruxes, is the role Marlow's *Nellie* audience plays in the novella. Indeed, what Seymour Gross wrote more than four decades ago is no less true today: "Despite the frequency with which Conrad's 'Heart of Darkness' has been discussed, the function of the frame in the novelette—the four men who sit on the deck of the *Nellie* and listen to Marlow's tale—has either been ignored or [. . .] misconstrued" (167). Although ostensibly peripheral, this narrative frame is central to the novella. In coming to grips with the significance of Marlow's audience to the narrative's meanings and implications, students may begin the process of determining their own angle of vision on and ideological relation to Conrad's narrative.

Many classroom discussions of Conrad's use of a frame narrative quickly move on to a consideration of the novella's critique of imperialism without giving the first matter the attention it deserves. It is useful to remind students, as Cedric Watts notes, that the device of the narrative frame can be traced via Brontë's *Wuthering Heights* to Coleridge's "Rime of the Ancient Mariner" ("Heart" 47–48) and that the convention of the tale within the tale was employed by many authors of the period whom Conrad read and admired: Turgenev, Maupassant, James, Kipling, Crane, Cunninghame Graham, and Wells. "This convention," Watts writes,

> was not only a reflection of the social customs of an age of gentlemen's clubs and semi-formal social gatherings at which travelers would meet to compare notes and exchange yarns about foreign experiences. It also emphasized the interplay of personal and social experience, [. . .] dramatizing relativism of perception [and the] limitations of knowledge [. . .].
>
> (46)

But Conrad exploits this narrative device in yet another way. For besides playing all these roles, Marlow's audience is a subtle commentator on the reception by Conrad's turn-of-the-century British audience of "Heart of Darkness" and British imperialism. As Owen Knowles puts it, "In Conrad's hands, this frame, with its English narrator and audience, may initially promise detachment and security, but these both soon prove to be illusory" ("Conrad's Life" 13). In fact, the frame allows Conrad to add another dimension to the novella—its stealthy commentary on its contemporary readers—that otherwise would not exist.

To pass the time before setting sail, Charlie Marlow tells his tale to the *Nellie's* passengers: a lawyer, "the best of old fellows"; an accountant, who carries a box of dominoes; a Director of Companies, who plays the role of both captain and host on this occasion; and the unnamed narrator, a merchant seaman (7). In class, the following questions tend to arise: Why does Conrad include a specified audience for Marlow at all? What does his building an audience into the narrative allow Conrad to accomplish that he could not otherwise achieve? Some students already will have glimpsed an answer: Marlow's English audience is a mirror of the European colonizers who do the "civilizing work" in Africa. Most obviously, the accountant aboard the *Nellie* mirrors the accountant at the outer station who proudly keeps his books "in apple-pie order" (21) despite the chaotic, "uncivilized" atmosphere in which he must work. That the *Nellie* accountant toys "architecturally with the bones" (7), a reference to the dominoes he has brought aboard, which presumably are made of ivory, the commodity for which the Europeans plunder Africa ("The word 'ivory' would ring in the air" [36]), only reinforces the connection between Marlow's audience, "English stockholders all, the investors that made empire possible" (A. White, "Conrad" 192), and the European imperialists whom Marlow encounters in the Belgian Congo.

The connections between the frame and central narratives do not end here. Just as Marlow postures as someone who does not see eye to eye with the European trading company's attitudes and policies in Africa—as he presents himself as seeing through the "philanthropic pretense of the whole concern" (27)—so too does he sit apart from the others on board the *Nellie*, in a posture that suggests his self-conscious mental (and moral) distance from his listeners. Initially he resembles an "idol" (7); at the end of the tale he sits "in the pose of a meditating Buddha" (76). His physical position on the yawl implies that he stands aloof from the worldview (and narrative expectations) of his established English audience. (Earlier, on returning to Europe, he dismisses the people he meets as "intruders whose knowledge of life" was merely "an irritating pretense"[70].)

The most important difference in attitude between Marlow and his audience is expressed in the gap between the narrator, who appears to be a straightforward adherent of imperialism, and Marlow, who would have us take him for a skeptic. The narrator smugly approves of the colonial triumphs of the English, which originate on the River Thames:

> Hunters for gold or pursuers of fame they all had gone out on that stream, bearing the sword, and often the torch, messengers of the might within the land, bearers of a spark from the sacred fire. What greatness had not floated on the ebb of that river into the mystery of an unknown

earth? . . . The dreams of men, the seed of commonwealths, the germ of empires.   (8)

Marlow, as if reading the narrator's mind, shortly thereafter interjects, "And this also [. . .] has been one of the dark places of the earth" (9). Marlow then launches into his Roman analogy, in which he implies that the antique Romans in Britain, and by implication the modern Europeans in Africa, were merely

> conquerors, and for that you want only brute force—nothing to boast of, when you have it, since your strength is just an accident arising from the weakness of others. They grabbed what they could get for the sake of what was to be got. It was just robbery with violence, aggravated murder on a great scale, and men going at it blind—as is very proper for those who tackle a darkness.   (10)

His image of a conquering civilization is sharply divergent from the narrator's (and presumably from that of the other *Nellie* auditors). Marlow hints that the Europeans wrongly conflate their evident military superiority with an imagined moral one.

At this point if not earlier in class discussion, I remind students that the novella was initially published serially, in *Blackwood's Edinburgh Magazine*. An understanding of the readership of this journal helps clarify the connections between the novella's frame and its central narratives and between the novella as a whole and its initial readership. Indeed, Conrad uses *Blackwood's* (popularly known as *Maga*) as a means of subtly ironizing his readers, both by building them into the narrative and by implicating them in its action. "Heart of Darkness" was published from February to April 1899 in *Maga*, "a conservative, traditionalist magazine that liked to give its readers good fare in masculine story-telling" (Baines 281). Ian Watt describes *Blackwood's* as "rather traditional in its literary tastes" and "very conservative and masculine in tone" (*Conrad* 131). This description is also apt for the tone Marlow adopts with his *Nellie* audience. Indeed, in writing for *Blackwood's*, Conrad could envision for his novella a particular audience, "middle-class Englishmen, officers in the forces or civil servants in the empire" (Batchelor 100)—precisely the kind of men Marlow addresses aboard the *Nellie*. As Conrad later commented, "One was in decent company [in *Blackwood's*] and had a good sort of public. There isn't a single club and messroom and man-of-war in the British Seas and Dominions which hasn't its copy of Maga" (qtd. in Watt, *Conrad* 131). In short, the congruence between Conrad's imagined *Blackwood's* audience and Marlow's *Nellie* audience was significant and intentional.

Put simply, Conrad intentionally constructs an audience for Marlow that *misses* his story's subversive suggestions and that instead views the remembered story, as so many readers have viewed "Heart of Darkness" itself, as just one more popular, exotic, masculine adventure tale (see Ruppel). Indeed, there is little evidence to suggest that Marlow's *Nellie* audience grasps the implications of his story—implications that address this group directly as a beneficiary of colonialism. "Do you see him [Kurtz]? Do you see the story? Do you see anything?" Marlow at one point asks his audience, continuing: "Of course in this you fellows see more than I could then. You see me, whom you know. . . ." The narrator then reports, "It had become so pitch dark that we listeners could hardly see one another. [. . .] There was not a word from anybody. The others might have been asleep [. . .]" (30). The implication of this juxtaposition of Marlow's questions and the narrator's answer is clear: not only do the members of Marlow's audience here fail to see him and his story, they may no longer even be listening. That Marlow's tale inspires only a "faint uneasiness" in the narrator (30) further suggests that this narrator and certainly Marlow's other listeners receive the tale more as an unsuccessful entertainment, for purposes of passing the time, than as a narrative with any unsettling political or ethical relevance to their own situations or world. Earlier, for example, when Marlow first breaks into the narrator's thoughts, the narrator comments, "His remark did not seem at all surprising. It was just like Marlow. It was accepted in silence. No one took the trouble to grunt, even" (9). The narrator later adds that Marlow, in telling his story, reveals the "weakness of many tellers of tales who seem so often unaware of what their audience would best like to hear" (11). In this way the narrator distinguishes Marlow from other seamen—because his mind is not of the "stay-at-home order" and his story is not one of "direct simplicity"—who tell their audiences more conventional, less challenging tales, "the whole meaning of which lies within the shell of a cracked nut" (9). Unfortunately for Marlow's silent and probably uncomprehending audience, it is "fated" instead, as the narrator puts it, "to hear about one of Marlow's inconclusive experiences" (11). Robert O. Evans is correct to remark that members of Marlow's audience are probably "incapable of understanding" his narrative (59); but to make matters still worse, they may not be taking it seriously or even listening.

At one point, Marlow seems aware of his audience's inability to grasp his tale's more subversive suggestions. He believes that he hears "somebody" on board the *Nellie* (he cannot identify the speaker in the pitch darkness) mutter "absurd" in response to something he has said. He then asks, "You can't understand? How could you—with solid pavement under your feet, surrounded by kind neighbours [. . .], stepping delicately between the butcher and the policeman, in the holy terror of scandal and gallows and lunatic asylums—[. . .] too dull even to know you are being assaulted by the powers of darkness" (49–50). This argument would appear to explain, for Marlow, why his middle-class audience misses his narrative's more disturbing implications.

At this point in class I return to the novella's two accountants in order to forge a final and more penetrating connection between them. This connection pertains less to the outer station accountant's surprising "clerical" precision than to his even more surprising and equally polished physical appearance—

his "varnished boots," "brushed hair," "starched collars and got-up shirt-fronts." When Marlow asks him how he "managed to sport such linen" given "the great demoralisation of the land" in which he has been living for "nearly three years," the accountant "had just the faintest blush and said modestly, 'I've been teaching one of the native women about the station. It was difficult. She had a distaste for the work'" (21). One implication of this passage is that the accountant has been teaching the native woman to provide him with sexual as well as laundry services, as the blush, the distasteful work, and the dirty laundry all function euphemistically. Conrad here introduces the rape-of-Africa motif, which is reiterated frequently in the text (e.g., Africa is figured as a female body violated by male Europeans: "To tear treasure out of the bowels of the land was their desire, with no more moral purpose at the back of it than there is in burglars breaking into a safe" [32–33]). This plundering of African ivory and violating of African women also echoes in the rapacious Kurtz, who possesses a strong "appetite" both for "ivory" and for women: "Mr. Kurtz lacked restraint in the gratification of his various lusts" (57). Marlow also subtly relates Kurtz and the accountant to other Europeans he encounters, including the passengers aboard the *Nellie*, who are said to possess appetites and who presumably profit from the economic rape of Africa: "Here you all are[,] each moored with two good addresses like a hulk with two anchors [note that the *Nellie* is anchored as Marlow tells his tale], a butcher round one corner, a policeman round another, excellent *appetites* [. . .] from year's end to year's end" (48; emphasis mine). It is significant that Marlow tells his story of Europeans in Africa to the *Nellie* passengers against the physical backdrop of London, "the biggest, and the greatest, town on earth" (7) and the heart of the British Empire, even if the "monstrous town" is imaged only indirectly and in the distance as a "brooding gloom in sunshine, a lurid glare under the stars" (9). "Heart of Darkness" makes its points in a similarly oblique and subtle fashion.

As for Conrad's original readers, how different were their responses to Marlow's narrative from those of Marlow's *Nellie* audience? The outlook of many *Blackwood's* readers would have been the same as Marlow's exclusively male, middle-class, and professional audience. Conrad himself seemed to think that few of his readers would grasp the novella's subversive dimensions. Writing to fellow world traveler Robert Bontine Cunninghame Graham, whom Conrad took to be an unusually perceptive reader and kindred spirit, the author cautioned Cunninghame Graham, following the latter's kind words on the publication of part 1 of "Heart of Darkness," "There are two more installments in which the idea is so wrapped up in secondary notions that You—even You!—may miss it" (*Collected Letters* 2: 157). Even as astute a reader as Edward Garnett, the man credited with having discovered Conrad's talent, spoke of "Heart of Darkness" as presenting "the meaning or meaninglessness of the white man in uncivilised Africa" (Sherry, *Critical Heritage* 133). And an anonymous reviewer for the *Manchester Guardian* entirely missed the point when he wrote, "It must not be supposed that Mr. Conrad makes attack upon colonisation, expansion, even upon Imperialism. In no one is the adventurous spirit more instinctive" (135). By the same token, the members of Marlow's *Nellie* audience appear to misconstrue his tale, viewing it as a conformist (if also unsuccessful) adventure romance rather than as a critique of British popular prejudices and European imperial practices.

It might be argued in class, then, that Marlow's audience is built into the tale in order to implicate Conrad's readers in the imperial crimes and hypocritical habits of mind that the novella sometimes subtly, sometimes directly, reveals. Marlow's audience is also there to demonstrate this readership's denial of its implication in these crimes. In this way, "Heart of Darkness" surreptitiously attacks its readers' unwitting—or, worse still, apathetic—culpability in the murderous business of empire.

Students may ask why Conrad enacts this critique so subtly, behind the backs of his readers. Three answers suggest themselves, all of which pertain to what Knowles calls Conrad's "struggle to negotiate with his English cultural identity and audience" ("Conrad's Life" 13). The first is rhetorical and is suggested by Conrad in an 1897 letter to William Blackwood: "[A] sweeping assertion is always wrong, since men are infinitely varied; and hard words are useless because they cannot combat ideas. And the ideas (that live) should be combated, not the men who die" (qtd. in Hay 111–12). That is to say, Conrad believed that an open indictment of benighted individuals, using "hard words," would make less of an impact than would an oblique criticism of the society's reigning ideas (convictions); because readers, if affronted, would stop reading. The second reason, as Zdzislaw Najder notes, is that Conrad "wanted to belong to English literature and to England" yet was "never fully successful in his attempts; something would always give away his foreignness" (*Joseph Conrad* 231). A frontal assault on his readers would neither win them over nor make him appear any less foreign in their eyes. As Eloise Knapp Hay argues, Conrad intentionally wrote over the heads of his readers because these "readers, coming to the story in 1899, were poorly equipped to penetrate its whole meaning" (111–12). A surreptitious rather than an open critique, paradoxically, would be better digested by and therefore make a greater impact on readers. The third reason is perhaps the most obvious one: too harsh a treatment of Conrad's topic would have precluded the novella's being published at all—certainly in the respectable *Blackwood's*.

Finally, what about Conrad's present-day audience, specifically the students in our classrooms? There is perhaps some danger that *Apocalypse Now* and other attacks on United States imperialism may obscure Conrad's broader, subtler, more penetrating analysis. But the greater danger is that students will not see the story any more than did Marlow's (or Conrad's) immediate audience. Focusing on the role Marlow's audience plays in "Heart of Darkness" will help sensitize students to the ways in which Conrad's novella challenges the Western presumption of moral and intellectual superiority and will help suggest why this novella even now endures, in Watt's words, "as the most powerful lit-

erary indictment of imperialism" (*Conrad* 161; also see Shaffer, "Rebarbarizing" and *Torch*). It will move students beyond a conception of the story as merely a physical and psychological journey, a romance that confirms the legitimacy of the "adventurous spirit," however costly that spirit is to others. The story also will suggest to them how the "adventurous spirit" is morally and intellectually dishonest, one of those deadly lies to which Marlow frequently alludes but fails to evade himself. Perhaps in more fully grasping the role Marlow's audience plays in "Heart of Darkness," we may avoid the obliviousness of the smug, self-deceived, blind *Nellie* audience—which ends up sitting in a darkness that is not only visual but epistemological and moral as well—as to the ills its civilization inflicts on so many nameless, faceless others beyond its pale.

"He Was Not a Bit like Me, Really": Narrators and Audiences in "The Secret Sharer"

Brian Richardson

"The Secret Sharer" is deservedly reputed for inviting a wide range of critical interpretations, and in the undergraduate classroom the range of suggested meanings is even greater. Every hypothesis seems (at least at first glance) to be equally possible, from the old red herring "I think he dreamed the whole thing" to the concerned student who worries, "How does he know Leggatt won't kill them all as soon as he has a chance?" Narrative theory can provide a helpful way to sort through the often bewildering array of interpretative options, and this tale demands a close look at the various narrators in the text and the multiple audiences both within and outside the story. Such a look generally produces a keener sense of the issues at stake in the work, an exemplary instance for discussion of larger issues of narrative interpretation, and a good introduction to modernist literary strategies.

In my classes, I often begin by having the students write a summary of the main events of the story. Then we go over the sources of our beliefs as to what actually happened. Quickly, we identify the main narrators and go on to discuss the evidence for their claims along with the motives for their particular versions; we ask whether any other accounts corroborate or contradict the primary explanatory framework. When we focus on the motives and reliability of the various narrators, a distinct pattern emerges.

For the most part, all we know of Leggatt is what he says himself, and all we know of the surrounding events is what the captain-narrator provides. But these two narrative transmissions deserve a certain degree of suspicion, since they produce a framework that begs for significant distortion. Leggatt has, after all, killed a man. He provides himself with an exculpatory narrative: striking the man (a worthless shirker who endangered the safety of the ship) actually saved the entire crew in the middle of a deadly storm. The seaman wound up dead, and Leggatt, who should have been treated like a hero, was instead thrown in the brig and treated like a common criminal according to the clearly inappropriate letter of the law.

It is not surprising that a killer has a story that exonerates him; most killers do. The motive for his story—saving his neck—is clear. What is unusual is how the narrator believes without question whatever Leggatt says and even helps him produce this rather romantic narrative. Just after Leggatt has come on board and is given the captain's spare sleeping suit, he starts to tell his story, mentioning that he is, or rather was, the first mate of the *Sephora*. But at a crucial moment in Leggatt's story, just as he is about to explain the circumstances of the homicide, the narrator interrupts to say, "'Fit of temper,' I suggested,

confidently." At this comment, Leggatt's dark head, in the night, "seemed to nod imperceptibly." This is the faintest description of a nod of affirmation that most readers will ever encounter. So what is his story? That's hard to say precisely. The narrator admits he "did not think of asking him for details, and he told me the story roughly in brusque, disconnected sentences. I needed no more" (31).[1]

Though the vast majority of critics have, like the narrator, been fairly satisfied with Leggatt's account, other involved parties in "The Secret Sharer" tell a different story. One of these of course is Archbold, the captain of the *Sephora*, the ship that Leggatt fled. He is certainly someone who could provide important contextualizations and revealing details of the situation, and one would normally assume that one captain would give weight to the perspective of another. What is Archbold's story? We don't know, since our captain-narrator claims, "It is not worth while to record that version" (42). Nevertheless, the moral outrage that Archbold feels about the homicide ("I've never heard of such a thing happening in an English ship" [42]) does not jibe at all with the rather Byronic narrative told by Leggatt.

There is another source of alternative narratives: the crew of the *Sephora*. They were there, knew the circumstances, and witnessed the act. The killing is mentioned by the narrator's chief mate: "His boat's crew told our chaps a very extraordinary story, if what I am told by the steward is true" (45). The sagacious mate (who "'liked to account to himself' for practically everything that came his way" [26])—and no doubt was used to the exaggerations and self-serving nature of personal narratives—is hoping for additional information that might confirm or qualify what he has heard. Not getting any significant response, he goes on to add the provocative comment, "Beats all these tales we hear about murders in Yankee ships" (46). But the captain-narrator, quite credulous by contrast, simply denies the comparison without knowing any of its particulars.

We never learn these details, though it is fair to assume they were awful, given the brutalities common on American ships in the 1880s—brutalities often exacerbated by class struggle, as recruitment for seamen's unions was vigorous at this time. But whatever they were, they too fail to square with Leggatt's self-justifying version of the events.[2] Discussing this history, I invariably turn to the students and ask them whether they prefer to read like the old sailor or the young captain, a question that enhances the text's own opposition between power and knowledge.

At this point we look at the evidence the captain offers to justify his identification with the mysterious Leggatt. It turns out to be quite insubstantial. Leggatt is said to have a good voice, self-possession, and youth, A "mysterious communication" was immediately established between them (how?). They both attended the same naval training school (if what Leggatt says is correct—their years there did not overlap). After hearing the brief articulation of the basic facts of the case, the narrator concludes, "I knew well enough [. . .] that my double there was no homicidal ruffian." How does he know? Later, however, he

fears the man may have throttled the steward, and Leggatt notes his own potential for additional violence ("I didn't mean to go back . . . Somebody would have got killed for certain" [37]). The fear of the student I mentioned at the beginning of this paper, for the lives of the others onboard, turns out not to be so far-fetched after all.

A close look at the often remarked-on physical resemblances between Leggatt and the captain is quite revealing. The following statement is representative of this discourse: "as we stood leaning over my bed-place, whispering side by side, with our dark heads together and our backs to the door, anybody bold enough to open it stealthily would have been treated to the uncanny sight of a double captain busy talking in whispers with his other self" (34). But just what kind of visual image is this, especially when we remember that for Conrad, the ability to see is always paramount? All that would be visible from such a vantage point would be the backs of two heads and two sleeping suits. Not much here to make a case for identity. But even stranger is the line that precedes this description: "He was not a bit like me, really." The captain's assertions of physical resemblance are thus gratuitous projections; so, one must suspect, are the claims for psychological similarity.

This misidentification in turn leads to the question of motive: why would the narrator trust and identify with a self-confessed killer running from the authorities, a man whom he found naked, hanging on to the ship's ladder, in the middle of the night? Critics have long agreed that the narrator-captain is isolated, inexperienced, and unsure of himself; he readily identifies with and seeks companionship from another young officer in a difficult situation. Cedric Watts has pointed out that as Conway boys, both would be "members of a British social and maritime elite; both have the tone, style, phraseology and assumptions of gentlemen rather than the working class" ("Mirror Tale" 27). Class prejudice and psychological isolation thus combine to fashion a sympathetic Leggatt. Earlier criticism has not fully understood the degree to which the narrator invents his dubious companion on highly questionable grounds of alleged similarity. Close scrutiny of the text's various narrators and their motives discloses how fragile the truth of this situation is and how easily it is lost in transmission.

Another important aspect of this text is the question of its reception, that is, who are the audiences in and of this work? As we have seen, there is one major interpretive division among the story's characters, and that is between the narrator and his crew, who persistently misunderstand each other and who have very different readings of the same sets of events. In many cases, the divergent interpretations are due to differences in knowledge; often, though, they go deeper and reflect opposed kinds of judgment. Thus, the crew thinks the captain has lost his senses for sailing foolishly close to the shore; they can't know that he's done it to enable Leggatt to escape more easily. But even if they had known of the stowaway's presence and approved of the captain's attempts to save him, they still may have felt it was not sane to risk the ship just to reduce the distance for a man who claimed to be a champion swimmer.

Similarly, Leggatt's shipboard incident as described by the crew of the *Sephora* is judged to be a "very horrible affair" (46), and Leggatt himself states that his captain asked him how he could sleep at night after what he'd done. Though we will never be able to know exactly what did happen, we can be sure that these two responses by witnesses of the events are entirely inconsistent with Leggatt's version of his story: the crew and Leggatt's captain would seem to have seen something quite different. There are two incompatible audiences in the story—one middle-class, uncritical, and romantic; the other working-class, skeptical, and realistic—and they remain unreconciled throughout the work. From an ideological vantage point, Conrad's sympathetic presentation of working-class perceptions and sensibilities here may partially compensate for his perceived indifference elsewhere to potential female readers and their likely responses.

Reader-response theory presents us with additional tools. Our best guide here is Peter Rabinowitz, who differentiates among the narrative audience, which shares the assumptions of the narrator; the authorial audience, the hypothetical readers whom the author imagines writing for, who can see through unreliable narrators and get the author's jokes; and the actual, flesh-and-blood audience, whose hands turn the pages. The narrative analysis pursued above indicates that the tale's troubled, idealistic narrator is utterly different from the work's more skeptical, implied author and that the authorial audience (or what Iser and others have termed the "implied reader") should doubt much of what the narrative audience is expected to believe. Thus, when the narrator notes early in the story that he left Leggatt alone on deck while he went below to fetch some clothing, he thereby gives away his irresponsibility, since, as J. D. O'Hara points out, such an action is "wildly improbable as a description of an English captain coping with a strange visitor in a foreign land" (447). This inference is just the kind an authorial audience is expected to make and a narrative audience is constructed to miss. The two conceptions are widely opposed in this work, as they are in novels by William Faulkner and by Vladimir Nabokov.

What is particularly interesting in this context is that historical readers, practicing critics, and undergraduate students all typically differ widely on just how close these two audiences are, as the interpretive opposition described in the book is reenacted by its various readers. Once again, this situation presents an excellent opportunity for understanding the motives and consequences of different interpretive acts, including their epistemic foundations and social bases. A good assignment to bring this home is to ask students to retell the main events from the perspective of one of the crewmen of either ship.

The consequences of a narrative analysis of this work suggest that the text is much more ironic and the narrator vastly more unreliable than has previously been proposed. This insight makes the work much more central in the modernist tradition of confused, mistaken, and unusual narrators that include the nameless narrator of the Cyclops episode in *Ulysses* and Benjy in *The Sound and the Fury*. It also reveals a hermeneutical subtlety concerning the depths in which the secrets of work are cached, though here too there is an interesting irony: one needs to be either a modernist sophisticate with a keen eye for interpretive incongruity or an experienced seaman to properly read the hieroglyphics of this text. Finally, this narrative approach urges us to be quite cautious about any assumed biographical correspondences between the captain and the young Conrad; it suggests instead that authorial and narrative audiences are entirely opposed here, making the story a very unlikely repository for autobiographical material. "The Secret Sharer" is not a disguised confession but, rather, a great yarn.

At a more general level, this work is an excellent medium for analyzing and theorizing the role of narrators, the importance of multiple points of view, and the material consequences of each narrator's position. It reveals much about audience response, modernist play with readers, and the ideological assumptions that readers necessarily bring to the text. Pedagogically, it can help us talk usefully about effective literary interpretation in general as well as of the importance of evidence, consistency, and comprehensiveness in narrative analysis—whether done by characters in a novel, critics in a journal, or students in a classroom.

NOTES

[1]The first critic to point out the narrator's unreliability was J. D. O'Hara, himself a former seaman.

[2]For a sustained discussion of general interpretive issues in the text as well as historical and intertextual situating, see my article "Construing Conrad's 'The Secret Sharer.'"

Creating a Second Self:
Transference as Narrative Form in
"The Secret Sharer"

Daniel Schwarz

I approach the "The Secret Sharer" as a radical example of the Conradian theme, dramatized in the Marlow tales, that we all interpret experience according to our emotional and moral needs. The captain's creation of Leggatt is very much part of his experience. By "creation," I am suggesting not that the captain invents or dreams up Leggatt but that he constructs Leggatt for his own psychological purposes. Self-doubt and anxiety create an illogical identification with Leggatt as his double.

In discussing "The Secret Sharer," we need to differentiate between how the captain responds to the originating events—his first command, his encounters with Leggatt and the man he remembers as Archbold—and the retrospective narrative at a distance of years. Specifically, we need understand that we are listening to a retrospective telling, but that the captain-speaker often ingenuously disguises it as his immediate response.

In my thirty-five years of teaching "The Secret Sharer," I find students respond best when they identify with the speaker as a young adult undertaking a challenging yet frightening responsibility and when they understand the story as a drama about making meaning from a confusing past experience. They respond to the "The Secret Sharer" as a radical example of the discrepancy between what actually happened and how we remember what happened and of the concomitant discrepancy between how we remember an event and how we narrate it.

A pedagogical note: at times I shall use the interrogative mode to encourage openness to discussion and the dialogic nature of my readings. When we get an intimation of what seems true or right by examining evidence and developing reasoned arguments, we should want to express it for others and ourselves in the spirit of participating in a community of inquiry. When we attend to what others are saying and writing, we are learning; when we argue about meaning (as Plato knew), we come to understand how we know what we know. Thus I divide my inquiry here into a number of questions that shape my teaching.

How is the captain-narrator's telling crucial to our understanding?

"The Secret Sharer" is personal in the way great lyrical poetry is personal, drawing from experience that is at once individual (Conrad became captain of the *Otago* in 1888) and representative of the deepest strains of human experience: fear and self-doubt in the face of challenge. Although in this period of renewed personal and financial turmoil for Conrad his imagination turns nostalgically to life at sea, the sea is no longer the simplified world of "Typhoon" or "The End of the Tether" where moral distinctions are clear. In "The Secret Sharer," a young captain is faced with circumstances and emotional traumas for which neither the maritime code nor his experience has prepared him.

The captain-narrator recounts a tale of initiation in which he successfully overcame debilitating emotional insecurity to command his ship. The significance of the events for the sensitive and intelligent captain is that he discovered within himself the ability to act decisively that he had lacked. As a younger man, the captain doubted himself, felt a "stranger" to the community to which he belonged, and wondered if he should "turn out faithful to that ideal conception of one's personality every man sets up for himself secretly" (26). His concern *now* is to present the issues in terms of what Leggatt meant to him. Although he certainly knows that harboring an escaped murderer represents a threat to maritime civilization and a violation of his own legal and moral commitment, his retelling ignores this. In our psychological critique of "The Secret Sharer" we need to explore the complex psyche and values of the captain-narrator and to understand not only why he behaves as he does but also how the original experience is reflected, refracted, displaced, and projected in the retrospective telling.

Henry James's and Conrad's experiments with the dramatized narrator show how modernism shifts the emphasis from the subject to the perceiver's mind in the act of interpreting the subject; the observers are the subjects as much as what they observe. Conrad's "The Secret Sharer," like James's *The Turn of the Screw* (1898), is about seeing and being seen. Leggatt likes to be looked at: "When I saw a man's head looking over I thought I would swim away presently and leave him shouting—in whatever language it was. I didn't mind being looked at. I—I liked it. And then you speaking to me so quietly—as if you had expected me—made me hold on a little longer" (37). Self-reflection and even narcissism are troped in the verbal style of both the captain and Leggatt. Here the "I" is not the "I" of a strong ego; rather, as the *object* of observation, "I" becomes the subject.

Memory is another kind of seeing—retrospective seeing—and, as we know, memory creates its own distortions. The captain-narrator, separated by a "distance of years" from the meeting with Leggatt, delivers a retrospective monologue:

> On my right hand there were lines of fishing-stakes resembling a mysterious system of half-submerged bamboo fences, incomprehensible in its division of the domain of tropical fishes, and crazy of aspect as if abandoned for ever by some nomad tribe of fishermen now gone to the other end of the ocean; for there was no sign of human habitation as far as the eye could reach. (24)

But, despite the past tense, readers often forget that the events have already occurred; the nominal narrative past becomes a harrowing living present, which readers find themselves exploring along with the narrator.

The oblique style disguises as much as it reveals. It is as if the very specificity of the details were circumventing the issues: the "fishing stakes resembling a mysterious system of half submerged fences" anticipate the headless corpses that he pulls out of the water when he leaves the ladder in the water while on the watch. When Leggatt appears, he is "silvery, fishlike. He remained as mute as a fish, too" (29). Leggatt is aligned with the atavistic and primitive, while the captain is a hyperconscious modern man, retreating to his psychic laboratory to sift through his feelings. Appropriately, at the end Leggatt asks to be abandoned to the primitive world beyond the pale. Words like "incomprehensible" and "crazy" are the available and feeble semiotic tools with which the captain is trying to come to terms with his behavior, a behavior that even at the distance of years since his first command eludes explanation. For he is well aware now of the importance of these events and knows that in the past he jeopardized his future by harboring an escaped murderer; for Leggatt violated every tenet of the maritime code, and, as first mate, he strangled a man under his command.

We need to understand that the retrospective telling is a *painful* act of memory that has potential to be deeply disruptive to the captain's current sense of self. In a sense we are in the position of an analyst hearing the analysand and sorting through an incomprehensible, even traumatic experience. Indeed, we might recall Freud's discussion of the "repetition-compulsion": telling is a version of the repetition compulsion described in his 1920 essay "Beyond the Pleasure Principle":

> It must be explained that we are able to postulate the principle of a repetition-compulsion in the unconscious mind, based upon instinctual activity and inherent in the very nature of the instincts—a principle powerful enough to overrule the pleasure-principle, lending to certain aspects of the mind their daemonic character, and still very clearly expressed in the tendencies of small children; a principle, too, which is responsible for a part of the course taken by the analysis of neurotic patients. Taken in all, the foregoing prepares us for the discovery that whatever reminds us of this inner repetition-compulsion is perceived as uncanny.   (qtd. in Hertz 300)

Freud is describing a patient's need to repeat partly forgotten and repressed material. In "The Secret Sharer" the speaker has a burden of guilt because he has broken the seaman's code. His excuses make up much of the story, and his narrative telling iterates that he is still a stranger to himself. In a sense, the captain's telling is an iteration of the original experience of his creating a double from a man to whom he bears in terms of values only the most superficial resemblance. Neil Hertz observes in his discussion of trauma in "Freud and the Sandman":

> Repetition becomes "visible" when it is colored or tinged by something being repeated, which itself functions like vivid or heightened language, lending a kind of rhetorical consistency to what is otherwise quite literally

unspeakable. Whatever it is that is repeated—an obsessive ritual, perhaps, or a bit of acting-out in relation to one's analyst—will, then, feel most compellingly uncanny when it is seen as *merely* coloring, that is, when it comes to seem most gratuitously rhetorical.   (Hertz 301)

What shapes the captain's response to Leggatt?

Because one's version of events reflects an interaction between, on the one hand, experience and perception and, on the other, memories and psychic needs, interpretation always has a subjective element. The captain's interpretation of his experience dramatizes the process of his coming to terms with what Leggatt symbolizes. In somewhat reductive but apt Freudian terms, Leggatt is a man of unrestrained id and underdeveloped superego. The captain, an example of hyperconscious modern man who fastidiously thinks of the consequences of every action to the point where he cannot do anything, is his opposite. The captain's self-doubt and anxiety create an illogical identification with Leggatt as his double. The captain risks his future to hide the man he regards as his "second self" (58). To avoid discovery, he begins to act desperately and instinctively, without conscious examination of the consequences of each action. Leggatt's presence creates situations where the luxury of introspection is no longer possible. Symbolically, the captain completes himself. He finds within himself the potential to act instinctively and boldly that his double exemplifies. It can be said that his adult ego is created by his appeasing the contradictory demands of the id and superego. Listening to the narrator, we tentatively suspend our moral perspective and fail to condemn him for giving refuge to a suspected murderer. We suspend our moral perspective because, as his words engage us and as we become implicated as his confessor, we come partially to share his perspective.

In my teaching I stress how Conrad wishes us to perceive Leggatt and the captain as representatives of a split in modern humans between mind and instinct. Leggatt's presence disrupts the ship's community and raises further doubts among the officers about the captain's self-control and sanity. Because the captain has to consider whether his every word might reveal his secret, he becomes more neurotic. He now has twin loyalties, mutually exclusive: to the man he is harboring and with whom he identifies and to his ship. Paradoxically, the desperation of his paranoia, of his belief that he is constantly being scrutinized by his subordinates, leads him to give his "first particular order." When threatened, he feels "the need of asserting myself." The pressure of circumstances makes it increasingly difficult for him to distinguish between himself and Leggatt:

[A]ll the time the dual working of my mind distracted me almost to the point of insanity. I was constantly watching myself, my secret self, as dependent on my actions as my own personality, sleeping in that bed,

behind the door which faced me as I sat at the head of the table. It was very much like being mad, only it was worse because one was aware of it.
(40)

The captain's distinction between self and other threatens to collapse: "That mental feeling of being in two places at once affected me physically as if the mood of secrecy had penetrated my very soul" (48). Like T. S. Eliot's J. Alfred Prufrock and James Joyce's Gabriel Conroy—other paralytically self-conscious modern characters—the captain has a personality whose integrity is threatened by a disbelief in the authenticity of self. If R. D. Laing's *The Divided Self* aptly describes a phenomenon of modern literature, it is because the terms in which existential psychology describes schizoid conditions are directly related to the crisis of identity that Eliot, Joyce, and Conrad analyze:

> If one experiences the other as a free agent, one is open to the possibility of experiencing oneself as an *object* of his experience and thereby of feeling one's own subjectivity drained away. One is threatened with the possibility of becoming no more than a thing in the world of the other, without any life for oneself, without any being for oneself [. . .]. One may find oneself enlivened and the sense of one's own being enhanced by the other, or one may experience the other as deadening and impoverishing.
> (Laing 47)

Retrospectively it is clear that the captain has been "enlivened" by his experience of Leggatt, although at first Leggatt's appearance—like the presence of the threatening first mate, whose whiskers and manner intimidate the captain—has a "deadening" effect.

The captain's creation of Leggatt is a major part of the original experience. By *creation*, I do not mean that the captain invents or dreams up Leggatt but that he constructs him for his own psychological purposes, which are at odds with the real Leggatt. Before Leggatt's appearance, the captain is immobilized by self-consciousness and self-doubt: "My position was that of the only *stranger* on board. I mention this because it has some bearing on what is to follow. But what I felt most was my being a *stranger* to the ship; and if all the truth must be told, I was somewhat a *stranger* to myself" (26; emphasis mine). That "stranger" carries the meaning of "alien" and "outside" from the French word *étranger* is an instance of how the richness of Conrad's language is occasionally increased by his appropriating French definitions for similarly spelled English words.

Humorless, insecure, and claustrophobic, the captain needs to be on deck to avoid the discomfort and awkwardness that his feelings of inadequacy feed. The character of Leggatt is a function of the captain's need for someone to share the burdens of loneliness and anxiety. The captain's impulse is to integrate completely his newfound companion into his social and moral fabric and to totemize him as part of himself. But Leggatt is one of what Herman Melville calls Isolatoes, those who "not acknowledging the common continent of men [. . . live] on a separate continent of [their] own" (*Moby-Dick* 108; ch. 27). When he hears of Leggatt's alternatives (to keep swimming until he drowns or is welcomed on board the captain's ship), he responds, "I felt this was no mere formula of desperate speech, but a real alternative in the view of a strong soul. [. . .] A mysterious communication was established already between us two—in the face of that silent, darkened tropical sea" (30). The captain recalls that "the voice was calm and resolute. A good voice. The *self-possession* of that man had somehow induced a corresponding state in myself" (30; emphasis mine).

But the captain's statement contrasts with his original response of seconds before: "He seemed to struggle with himself, for I heard something like the low, bitter murmur of doubt. 'What's the good?' His next words came out with a hesitating effort" (29). Jumping from one assertion to another without empirical data, the captain continues to convince himself of Leggatt's resemblance to him on such flimsy grounds as that they are both young. Although he tells us that they looked identical, he later admits that Leggatt "was not a bit like me, really" (34). His original, flattering description of Leggatt is continually modified until it is almost contradicted. Before Leggatt even begins to explain how he killed a man, the captain has excused him: "'Fit of temper,' I suggested, confidently" (31). Insisting on the value of his second self enables the captain to discover himself morally and psychologically. But the process of idealizing his double, his other self, into a model of self-control, self-confidence, and sanity is arbitrary and noncognitive. Perhaps we better understand the extent of the narrator's surrender of self if we recall Laing's analysis of a man who suffered what he calls "ontological insecurity": "In contrast to his own belittlement of uncertainty about himself, he was always on the brink of being overawed and crushed by the formidable reality that other people contained. In contrast to his own [. . .] uncertainty, and insubstantiality, *they* were solid, decisive, emphatic, and substantial" (48). Despite the evidence that Leggatt murdered another man in a fit of passion, the captain holds to a belief in Leggatt's control and sanity and insists that the killing was an act of duty. But the reader does not forget that Leggatt committed a horribly immoral act and that he does not regret it.

Conrad emphasizes how the destructive relationship between the doubting crew and the insecure captain creates the captain's attitude to Leggatt. The captain never criticizes Leggatt, despite his penchant for criticizing everybody else, from the ratiocinative first mate to the impudent second mate to the "unintelligent" Captain Archbold (42), because, believing himself a stranger and an alien on the ship, he desperately needs an ally against self-doubt and the hostility of the crew. He identifies with Leggatt not as a criminal but as an outcast: "I felt that it would take very little to make me a suspect person in the eyes of the ship's company" (37). Because in the captain's mind Leggatt is the picture of resolute self-confidence, Leggatt becomes in some respects an ideal to be studied: "And yet, haggard as he *appeared*, he *looked* always perfectly self-controlled, more than calm—almost invulnerable" (48–49; emphasis mine). The fetal position that Leggatt assumes as he hides in the cabin hardly suggests invulnerability. Indeed, it suggests his moral immaturity and his inability to distinguish between self and world from an ethical or psychological perspective. Yet the now mature captain believes he learned from this second self qualities of courage, self-confidence, and psychological wholeness—qualities that became his means of achieving maturity.

How does the captain's identification with Leggatt shape his response to the captain of the *Sephora*, whose name he remembers as Archbold?

Now let us turn to how the captain-narrator creates the *other* captain, Archbold. As an embodiment of the maritime tradition of authority, Archbold—the captain of the *Sephora*, the boat on which Leggatt killed a man—represents a father figure whom the captain is oedipally rejecting. Paradoxically, Leggatt disrupts the captain's psychic health, and hence the order of the ship, at the same time that he is a catalyst for a more efficient integration of both the captain's personality and his fitness to command. As we have seen, the captain projects on Leggatt a confidence he himself lacks and an ability to face crises he does not yet possess. Yet Leggatt's struggle with the crewman came when he was himself highly excited, and he shows considerable emotion several times in discussions with the captain.

While experiencing Leggatt's objective world, the captain adopts Leggatt's perspective. Therefore he has no hesitation or ambivalence in his attitude to Archbold. Not only does he compare the man—who stands, however poignantly, as an upholder of the moral order—to a criminal but in addition he describes him as "a tenacious beast." Speaking of an exchange with Archbold, the captain recalled, "I had been too frightened not to feel *vengeful*; I felt I had him on the run, and I meant to keep him on the run. My polite insistence must have had something menacing in it, because he gave in suddenly" (45; emphasis mine). However, the reader knows that the captain's judgment of Archbold is really Leggatt's and cannot exclude the possibility—indeed the probability—that Archbold is everything he says he is.

Nor can we accept the distinctions so essential to the captain that Leggatt deserves the allegorical identity of Truth and Captain Archbold that of Falsehood. His recollection of Leggatt's captain is consistent with his present myth-making. Although he does not remember the man's name, he assigns a pejorative name that we realize would be far more appropriate to Leggatt, whose *arch boldness* defies conventional morality: "He mumbled to me as if he were ashamed of what he was saying; gave his name (it was something like Archbold—but at this distance of years I hardly am sure), his ship's name, and a few other particulars of that sort, in the manner of a criminal making a reluctant and doleful confession" (41). Although he is certain that the captain suspects him, he offers no real evidence to support this notion; after all, he has told us how *different* from Leggatt he looked: "I had become so connected in thoughts and impressions with the secret sharer of my cabin that I felt as if I, personally, were being given to understand that I, too, was not the sort that would have done for the chief mate of a ship like the *Sephora*. I had no doubt of it in my mind" (43). Conrad hardly expected his readers to believe the captain's assertion that he reminded Archbold of Leggatt.

What is the effect of Leggatt's presence on the captain—and what is the effect of the captain on Leggatt?

The captain is as much Leggatt's secret sharer as Leggatt is the captain's. Put another way, each plays the role of analyst and analysand. Indeed, each of the two men has a partial understanding of the other, but each believes the other's partial understanding to be complete. In this sense, too, Leggatt is the captain's double. Leggatt says, "As long as I know that you understand," before adding, "But of course you do," because he too needs to believe he is understood (52). Leggatt desperately reaches out for someone to share his psychic burden. He likes to be looked at and spoken to, and even stammers when recalling their first meeting. At one point he says, "I wanted to be seen, to talk with somebody, before I went on" (38). Both men create a buffer to protect themselves from their feelings of excruciating loneliness in a hostile world. In each other, they find the intimacy of a captain-mate relationship that both pathetically lack in their professional capacities. For the first mate's suspicion of the captain echoes Leggatt's opinion of *his* captain. And Archbold—or, rather, Leggatt's and the captain's shared version of him—is the very type of captain that the narrator might have become if he had not engaged in this process of self-development.

Leggatt hides in the captain's L-shaped room. As Barbara Johnson and Marjorie Garber remark in "Secret Sharing: Reading Conrad Psychoanalytically":

> The cabin is L-shaped. It is shaped like a signifier, and what it signifies is what it contains and what contains it, the man whose name begins with L: Leggatt. Even Leggatt's name is doubled, two g's, two t's, two vowels— only the L stands alone, and it too is doubled in the form of the cabin. The capital L stands for Leggatt, but also for letter, for the "agency of the letter in the unconscious" (Lacan), for the fact that what is innermost (concealed) in the mind is in a sense its other.   (636)

Following our insistence that "The Secret Sharer" be regarded as a drama about the problems and interrelationships of people, we must ask why Leggatt requests to be abandoned. Does he sense that the captain cannot continue to operate as a split personality? Probably, but defined by his murderous impulsive act, Leggatt also needs to assert his own independence and to accept the role of exiled wanderer, as outcast to the universe where civilized values, embodied by the benign autocracy of the maritime, prevail. The narrator, of course, puts the best possible interpretation on Leggatt's behavior and implicitly invites us to do the same. Certainly, when the character with whom we identify and whose judgment is practically beyond reproach enlists our sympathy, it is not surprising that our first response is to accept his evaluation. The captain admires Leggatt both as a man of self-control who can accept the consequences of his actions and as a man whose instinctive behavior saved the *Sephora*. For him, Leggatt is not a mutineer and a murderer but an effective officer who is the victim of circumstances beyond his control.

The captain's recollection of his final view of Leggatt is significant: "[. . .] I was in time to catch an evanescent glimpse of my white hat left behind to mark the spot where the secret sharer of my cabin and of my thoughts, as though he were my second self, had lowered himself into the water to take his punishment: a *free* man, a *proud* swimmer striking out for a new destiny" (60; emphasis mine). The only way for the captain to satisfy his conscience, now that he has cast Leggatt from his boat, is to create the myth of a triumphant departure, for even retrospectively he cannot admit that he might have sacrificed Leggatt in order to preserve his own position. Yet, for the reader, Leggatt is a tragic, lonesome figure, branded as an outsider destined to wander the earth not only by the standards of civilization but by the captain himself.

Why does the captain take him so close to land? For one thing, he needs to assuage his conscience; for another, he has to prove to himself that he has grown into the role of captain; he needs to assert himself in the role of command. Indeed, the telling is that of a retrospective analysand probing into a crucial crossing from youth to maturity. While we cannot be sure of the tale's authenticity, its value as narrative to the speaker is incontestable.

It is the teller who has fulfilled the implied prophecy of a new destiny. He has lived up to an ideal conception of himself by proving his ability to command and by establishing his hierarchical position as captain. And Leggatt, abandoned to a world where the captain's epistemology is irrelevant, no longer exists within the civilized community except as part of the captain's consciousness. As soon as Leggatt departed, the captain "hardly thought of my other self, now gone from the ship, to be hidden forever from all friendly faces, to be a fugitive and a vagabond on the earth, with no brand of the curse on his sane forehead to stay a slaying hand . . . too proud to explain" (59). It is almost as if the captain can now cast aside the man who once threatened his identity, although the telling shows that he regards the experience as crucial to his personal development.

In retrospect it seems that Leggatt represents to the captain the captain's own potential for evil, a potential that must be expurgated before the captain can become morally as well as psychologically whole. The narrator clearly knows that, when confronted with a similar situation, he has behaved quite differently from the man he regarded as a double. When we as readers finish the story, we understand its iterative structure. As Louis H. Leiter perceptively argues:

> Leggatt seizes the man by the throat at the climax of his archetypal trial by storm and kills him in a fit of uncontrolled passion; the narrator also seizes the Chief Mate under similar circumstances, his archetypal trial by silence, but by controlling himself, controlling the frightened, disbelieving man, he controls the ship and consequently saves her from destruction, while saving his reputation and winning the respect of his crew.   (142)

The captain found in himself the confidence to act entirely without the paralytic self-consciousness that interfered at the outset with his ability to command the ship.

Leggatt, the captain-narrator recalls, is flippantly conscious of the possible analogy between Cain and himself: "The 'brand of Cain' business, don't you see. That's all right. I was ready enough to go off wandering on the face of the earth—and that was price enough to pay for an Abel of that sort" (107). Ironically, although Leggatt proclaims indifference to legal and religious standards, he cannot avoid responding to them:

> You don't suppose I am afraid of what can be done to me? [. . .] You don't see me coming back to explain such things to an old fellow in a wig and twelve respectable tradesmen, do you? What can they know whether I am guilty or not—or of *what* I am guilty, either? That's my affair. What does the Bible say? "Driven off the face of the earth!" Very well. I am off the face of the earth now.   (52)

It disturbs the conventional morality of the reminiscing captain to be on the side of Cain: "The very trust in Providence was, I suppose, denied to his guilt. Shall I confess that this thought cast me down very much?" (46). But most of the time his telling stresses his role as an Abel figure—his brother's keeper—in protecting his double, Leggatt. Yet it is clear to the reader that both men contain Cain and Abel elements. Leggatt plays the role of Abel when he willingly leaves the ship and thus helps the captain through the crisis. The captain's Cain identity derives from our realization that, to fulfill his own aspirations, he must abandon Leggatt.

The captain's use of Leggatt has its analogy in the creative process of art. Leggatt comes into his experience as a fact of the objective world; the captain transforms him into a fiction only partially congruent with the objective data of Leggatt's identity; then he releases him back into the objective world. Unwilling to risk his future, the captain sacrifices Leggatt for the unity of his own personality, just as the artist may sacrifice moral engagement for artistic purposes. Conrad believed that all people have a Cain aspect in their personalities in the sense that physical and psychic survival is dependent on conscious and unconscious decisions that may jeopardize the best interests of others. The artist is a radical example, because the creative process is a kind of withdrawal into the imagination at the expense of immediate participation in the community. The persistent allusions to the Cain-Abel myth suggest that each person must continually confront an unresolvable conflict between self-fulfillment and commitment to others. In an early letter to Mme Poradowska, Conrad had written, "Charity [. . .] is a gift straight from the Eternal to the elect. [. . .] For Charity is eternal and universal Love, the divine virtue, the sole manifestation of the Almighty which may in some manner justify the act of creation." But later in the same letter he wrote: "Abnegation carried to an extreme [. . .] becomes not a fault but a crime, and to return good for evil is not only profoundly immoral but dangerous, in that it sharpens the appetite for evil in the malevolent and develops (perhaps unconsciously) that latent human tendency towards hypocrisy in the [. . .] let us say, benevolent" (*Letters* 42; 5 Mar. 1892). The captain understands that it would be a "sham sentiment" (*Secret Sharer* 52)—what Conrad called "abnegation carried to an extreme"—to sacrifice his future by indefinitely harboring Leggatt.

NOTE

This essay is adapted from my 1997 essay "'The Secret Sharer' as an Act of Memory," which appears in my edition of Conrad's "The Secret Sharer" in the Bedford–St. Martin's series Case Studies in Contemporary Criticism.

"Heart of Darkness" and Others

Marianne DeKoven

One of the most important informing contexts in which Conrad wrote "Heart of Darkness" was the turn-of-the-century shift in gender relations so memorably noted by Virginia Woolf in her essay "Mr. Bennett and Mrs. Brown": "on or about December, 1910, human character changed" (96). Teaching "Heart of Darkness" in relation to this context in general, and in juxtaposition with Woolf's early work in particular, reveals structures and meanings in the text that are not otherwise apparent.

The period from 1880 to 1920, in which modernism emerged and rose to preeminence as the dominant art form in the West, was also the heyday of the first wave of feminism, consolidated in the woman suffrage movement. The radical implications of the social-cultural changes feminism advocated produced in modernist writing an unprecedented preoccupation with gender, both thematic and formal. Much of this preoccupation expressed a male modernist fear of women's new power and resulted in the combination of misogyny and triumphal masculinism that many critics see as central, defining features of modernist work by men. Conrad's work is often seen as a characteristic, even extreme, instance of modernist misogyny. This masculinist misogyny, however, was almost universally accompanied, and was particularly so for Conrad, by its dialectical twin: a fascination and strong identification with an empowered femininity. The result was an irresolvable ambivalence toward powerful femininity that forged many of modernism's and Conrad's most characteristic formal innovations. This ambivalence was felt by female as well as male modernist writers. While male modernists like Conrad feared the destructive power of the radical cultural change they desired—egalitarian change often embodied in various figurations of empowered femininity—the female modernists generally feared punishment for desiring that change (see my *Rich and Strange* for a book-length treatment of this idea).

Conrad's oeuvre is indeed profoundly masculine. He works primarily in and against the masculine tradition of adventure fiction. There are few women characters in his novels and stories, major or minor, and those who do appear are consistently flatter, more stereotypical, less fully realized than his great masculine characters. Nonetheless, the empowered maternal feminine is at the heart of Conrad's invention of modernism. In *The Nigger of the "Narcissus"* (1897), in many ways Conrad's first real step into the twentieth century (as Gertrude Stein says of her "Melanctha" in *The Autobiography of Alice B. Toklas* [50]), the dying black sailor James Wait is a figure of moral and narrative undecidability who pushes the text beyond the boundaries of realism. The rescue of Wait in the storm, which is at the center of this story, is narrated very explicitly in childbirth imagery: "he [Wait] pressed his head to it [a hole in the bulkhead beneath which he is trapped in a tiny room], trying madly to get out through that opening one inch wide and three inches long." He is "crowning." Finally, after much struggle, "suddenly Jimmy's head and shoulders appeared. He stuck halfway, and with rolling eyes foamed at our feet [. . .] all at once he came away in our hands as though somebody had let go his legs. With the same movement, without a pause, we swung him up. His breath whistled, he kicked our upturned faces" (43). The text as maternal womb gives birth to Wait, the embodiment of the powerful, dark complexities of modernism. As black and working class, he also embodies the central conflation in modernist figuration of the maternal with the "darker" races and "lower" classes implied by the crucially symbolic positioning of the womb, darker and lower down (Luce Irigaray brilliantly elaborates the masculinist Platonic parable of the cave as repudiated maternal womb in her chapter of *Speculum of the Other Woman* entitled "Plato's Hystera"). This conflation of erupting, newly empowered femininity, darker races, and lower classes, precisely that suggested by the political contiguity of socialism and feminism in turn-of-the-century radicalism, reappears throughout modernism.

In "Heart of Darkness," it is Africa itself that becomes the undecidable locus of empowerment of the maternal feminine as racially and geographically darker and lower down (the birth sequence in *The Nigger of the "Narcissus"* occurs as the ship passes through a gale in the Cape of Good Hope, at the southern tip of Africa). Conrad's representation of Africa is rife with maternal imagery. The "dark continent" is notoriously a figural conflation of racial and female-maternal otherness in relation to white Western masculinity. In Conrad's upriver journey into modernism, the dark continent begins stereotypically as terrifying, death dealing, devouring, the locus of illusion. But as Marlow gradually shifts his allegiance from the civilized (actually cruelly barbaric) European imperialism of the Company and its "faithless pilgrims" (26) to what becomes the truth of the African wilderness, the heart of moral darkness shifts in the text from Africa to Kurtz, embodiment of the monstrous failure of Europe's civilizing mission. The deepest informing truth of the novella, a truth associated with the modernist forms of symbolism and the dream—and with the unreliable first-person narration that, more than anything else, marks this text as a founding work of modernism—resides in the undecidable (at once deathly and empowering) maternal African wilderness.

Among the female modernists, Woolf is of course exemplary, in the quality, depth, and myriad importance of her oeuvre as well as of her cultural and intellectual presence. She thought and wrote extensively about questions of gender. In addition to her novels and stories constructed around the primacy of gender, her books *A Room of One's Own* and *Three Guineas*, as well as her numerous essays, diary entries, and letters touching on gender issues, remain a resource of the first importance for discussions of gender and modernism as well as for feminist theory and history in general. Woolf revised the predominant association of modernism with masculinity by associating it with femininity instead.

Her arguments (most notably in "Modern Fiction" [1919], "Mr. Bennett and Mrs. Brown" [1924], and *A Room of One's Own*), for the subversiveness of modernist form, its ability to penetrate and represent the underlying, multiplicitous truths of consciousness and psyche beneath the outward, unitary, coherent appearances of social and realist fictional convention, connect with Irigaray's linkage of repressed maternal femininity to the Freudian unconscious. Beginning with her first novel, *The Voyage Out*, where the New Woman–inspired heroine Rachel Vinrace attempts to "voyage out" of Europe and thereby out of its patriarchal-imperialist gender relations but ultimately is defeated by the community's translation of heterosexual love into patriarchal marriage, Woolf used literary form throughout her career to explore the possibility of releasing into representation the subversiveness of a culturally suppressed and repressed femininity. At the same time, in ways that the New Critics miraculously entirely missed, Woolf wrote directly about the great social and political issues of the twentieth century. A socialist, she always aligned herself with democratic egalitarian hope, even if she was not always in control of the upper-middle-class British ideologies of her upbringing.

Woolf admired Conrad greatly—she saw him as one of the few who were forging the way for the new writing of the twentieth century. *The Voyage Out*, particularly its pivotal river journey sequence, is obviously inspired by "Heart of Darkness." The river journey occupies most of Conrad's novella and only a short segment of Woolf's novel, but the parallels between the two texts, structural and stylistic as well as thematic, are much more extensive than that disproportion suggests. Those parallels are not particularly evident at first glance. "Heart of Darkness" is as commonly read and well-known a work as any in the canon of world literature in English, while *The Voyage Out* is relatively obscure and little read compared with Woolf's later novels. Nonetheless, the overall structure of each narrative is much the same. An opening section set in London and dominated by the Thames introduces an ocean voyage to the Third

World; a second section (much longer and more important in *The Voyage Out*) narrates the ocean voyage; a third section establishes the colonial setting and the relationships between protagonist and secondary characters; a fourth section narrates the river passage, with its climactic episode of arrival at the upriver destination; and a final section of return and its aftermath is marked by death and failed marriage.

In each text, the opening section posits hegemonic gender, economic, and narrative structures, emphasizing the malaise they have generated. The first page of *The Voyage Out* establishes a nexus of marriage, the social dominance of the middle class and the gender dominance of the male, conventional realist narrative, and sorrow. The setting for this nexus is Thameside London. As protagonists of bourgeois-realist narrative, Ridley and Helen Ambrose tower above the "lawyers' clerks" and "young lady typists," the "small, agitated figures–for in comparison with this couple most people looked small—decorated with fountain pens, and burdened with despatch-boxes," who "had appointments to keep, and drew a weekly salary" (9). But this towering and the marriage that supports it are immediately made problematic: the first sentence tells us that the Embankment streets are too narrow for the Ambroses to be able to walk arm in arm, an obvious symbol of their married state, without antagonizing the people over whom they tower, whose "angry glances struck their backs" (9). The narrative immediately proceeds to discuss Helen Ambrose's "sorrow," which seems to attach at once to non–West End London and to her regret at leaving her children: simultaneous class and gender references.

As it is for Conrad in the opening of "Heart of Darkness," London is for Woolf here a smothering darkness, a blot, a "vast black cloak." It is also home of the "poor who were unhappy and rightly malignant" (12). Conrad's opening section, like Woolf's, is dominated by an ominous gender polarity, by the gloom (Woolf's sorrow is Conrad's gloom) of turn-of-the-century urban capitalism, and by the ambiguous mysteriousness of the Thames. It is crucial that the "meaning" of Marlow's tale, in the framing narrator's well-known formulation, resides in the realm of the feminine, "outside" the "cracked nut" of the conventional seaman's narrative, in the "enveloping [. . .] misty [. . .] moonshine" (9). The framing narrator, in separating the "gloom" of London from the "exquisite brilliance" of the "mist on the Essex marshes," with its "gaudy and radiant fabric" (7, 8) maintains the clear gender polarity that Conrad as modernist, through his narrator Marlow, will undo.

Enter Marlow with his famous opening: "'And this also,' said Marlow suddenly, 'has been one of the dark places of the earth'" (9). The first narrator's neat, comfortable dualism, separating the gloom of modern London from the shining heroic "great spirit of the past" (8) of British imperial might, is collapsed in a stroke, as we move through Marlow into modernist narrative. Marlow insists, through his fantasy of the Roman conqueror facing the dark horror of the Thames, clearly foreshadowing the Congo journey, that the darkness is always already part of the brilliant, shining power of Britannia.

The maternal heart of darkness, the African jungle, repeatedly associated at the beginning of the narrative with lies, with conventional narrative, and with strict gender dualism, shifts in the course of the novella to become the locus of truth, while the truth of imperialism, and of high bourgeois European civilization in general, becomes the lie of the "faithless pilgrims" (26) and of the grotesque betrayals of Kurtz. The valence of the maternal feminine symbolism associated with Conrad's remarkable descriptions of the African wilderness shifts, in the course of the novella, from purely alien, terrifying, engulfing, deathly to that of a fecund life-origin whose integrity has been violated, ravished, by the onslaught of European imperialism. In general, through rich, dense, brilliant articulations of connotation and imagery, Conrad shifts his allegiance, in the course of "Heart of Darkness," from male-dominated European bourgeois capitalism, with its allied form of realist narrative, to a subversive modernism allied with anti-imperialism and the empowered feminine, which is in turn linked to "lower" class and "darker" race.

In *The Voyage Out*, as the title indicates, the main idea is to get out of the old order rather than to get to another, which Woolf cannot quite yet conceive. Woolf's South America is a fantasy location outside Europe in which the oppressive class and gender structure of European culture is nakedly revealed. In "Heart of Darkness," Conrad is much more concerned with what he is voyaging to: "I felt as though instead of going to the centre of a continent I were about to set off for the centre of the earth" (16): the dark continent is the maternal womb of all life. Marlow's initial description of Africa, again, is entirely negative. The African coast is "almost featureless [. . .] with an aspect of monotonous grimness. [. . . A] God-forsaken wilderness [. . .]. [W]e passed various places—trading places—with names [. . .] that seemed to belong to some sordid farce acted in front of a sinister back-cloth" (16–17). Moreover, Africa "seemed to keep me [Marlow] away from the truth of things within the toil of a mournful and senseless delusion" (17). Marlow is now himself entering the position he so blithely assigned to women before he left for Africa, the position of being separated from "the truth of things": "It's queer how out of touch with truth women are!" (16).

The dominant tone of the ocean voyage in *The Voyage Out* is opposite to that of Marlow's brief ocean journey: Woolf's narrative seems exuberant, triumphant, at leaving England behind. The ship on which this novel voyages out is called the *Euphrosyne*, the Grace of joyfulness. However, the liberating ocean contains psychic and political monsters ("the great white monsters of the lower waters," "white, hairless, blind monsters lying curled on the ridges of sand at the bottom of the sea" [22, 23]), monsters associated with the Old World economic and gender systems that it is impossible for Woolf to leave behind. As they will be on the Amazon passage, the bourgeois proprieties of proper dining, and in general the rigid, paternalist laws of sociability, are very much preserved aboard the *Euphrosyne*. Further, the ship becomes the temporary residence of the echt-imperialist Richard Dalloway, who assaults Rachel sexually following a long speech in which he extols the virtues of the British Empire, and of his ultra-feminine wife Clarissa (the prototype of the greatly evolved protagonist of *Mrs. Dalloway*), who is horrified by the idea of votes for women.

The South American section of *The Voyage Out* preceding the Amazon journey suppresses, for the most part, the Third World colonial setting. We feel that this group of privileged English people has been transported to another planet, or to a fictive space in which setting serves mainly to detach them from the context in which their behavior appears normal and inevitable. In Conrad's third section, Marlow's arrival and pre-river-passage sojourn in Africa, setting is heightened as much as it is suppressed in Woolf's. At the first Company station, we see immediately and unequivocally the truth of imperialism. All pretense of a redeeming idea is shattered by the horror of the hypocrisy, exploitation, and suffering Marlow encounters there, all for the "precious trickle of ivory" (21). As the miraculously starched and snowy-white monster, the Company chief accountant, says, within sight of the appalling "grove of death," "When one has got to make correct entries one comes to hate those savages–hate them to the death" (22).

It is after Marlow's two-hundred-mile tramp through the interior to the Central Station, where he finds his steamer "at the bottom of the river" (24), that Conrad's descriptions of the jungle darkness change utterly. First, Conrad emphasizes imagistically the feminine gendering, and association with maternal origin, of the African wilderness: "The smell of mud, of primeval mud by Jove, was in my nostrils [. . .]. The moon had spread over everything a thin layer of silver—over the rank grass, over the mud, upon the wall of matted vegetation," divided in two by "the great river I could see through a sombre gap." This "great, expectant, mute [. . .] immensity" of wilderness, "confound-edly big," that "couldn't talk and perhaps was deaf as well" (29), corresponds powerfully to Irigaray's account of the maternal origin, vast, vaginal, abjected, material, silenced and suppressed by patriarchal culture.

The crucial terms *fact* and *truth* shift again at this point in the text, this time from connection to the profit motive to connection to the heart of darkness itself. The feminine wilderness is now the locus of fact and truth, while the male European emissaries of profit construct the world of illusion: " I've never seen anything so unreal in my life [as the Station]" (26); "There was an air of plotting about that station, but nothing came of it, of course. It was as unreal as everything else—as the philanthropic pretence of the whole concern" (27). But "outside, the silent wilderness surrounding this cleared speck on the earth struck me as something great and invincible, like evil or truth, waiting patiently for the passing away of this fantastic invasion" (26). The maternal origin of life is ambiguous, resembling evil as well as truth. Conrad, like all modernists, is ambivalent about the possibility of the utter political and cultural change promised/threatened by the radical turn-of-the-century movements for gender, class, and racial equality. Nonetheless, truth and invincibility now reside in the African female wilderness, while white male imperialist European culture, as we see most powerfully in that ultimate imperialist Kurtz, is the home of unreality, hypocrisy, rapacity, absurdity, faithlessness, lies.

Woolf is equally ambivalent. Rachel journeys up the Amazon to find in its maternal wilderness, clearly derived from Conrad's, a true, authentic contact with her lover, Terence Hewet, unlike the inauthentic, rule-bound British upper-middle-class social relations Woolf satirizes and impugns throughout the rest of the novel. Terence is the ideal companion for the struggling New Woman: a novelist who wants to write about the truths embedded in silence, the "things people don't say" (216); who encourages Rachel to be independent; and who professes to believe in the equality of women. However, their sexualized encounter in the feminine wilderness, presided over by the highly ambiguous maternal figure Helen, is rough and frightening as well as authentic and liberating, and in its aftermath, when they return down the river to the hotel, Rachel falls ill and dies. Just before the onset of her illness, when she and Terence are a formally acknowledged betrothed couple, Woolf enacts the narrative and social power, not yet to be resisted successfully, of bourgeois patriarchal gender relations. Terence is utterly transformed, without warning, into a conventional man—bullying and deprecating Rachel and insisting that she follow strictly the rules and forms of bourgeois marriage, writing notes acknowledging congratulations rather than playing the notes of Beethoven (fairly inarticulate, she is nonetheless an accomplished musician—music is her particular means of intellectual, spiritual seriousness as well as of ardent self-expression). If this is her future, a return to the sorrowful London condition of bourgeois marriage in which the novel begins, Woolf would rather she died. The ending of *The Voyage Out* is just as bitter, just as defeated, as the ending of "Heart of Darkness," with its capitulation to the Intended's white, virginal (antimaternal) delusions in the "sepulchral city" of imperialism (27), antithesis as she is to the African lover spreading her arms out over the river as Marlow sails away with the moribund body of Kurtzian deceit and horror. The passage to a different order of gender, culture, and narrative, however, was opened, and through it two modernist narratives were born.

Women's Caring and Men's Secret Sharing: Constructions of Gender and Sexuality in "Heart of Darkness" and "The Secret Sharer"

Carola M. Kaplan

Two questions my students raise when I teach "Heart of Darkness" and "The Secret Sharer" are, Where are the women? and Why does the male protagonist risk his life for such a questionable friend (i.e., Kurtz and Leggatt, respectively)? I find these questions a good starting point for a discussion of the two texts, most particularly for considering issues of gender and sexuality. In class, I begin by suggesting that the two questions are closely related and that any answers we posit must be linked as well. In this way, I encourage my students to consider the connection between the marginalization of women and the intensity of homosocial bonding in the two works.

I teach "Heart of Darkness" and "The Secret Sharer" in sequence, in an upper-division course in twentieth-century British literature for English majors, most of whom are women. Predictably, students immediately comment on the marginalization of women in the first work and the apparent absence of women in the second. A consideration of issues of sexuality and gender raised by these two pieces is therefore imperative at the very outset of class discussion. Because their relative brevity makes possible a very close reading, I center class discussion on in-depth analysis of specific passages that deal with these issues. By paying careful attention to the details and ambiguities of these passages, students are able to discover that the two works consider issues of gender and sexuality with far greater complexity than the respective first-person male narrators acknowledge.

In both narrative and language, "Heart of Darkness" and "The Secret Sharer" consider the roles of women and the relationships between men. "Heart of Darkness" does so explicitly; "The Secret Sharer," implicitly. What they have to say on these subjects, as students come to realize, is contradictory. In each story, what the narrative denies, the language affirms.

On a narrative level, both texts deny the importance of women and insist on the supremacy of men. In "Heart of Darkness," Marlow maintains, "the women [. . .] are out of it" (49), and in his narrative he relegates them to the sidelines. Accordingly, the aunt, the knitting women, the African mistress, and the Intended have no names, play minor parts, stay in place, and, by implication, know their place. Yet, as the story unfolds, Marlow's take on women reveals its blindnesses, just as Marlow, the narrator, reveals his unreliability. In "The Secret Sharer," the captain, who retrospectively tells the story of his first command, discloses through the language he employs—in particular, through its pervasive sexual imagery—the power of the feminine that his narrative so determinedly suppresses.

Because of the inconsistencies, omissions, and contradictions in their narration, these works prove to be excellent vehicles for students to explore the limited and shifting narrative perspectives characteristic of modernist literature. By paying attention to all the language of each text, students find they can arrive at conclusions that exceed the limited understanding of the narrator. In order to help students interpret language and details in these stories that their narrators ignore, I encourage them to enlist the ideas and insights of contemporary literary theory, to which they have been previously introduced in a lower-division course required of all English majors. Specifically, I include in the syllabus extracts from psychoanalytic, postcolonial, feminist, and queer theory (by Sigmund Freud ["From the History"], Jacques Lacan [*Ecrits, Feminine Sexuality*], Abdul R. JanMohamed, Marianne DeKoven, Eve Kosofsky Sedgwick [*Between Men, Epistemology*], and Judith Butler [*Bodies, Gender Trouble*]) and urge students to draw on these ideas in their interpretations. Students find particularly useful the awareness afforded by feminist theory of the social construction of gender and the power relations governing sexuality, the emphasis of psychoanalytic theory on the fragmentation of the self and on interpretation beyond the rational, and the resistance of queer theory to sexual schema and its reminder of the polyvalence of desire. By considering literature in light of theory, students gain not only a more inclusive understanding of literary texts but also some insight into the intellectual and ideological underpinnings of modernist techniques.

One modernist technique with which students must grapple in these works by Conrad is that of the unreliable narrator. Conrad's use of this device is particularly difficult for students to understand in that they must contend with narrators who are neither fully reliable nor completely unreliable but, rather, somewhat reliable. That is, they must go along with the decisions of both Marlow and the young captain if these stories are to make sense at all—but they must accept these narrators' perspectives only with considerable qualifications.

"Heart of Darkness" in particular is an excellent text for helping students deal with the complexities of the issue of narrative reliability. Minimally, they must trust Marlow's assigning importance to Kurtz and Marlow's choice of nightmare, that is, his preference of Kurtz's horror over the pilgrims' flabby cowardice. At the same time, students must appreciate the limitations of Marlow's interpretations. In particular, they are called on to question the binary oppositions that Marlow enlists to buttress his hegemonic assumptions and to justify his participation in the colonial enterprise.

Throughout the text, Marlow insists on the distinction between truth and lies; between men and women; between civilization and savagery; and, most of all, between self and other. Yet despite his insistence, all binary oppositions collapse in the course of his narrative: colonists prove to be conquerors, the gang of virtue is indistinguishable from the gang of greed, the illusions of women merely echo the illusions of men, and there is no clear distinction between lies and truth. Most important, the fundamental difference between self and other disappears and, with it, the unbridgeable gulf between men and women and between savage and civilized that sustains the power structure of Western civilization. But this awareness offered by the text eludes Marlow, for, enmeshed in his own culture, he would, as he himself admits, find this awareness "too dark—too dark altogether" (76).

Through close reading, students discover that the text of "Heart of Darkness" dismantles the distinctions that Marlow takes pains to establish. One of the chief of these is his distinction between the world of women and the world of men— the women's narrow and idealistic ("too beautiful" [16]), the men's broad and realistic. The narrative, as voiced through Marlow, attempts to contain, that is to say, confine women. Yet in the language of the text women everywhere overflow this narrative containment. Accordingly, when he downplays his aunt's importance, he inadvertently reveals his reliance on her. His aunt, who clearly wields more social power than he, is described patronizingly as "a dear enthusiastic soul" (12), although her influential recommendations of him haunt him along his Congo journey and serve to ally him with the similarly "gifted" Kurtz (15, 48). Likewise, Marlow's compelling but ambivalent description of Kurtz's African mistress enables the reader to see her power, authority, and unique attributes. As Marlow describes her, she is a distillation of alluring but frightening otherness. In her overt sexuality and aggressive claims on Kurtz's person, she is both enticing and menacing. Wearing a helmet, armor, and magic charms (60), she appears to belong to a matriarchal and polyandrous female warrior culture that reverses the sexual hierarchy of the West (Kaplan 328).

Perhaps most tellingly, Marlow's efforts to separate the soothing female world of illusions from the larger male world of shocking realities collapses in his interview with Kurtz's Intended. These worlds fuse in the nightmare atmosphere of the Intended's drawing room, inhabited by Kurtz's ghost, whose words echo and eerily combine with hers to form the ghastly chorus Marlow hears. This chorus suggests a terrifying intertwining of purpose between Kurtz and his Intended—a collusion between the "soul as translucently pure as a cliff of crystal" (70) and the "soul that knew no restraint, no faith, and no fear" (66). For this reason, when Marlow asserts, "I saw them together—I heard them together" in the drawing room, he experiences "a sensation of panic in my heart as though I had blundered into a place of cruel and absurd mysteries not fit for a human being to behold" (73). The phrase "cruel and absurd mysteries" eerily echoes the "unspeakable rites" (50) attributed to Kurtz in Africa.

In this scene, Marlow's language and observations suggest, although his panic and confusion indicate he does not consciously understand, that domestic bliss and female innocence in England are predicated on the exploitation of natives and the pilfering of ivory in the Congo; that marriages between ambitious young men of insufficient means with young women of substance are facilitated by the colonial enterprise, in which enterprising young men make good in the name of doing good. The details of this scene combine to point out that, although Kurtz is dead, his power continues to live on through his

Intended, who carries the torch of his ideas, a torch that casts a sinister light back on her. She, in her female innocence, colludes with global evil in death-dealing conspiracy.

From their classroom analysis of these key scenes, students generally conclude that Marlow fails miserably in his attempts to minimize the importance of women. I then ask them to consider why Marlow is so invested in denying female power and influence. To help students understand the underlying reasons for his denigration of women, I find it especially helpful to enlist Marianne DeKoven's idea of modernist *sous rature*, the unresolved contradiction or ineradicable ambivalence toward radical cultural change that is expressed in the works of male modernist writers (21). Employing this idea, I engage the class in a consideration of the simultaneous attraction and revulsion toward feminism that surfaces in disguised form in the text of "Heart of Darkness" (and, by extension, in "The Secret Sharer"). In their scrutiny of the text, students discover that Marlow's entire account of his journey is, as DeKoven points out, permeated by female sexual imagery (85–126) that serves to underscore the power of women that Marlow, in frightened recoil, attempts to deny.

As students become aware of Marlow's inadvertent acknowledgment of women's power and influence, they begin to understand the reasons for his investment in Kurtz—in particular, his identification with Kurtz's success in the exclusively male enterprise of imperialism. Although Marlow wants to see men as more powerful and more realistic than women, his initial experiences in the Congo bring him into contact exclusively with misfits, miscreants, and ne'er-do-wells. Unlike these crass and cowardly specimens, Kurtz does in fact seem to represent a separate male sphere distinguished and justified by its superior understanding. In allying himself with Kurtz, Marlow seeks not only refuge from female domination but also assurance of the rightness of the imperial project when backed by an "idea—something you can set up, and bow down before, and offer a sacrifice to" (10). In identifying himself with Kurtz, however much he will come to recoil from Kurtz's corruption, Marlow is able both to denounce and to participate in the triumphs and transgressions of patriarchy and colonialism. Since Kurtz represents both the utmost fulfillment and most extreme violation of the patriarchal and imperial project, he helps define Marlow and serves to delineate both the possibilities and limitations of male subjectivity in general.

In making these connections, students come to understand why Kurtz's seductive voice irresistibly beckons Marlow, both in the jungle and in the drawing room. They see as well that the sexual allure of both the African mistress and the Intended works so strongly on Marlow because these women are extensions of Kurtz, their power over Marlow an attenuation of the far greater attraction he feels to Kurtz himself. He identifies with and protects the man who loved them. Likewise, he identifies himself with them in their love for Kurtz. Through his experience of sexual power as polyvalent, Marlow in his journey charts a psychosexual terrain far more complex than the map of Africa he originally contemplated—one closer in its multiplicity to the map as modified by the incursions of colonialism. In this redrawn territory, desire cathects both male and female objects, which simultaneously threaten and help define the subject. Just as details of the narrative break down the divisions between male and female in the social sphere, so too the narrative erases the facile distinctions between male and female sexual roles and challenges the hegemony of heterosexuality. Arguably, the greatest love the text discloses, through the actions of its characters, is that of Marlow and of the harlequin for Kurtz: in their self-sacrificing care and protection of him, they exceed the devotion of both his African mistress and his Intended.

Once students have grappled with the complex issue of narrative reliability in "Heart of Darkness" and have looked beyond Marlow for the text's larger understanding of gender and sexuality, they are ready to tackle "The Secret Sharer" in its more extreme denial and consequently greater validation of the importance of women. Like "Heart of Darkness," "The Secret Sharer" presents the feminine within the *sous rature* of modernism. The story opens with a simple picture—an overly simple picture, akin in its condensation to the manifest content of a dream. I remind students of Freud's distinction between the manifest and latent content of dreams, then encourage them to discuss the dreamlike elements in "The Secret Sharer"—in particular, the initial descriptions of the inexperienced and unnamed captain, the unfamiliar boat, and the surprise visitation of the fugitive Leggatt, against the background of night. In addition, I discuss with them Freud's analysis of the Wolf Man's specimen dream (of a tree with silent wolves in its branches) ("From the History" 29–47). I then ask students whether there are any similarities between the Wolf Man's dream and the opening of "The Secret Sharer." In response, students venture that, as in the Wolf Man's dream, the uncanny stillness of the opening—the picture of a world becalmed with a still boat on a motionless sea—suggests the aftermath of violent movement: in "The Secret Sharer," the moment after birth. Yet students observe that the captain's life seems tenuous. In his inertia and uncertainty, he seems not yet born. He is, after all, still lodged in the body of the mother—the ship, which like a uterus is "very fine, very roomy for her size, and very inviting" (27). In this prenatal state, he is in danger. Indeed, he may prove to be stillborn.

At this point, I ask them to do some freewriting, encouraging them to respond associatively to the language of the opening scene. Influenced by our preceding discussions of "Heart of Darkness," they tend to comment on the sexual imagery of this scene. They note that the boat containing the young captain has emerged from the mouth of a river, depicted in language that suggests a birth canal (the description of the river mouth surrounded by small clumps of trees evokes a vagina fringed by pubic hair; the blue and brown water evoke amniotic fluid and blood).

They note also the captain's feelings of isolation, uncertainty, and vulnerability. He is a stranger to the "mysterious" world around him, "a stranger to the ship," and "somewhat of a stranger to myself" (24, 26). Left alone by the tug to embark on "a long and arduous enterprise," he seems to long for a companion—"my hand resting lightly on my ship's rail as if on the shoulder of a trusted friend" (25). Soon after, he spots Leggatt, his "double" or "other self" (34). From his first view of the vulnerable, naked, apparently decapitated body for which he will provide the problem-solving head, his survival is linked to Leggatt's. In this scene, students begin to discern that, only by facilitating the birth of his twin brother (his active, even violent self), still attached to the uterus by the umbilical cord, the "rope side-ladder" (28), can the captain himself become clearly viable. Prematurely thrust into a life for which he is not ready—that is, a position of leadership—he must in a sense birth or rebirth himself, through sheltering his brother-other in his "berth."

Once students have commented on the female sexual imagery of the first scene, I ask them whether there are any actual women in the story. After some thought, they remember the twice-discussed but unseen wife of the captain of the *Sephora*. I ask them, What is the attitude of the story toward her? They note the implied disapproval shared by the young captain and Leggatt, which forms part of the bond between these two former Conway boys, who share similarities in background, class, and education. The details Leggatt offers about the wife make her sound uncongenial: she is allied with her husband in conventionality and facile condemnation. The captain and Leggatt seem to agree that her presence on board the *Sephora* testifies to the captain's inadequacy: he is as afraid of her as of his men. Further, Leggatt suggests that her influence worked to exacerbate the harshness of his treatment in the aftermath of the murder.

In criticizing the captain for having his wife on board, the story points out that, while heterosexuality is the convention on land, the insular world aboard a working ship is generally homosocial. And in valorizing an intense friendship between two men that transcends even their duty as officers, the story challenges common practice and overturns the assumptions of heteronormativity. Certainly, the language that describes their alliance is distinctly homoerotic. They share extremely close quarters, communicate in whispers or "only with our eyes" (46), repeatedly touch, clasp hands. The captain refers to "the secret sharer of my life" (40) and to "our secret partnership" (46); he reports feeling "extremely tired, in a peculiarly intimate way, by the strain of stealthiness, by the effort of whispering and the general secrecy of this excitement" (38). In discussing this story with students, I draw on the ideas of queer theorists Judith Butler (*Gender Trouble*) and Eve Kosofsky Sedgwick (*Between Men*) to foster awareness of the social construction of gender and to question the inevitability of heterosexuality. Accordingly, we note that, in the context of "The Secret Sharer," the marital relation seems incongruous and intimacy between men both natural and necessary.

Then I ask students whether, given the unimportance of the actual woman in the story, there is any female figure or entity figured as female that is important. This question leads to a discussion of the centrality of the ship, which is throughout referred to as "she." From the first, the captain emphasizes his need to become familiar with the ship and, by extension, to gain mastery over her. In regard to his concern, I remind the class of our earlier consideration of the story's female sexual imagery, in which the ship was associated with the body of the mother. If the ship is the mother, students realize, then by extension the cabin the two men share is a kind of womb that shelters them until they can emerge into their separate and individual lives at the end of the story.

From this interpretation, students are better able to understand and therefore to accept the intimacy of the relationship between apparent strangers, which, on a realistic level, seems precipitous, excessive, and unwise (from the standpoint of the captain's responsibilities). For, according to the female sexual imagery of the story, the two men are symbolically infant brothers, in fact, fraternal twins. I encourage the students to consider the homoerotic bond between the two men from the perspective of Freud's essay "Leonardo Da Vinci and a Memory of His Childhood" (1910), in which Freud analyzes a childhood dream of the painter as revealing his homosexual longings. Students acknowledge that, in the dreamlike narrative of Conrad's story, the captain and Leggatt seem to enact the fantasy that Freud cites as the basis of homosexuality. That is, the captain's attachment to Leggatt may be seen as a form of narcissism in which, identifying himself with a nurturing mother, he chooses as love object a man who is a younger version of himself. In the love they share, they are both brothers and lovers, nurtured and protected by the fantasy mother who, in being supplanted, is yet perpetuated. Accordingly this story, while it apparently suppresses the feminine, in fact enacts a necessary immersion in it. By succumbing to the feminine, sheltering himself and his brotherother in it, the young captain both incorporates and obtains mastery over the mother (the body of the ship), thereby uniting potentially warring aspects of himself. Thus Leggatt fulfills the promise of his name: by entering the protagonist's berth-birth, he proves to be the ambassador or legate of the captain's distinct and complex subjectivity.

Such an extensive consideration of sexual roles and gender construction in these two works helps students refine their reading skills and develop a methodology for further literary interpretation. Equally important, their engagement in the double-pronged process of close reading accompanied by the application of critical theory gives them not only the tools but also the confidence to strike out on their own in the consideration of other challenging modernist texts. By guiding them through this process, the professor— in keeping with the female sexual imagery of "Heart of Darkness" and "The Secret Sharer"—may fittingly assist students, in their passage through the straits of modernist literature and facilitate their birth as independent literary critics.

Why I Teach Conrad and Achebe

Padmini Mongia

A few years ago, a colleague of mine remarked after teaching a class on "Heart of Darkness," "We discussed Achebe's perspective in class today. But I tried to give them both sides of the story. After all, imperialism was not only a bad thing. It brought roads, the railway, and electricity to Africa." I was stunned by my colleague's conflation of imperialism and modernization and wondered just how Chinua Achebe's perspective had been discussed in his class. Almost ten years have passed since this moment occurred, and I have thought of it often during that time. I have considered why my colleague felt the need to say anything to me; why he felt the need to discuss Achebe in his class; and how the reference to Achebe, in his comment to me, functioned to buttress and support his views conflating imperialism and modernization. This unremarkable encounter reminds us that Achebe is evoked or taught routinely alongside "Heart of Darkness," that to evoke or teach him signifies "dealing with race," and that there are more "balanced" views to take of imperialism. As I address these moments, I consider the larger question that shapes this inquiry: Why should and how can one teach a novella that is considered racist?

Canonizing Conrad and Achebe

Like many other famous classics taught in the North American academy, "Heart of Darkness" is a text that has been fought over, particularly through the 1980s, when the discussions over the "great books" and the decline of values in higher education were most virulent.[1] To deal with "Heart of Darkness" is always also to deal with its status as a high-culture text and one that has, at least in the United States, become the nexus of vehement arguments on the threatened condition of Western culture itself. Achebe reminds us that as far back as 1950, Albert Guerard called "Heart of Darkness" "among the half-dozen greatest short novels in the English language" ("Image" 252). Since then, Conrad's place in the canon of high literature has only become more secure. In 1998, the "Heart of Darkness" centenary conference organized in South Africa drew 130 delegates from nineteen countries, with fifty presentations devoted to the novella. Read and responded to constantly, the work might most usefully be considered hypercanonized, a concept Jonathan Arac uses in reference to *Huckleberry Finn*. Speaking of *Huckleberry Finn* and its status in the North American academy and popular media, Arac argues that the process of hypercanonization created Twain's novel as a "masterpiece of world literature and as the highest image of America" (6). This process ensured that critics laid out the terms whereby *Huckleberry Finn* could be approached and appreciated, so generations of students were taught how to read the work as a great American novel.

Hypercanonization creates the status of a text and the critical terms by which it is approached. In "Heart of Darkness," there have been two chief strains of critical inquiry: first, that the novella is an exposé of the ills of imperialism; second, that it is a profound meditation on one man's journey into his own dark soul.[2] Achebe's 1975 charge that the novella was "racist" (257) introduced a new set of concerns and threatened the terms established by mainstream critical approaches to Conrad's work. However, despite the shock waves produced by Achebe's essay, the hypercanonized status of "Heart of Darkness" ensured that his position could be contained, a point I return to later.[3] In fact, Achebe's essay itself became canonized and offered the most direct path whereby critical issues addressing race could be apprehended. In 1988, with the publication of the Norton "Heart of Darkness," which included Achebe's essay, his argument consolidated his status. More than twenty-five years have passed since Achebe's critique, yet responses to him appear steadily. Even this present volume is a case in point. In this quarter century, Achebe's essay has remained the single route whereby Conrad's late-century constructions of race need to be addressed. To the mainstream critical establishment, it seems besides the point that in these two decades many new works have been published that contextualize Conrad's construction of race in interesting and textured ways.[4]

As with *Huckleberry Finn,* charges of racism in "Heart of Darkness" have led to heated responses against its removal from school curricula. While Conrad's work has not generated quite as public a controversy as Twain's, no doubt in part because its iconic status is not as closely linked to definitions of national identity, it continues to generate anxious concern. Nor, indeed, is the concern limited to the academy. In 1995, David Denby, writing in *The New Yorker,* shared his experience with "Heart of Darkness" in Columbia's Literature Humanities course. His engagement with Conrad's construction of race also came about through Achebe's essay. Denby offers his experience as essentially therapeutic, because class discussions allowed for vehement and heated exchanges on questions of racism. He therefore suggests that Conrad's text enables an understanding of the 1890s and of our current moment, which helps with the process of sharing and healing that racial politics requires. For Denby, then, suggesting that the text not be read, as Achebe does, goes against not only his beliefs in free speech but also the belief that such censorship would do a great disservice to the project of literature as healing. Compelling as this argument is, let us not forget the disturbing replication, in student essays, of the oppositions between "savage" and "civilized" as standard features associated with particular places. They reveal, at the least, that "Heart of Darkness" and Achebe's essay are taught and read in many different ways. Can the mere fact that certain works are taught also determine the way they are disseminated and understood?

Dealing with Race

Conrad and Achebe are routinely taught alongside each other. I would venture to say that they are inseparably linked in the courses of the early-twenty-first-century teacher of Conrad, in widely flung academies—in the United States, India, and South Africa. Presumably, the mainstream academy engages with Conrad's construction of race and with Achebe's charge that the novella is racist. But Achebe's charge of racism has led not so much to an engagement with his argument as to the need for rejecting it and defending Conrad. While Achebe's essay rocked the boat in the 1970s, it did not produce substantive rethinking of the critical terms for approaching Conrad. It is therefore not surprising that Conradian critics still respond to Achebe with the need to defend Conrad. A quick glance at the responses published since 1975 reveal a structure posited on a model of defense and rescue.[5] Examining Conrad's constructions of race thus becomes a matter of answering back to Achebe, proving or disproving his point.

Addressing race in Conrad through Achebe's charge of racism can lend itself to an easy and neat marginalization of race as a critical concern. Ironically, his essay can enable an evasion of rather than an engagement with the issues. His polemical argument swiftly becomes, particularly in the North American academy, circumscribed by two perspectives: first, that his views represent an extreme position held by people of color who are embittered by their experience; second, that banning books goes against the very fundamentals of Americanness and is soundly to be rejected. Seen primarily through these two lenses, the essay can allow "race to be dealt with" without any substantive engagement with Achebe's more profound concerns.

In other words, teaching Achebe alongside Conrad need not mean anything more than teaching/presenting a position that is not regarded seriously. A quick glance at the adjectives used to describe Achebe's views will suffice to illustrate how easily Achebe has been dismissed: Cedric Watts finds his capacity for "fine discriminations [. . .] eroded by bitterness" and suggests that "spleen has clouded his judgement" ("Bloody Racist" 197). Denby refers to positions such as Achebe's and Edward Said's as "hostile and undermining" ("Jungle Fever" 120). That these adjectives inevitably accompany responses to Achebe reveal the space allocated to serious discussion of his positions. If Achebe's views can so easily be relegated to the realm of the hostile and embittered, then has it mattered that Achebe on Conrad has been read at all? I think not. Precisely because Achebe lends himself to analyses that can be approached as free speech issues, his positions can be contained, even dismissed. Given this scenario, why and how can one teach Conrad or Achebe?

Why Teach "Heart of Darkness" and Achebe?

In a discussion on the residual lives of imperialism, Said in *Culture and Imperialism* points to the growing feeling in the West, through the 1960s and 1970s and into the 1980s, that it was time for the ex-colonized to take responsibility for their present states instead of criticizing the West. "Was it not true, ran their new evaluation, that 'we' [Westerners] had given 'them' progress and modernization? Hadn't we provided them with order and a kind of stability that they haven't been able since to provide for themselves?" Said's reading of the 1980s further points to "an imagined history of Western endowments and free hand-outs, followed by a reprehensible sequence of ungrateful bitings of that grandly giving 'Western' hand. 'Why don't they appreciate us, after what we did for them?'" (22). This sort of backdrop describes the scene of teaching and reading "Heart of Darkness" on North American college campuses today. Because this is the scene, it is imperative that we *do* teach Conrad.

When I was taught Conrad's *Lord Jim* twenty years ago, as an undergraduate in Delhi, I completely identified with "one of us." It never occurred to me, that I, the sensitive reader, was not one of the charmed circle of "us." Now that I know I am not and never was, I am still shocked by the power of that vast machinery that ensured that hundreds of eager-eyed sixteen-year-old Indians—and their teachers—would read *Lord Jim* and never consider how racial difference shaped the story. Certainly, such reading no longer obtains in India or elsewhere.[6] Yet, it is possible, and perhaps even commonplace, that texts like "Heart of Darkness" be taught with no substantive engagement with race and gender constructions in the novel. To my mind, these are not optional interpretative concerns in literature classrooms. To others they are. So I must teach high-culture texts and offer some interventions in how my students understand the concerns that shape the works they are taught to value most.

I teach Conrad because teaching about race and empire cannot just be the business of courses with like titles; it needs to be part of the mainstream English curriculum. If such concerns are relegated to works by women or people of color, we are only creating new ghettos rather than offering new modes of learning. As a teacher, I must displace the readings that have approached "Heart of Darkness" as a novella exploring the journey into man's dark soul. I need to interject in the readings that say colonialism was not a totally "bad" thing since it brought "progress" and railways and electricity to Africa and other colonies. I teach "Heart of Darkness" because I must try to make my students realize that the literature of the nineteenth century contends with race, empire, and colony, whether or not that contending is touched on in other courses.

How to Teach "Heart of Darkness" and Achebe

"Heart of Darkness" routinely forms part of my Nineteenth Century and After course, my Colonial and Postcolonial Novel course, and my Introduction to Literature class. I teach it, then, to both majors and nonmajors and usually include Achebe's essay as part of the reading. The "Heart of Darkness" I teach focuses on two main aspects of Conrad's text. The first is Marlow's meditation on empires early in the novel, which culminates with his emphasis on the belief in the "idea" (10). My students have almost always missed this meditation. Our discussions articulating the idea spell out the links between empire and "civilizing" mission. To my students' minds, the former was a "bad thing, sadly believed in by those who had not progressed enough yet, as we have." The civilizing mission they are less certain of, since they share many aspects of its definition. Students are not so certain that bringing "civilization" to the Africans was not a noble burden borne by the white man. In order to problematize civilizing, I point out the role of missionaries and the spread of English education as part of its necessary features.[7] I try to link the civilizing mission with its residual lives today, whether it is the pope's call to convert Hindus in India or the Gulf War and stated American intentions to rescue Kuwait.

The second moment we focus on is Marlow's erasure of Kurtz's postscript. It allows us a chance to discuss how knowledge is shaped and disseminated and always interested. We approach this moment in the suggestive terms of James Clifford's essay "On Ethnographic Self-Fashioning." We discuss the advent of new branches of knowledge production such as anthropology, a child of colonialism; we discuss how anthropology produces its object of knowledge through the participant-observer; and we discuss knowledge as power. Students are quite struck with the suggestiveness of this little detail of Conrad's novella and become uncomfortable about the weight we so easily grant disciplines, canons, teachers, and other figures and modes of authority. Once these two moments have been dealt with, students approach Marlow's tale with less certainty and belief than they had granted it earlier. Depending on the course, other features come more or less into the foreground as we discuss what Kurtz means to Marlow, the ending of the novel and its denial of knowledge to women, the rendition of land as feminine and engulfing, and so forth.

The problem with teaching Achebe lies in trying to find a way around the difficult issue of banning Conrad. To my mind, Achebe's essay is significant for the large concern that opens it: that racism against Africa and Africans is so standard that its operations go completely undetected, in life and in literature. In Achebe's argument, Conrad's novel perpetuates rather than disbands received stereotypes. Achebe's charge of Conrad's racism usually results in the following response: "Well, that was back then. Everybody thought like that. But we shouldn't ban a book because of that. How will we learn, then?" Not surprisingly, Achebe's call to ban Conrad raises hackles; arguments on free speech are mounted with a pious insistence on some simple entity known as free speech. Even to include different views (racially or otherwise determined) is no easy task. Since my students are mostly white and affluent, they do not see race as their issue. Race and racism are someone else's issues, presumably those of people of color, because it must matter to them, and of whites who are racist. My students are sure they are neither.

In order to avoid being mired in a debate about whether or not Conrad was a racist, I focus instead on the beginning and end of Achebe's essay. I make students work at length with the two episodes that open his piece. His vignette—high school students in Yonkers, who associate tribes with Africa—resonates with the assumptions of my students. I make them proffer their stereotypical views of Africa and suggest that they are not alone in believing that Africa is a primitive, backward place, prone to famine, poverty, and mayhem. We undertake an exercise where I ask for adjectives students would associate with Africa; their responses, not surprisingly, are initially hesitant and embarrassed. As I encourage them to share their received images of Africa, the list on the board grows; students gain confidence and begin to see that their views are shaped by the worlds they inhabit and not the result of some deep inner racist flaw. After we have examined the two anecdotes Achebe opens with, we meditate on the slippage between language and dialect of which he reminds us at the end of his essay. My students are made uncomfortable by realizing that they share assumptions they never considered they had, in their certainty that they were not racist.

Finally, because we have just examined how knowledge is always interested knowledge, as demonstrated by Marlow's erasure of Kurtz's postscript, we are more ready for Achebe's demand that the book not be taught. This part of class discussion is always difficult, but I feel I have had a measure of success if I manage to make my students consider that what they are being taught is interested, just as how they are being taught is. This point is easier to grasp now that they realize how polemical and difficult the issues surrounding "Heart of Darkness" are. Further, the listing of words associated with Africa makes students wonder if Achebe's opening claim—that white racism against Africa is so standard that its operations go undetected—might not deserve more weight than they had initially granted it. While I have never had students agree to banning "Heart of Darkness," they have considered seriously Achebe's point regarding the undetected mechanisms of how power functions. As a result, class discussions on Achebe's call to ban the book have not been sterile.

"Heart of Darkness" is not an easy work for me to teach. While many students agree with the emphases I place on our reading, many more don't. I keep struggling to find a way to get my students to understand Achebe's larger frustrations, for it has always seemed to me that the strategy of his essay, in part, was to generate debate. If my students leave with a sense that Achebe cannot be dismissed (despite their disagreeing with his call to ban Conrad), I feel I have been very successful. However, I do wonder if by teaching Conrad I have not just perpetuated the very structures I wanted my students to question. The disheartening repetition associating savagery and the primitive with Africa is never very far from written or spoken responses to Conrad. Yet I must risk that repetition and trust that more often than not I have produced sufficient discomfort to generate questioning, a questioning that may well continue long after the course is over.

NOTES

My thanks to Hunt Hawkins for our fruitful three-year-long dialogue about "Heart of Darkness" and Achebe and for inviting me to contribute to this volume.

[1]Allan Bloom's *The Closing of the American Mind* was published in 1987. It was swiftly followed, in 1991, by Dinesh D'Souza's *Illiberal Education: The Politics of Race and Sex on Campus*. These works generated a great deal of public attention, although they are only two of many more instances charging higher education with the erosion of intellectual and cultural values.

[2]Nicolas Tredell's *Joseph Conrad: "Heart of Darkness"* offers a useful survey of the critical issues that have shaped approaches to the novella since its publication in 1899. Tredell shows that in the 1960s, when the novel reached the height of its reputation, two of the major readings—by Eloise Knapp Hay and by J. Hillis Miller—saw the novel as a critique of imperialism and as nihilistic (9). D. C. R. A. Goonetilleke's introduction to the Broadview "Heart of Darkness" also consolidates critical approaches to Conrad's novella in terms similar to those I use above (15).

[3]As Tredell suggests of the criticism of the 1970s, "these new voices [Achebe and Perry Meisel's deconstructive reading] did not drown out the tones of more conventional scholarship and criticism" (9).

[4]I am thinking of works such as Marianna Torgovnick's *Gone Primitive*, which approaches race through the lens of the "primitive" as constructed in the 1890s; Benita Parry's *Conrad and Imperialism*, which examines conventional notions associated with light and dark imagery to reveal Conrad's subversion and later confirmation of these associations; and Dorothy Hammond and Alta Jablow's *The Myth of Africa*, a work that examines narrative constructions of Africa at the turn of the century. Christopher Miller's *Blank Darkness* is also useful for its exploration of the tropes that defined discourse on Africa, as is Sandhya Shetty's article *"Heart of Darkness*: Out of Africa Some New Thing Rarely Comes." Patrick Brantlinger's *Rule of Darkness* and Edward Said's *Culture and Imperialism* are two more works addressing race, difference, and empire in Conrad's novella with a historicizing complexity.

[5]I discuss this structure more fully in my "The Rescue: Conrad, Achebe, and the Critics."

[6]I recently spoke on *Lord Jim* in Delhi University and marveled at how different the critical terrain looked. While syllabi in Delhi University have barely changed in these twenty years, modes of reading certainly have.

[7]In this regard, see Gauri Vishwanathan's *Masks of Conquest*, which links the development of English literary studies to the arena of empire.

Conrad and the N Word:
Responding to the Sensitivities and Politics
of the Contemporary Classroom

Joseph F. Militello

["Heart of Darkness" is] a book which parades in the
most vulgar fashion prejudices and insults from which a
section of mankind has suffered untold agonies and
atrocities in the past and continues to do so in many ways
and many places today [. . .] a story in which the very
humanity of black people is called into question.
>—Chinua Achebe, "An Image of Africa"

And so I smiled, but he poked out / His tongue and
called me, "Nigger." / I saw the whole of Baltimore /
From May until December: / Of all the things that
happened there / That's all that I remember.
>—Countee Cullen

Tanned boys I do not know / on their first proud harvest
/ wave from their father's tractor / one smiles as we drive
past / the other hollers / nigger / into cropped and
fragrant air.
>—Audre Lorde

Although the college classroom has traditionally been thought of as an ivory-tower sanctuary from the topical unrest of the larger society, a place of quiet reflection and contemplation, of academic debate and rational discussion predicated on the ideal of heuristic argumentation and the calm analysis of hypothetical textbook scenarios, my experience as a teacher in higher education for more than a decade has often demonstrated to me the fallacy, or at least naive oversimplification, of this ideal.

A student of mine in a freshman English class (at a historically black university in the Mississippi Delta, where I taught for four years) expressed outrage, for example, at Shakespeare's preference for "snow-white" women's breasts to those that were "dun." Her tone in questioning this verse of sonnet 130 was one of hostility, directed at me (her white professor), directed at Shakespeare, and directed at all of a white Europe that could promote such a preference, and perhaps at white academia for elevating Shakespeare and this racist poem to a place of such high esteem. My attempts at explaining in the most accessible terms Shakespeare's anti-Petrarchan motives for writing sonnet 130, which in fact challenge racist conventions of beauty, or the Elizabethan cultural context in which pallid women exempted from work under the bronzing sun were valued as socioeconomically attractive mates, were viewed by the class as laughably pedantic rationalizations. For many of these students, the reference to "black wires" on the head of Shakespeare's "mistress" struck a hypersensitive chord with their experience of a devalued African American feminine beauty in our society, the pain of which Shakespeare's seemingly patronizing sympathy did little to alleviate. I then remembered students in other classes who had made childhood experiences of mockery by white children of their "nasty nappy hair" the subject of intensely written personal narrative essays. While *Othello* can be taught as an ultimately antiracist play, one finds in Shakespeare's putative embrace of the institution of slavery in *The Tempest* and his pejorative references to "Indian beauty" in *The Merchant of Venice* (3.2.93; to say nothing of the arguably anti-Semitic thrust of the play) grounds for endorsing the condemnation of Shakespeare for racism. Such a starting point, however, is not auspicious for leading students to a nuanced and comprehensive appreciation of this great author's works. With the current social climate, such an approach may tend to shut down cerebral discussion rather than open up areas of analysis and debate.

That a single hateful racist epithet can create a traumatic experience for African Americans is amply evidenced by Countee Cullen's famous poem "Incident" (DiYanni 692) or the more recent "Every Traveler Has One Vermont Poem," by Audre Lorde (E. Roberts 962). These poems describe how a one-time exposure to the N word left the speakers wholly disenchanted with the entire city of Baltimore and the state of Vermont, respectively, despite otherwise positive experiences there. The use of the word is shown in both poems to shut down all rational discourse with its incapacitating power of dehumanization. Since the O. J. Simpson trial, in which Mark Fuhrman's alleged racist language played a major role in swaying the jury, the euphemistic term "N word," modeled on the polite term "F word," has gained currency in American public discourse. This usage reveals the referent as so inflammatory as to be unpronounceable even for nonracist heuristic and journalistic purposes. An adult student of mine in an evening class told of her attempt to have administrators remove a book from her niece's school that contained the racist word. She wrote in an essay on the subject, "My niece should not have heard that word in school, especially not from a teacher. A seven-year-old girl should not have heard this word under any circumstances because it ridicules her heritage, her ancestors, and her ethnic group as a whole." There has been a long-running debate over whether Mark Twain's repeated use of the word, even in the context of a presumably antislavery novel widely regarded as a seminal American classic, should be sufficient cause to remove *Huckleberry Finn* from high school curricula (Hurwitz).

Less debate has attended the use of texts containing such words or other offensive subject matter or language in college-level courses, since it is still widely assumed, except perhaps in colleges with narrow religious perspectives or other specific agendas, that American higher education is a final bastion of free expression. One may share this value of free discourse unfettered by censorship while still addressing with concern the reality that some highly charged texts may create a corrosive climate antithetical to the purposes of learning in the contemporary American classroom. Such a state of affairs requires particular sensitivity and skill on the part of today's college professor. As a teacher of literature, one must respect such emotional reactions and allow them a classroom airing, but one must also find constructive ways to present classic literary texts seemingly discredited by the taint of a presumptive racism. One should avoid giving in to mere defensive apologetics for the author's evident indiscretions or biases, yet one must also resist the outright censorship of removing an offending text, even voluntarily, from the curriculum.

Conrad's repeated use of the N word throughout his writing has attracted less attention than Twain's. For one thing, Twain uses the word over two hundred times in *Huckleberry Finn* (Hurwitz), while Conrad reverts to it only about a half dozen times in "Heart of Darkness." Twain's treatment of American, rather than African, history may have also been a factor in stirring early protest over his writing instead of Conrad's.

Since the 1970s, of course, "Heart of Darkness" has been a magnet for attacks by postcolonialist critics like Chinua Achebe and Frances B. Singh, who accuse Conrad of a virulent racism and of providing support for European imperialism in Africa by depicting that continent's native people as savages in need of the civilizing influence of European culture.

Despite the number of cogent critical responses by Conradian scholars at MLA conference sessions and in academic journals, which demonstrate in varying ways the antiracist, anti-imperialist intentions of the author of "Heart of Darkness," and even despite the admission by the African activist Ngugi wa Thiong'o that Conrad's novel has been an important contribution to anticolonialist literature (Sarvan 285), the problem of teaching Conrad to wary undergraduates for whom the mere appearance of a racist epithet signals bigotry and stupidity rather than literary excellence or profundity remains daunting.

Achebe still holds to his labeling of Conrad as "a thoroughgoing racist" ("Image" 257), and his discussion of Conrad's deep-rooted psychological "antipathy to black people" (258), which he claims went well beyond the normal prejudices of his time, may have validity even if one acknowledges Conrad's larger political intentions in "Heart of Darkness" and other works as constituting a critique of colonialism.

For my recent seminar Nineteenth-Century British Literature, I used volume 2 of the *Norton Anthology of English Literature* (Abrams). Opening to the section on Conrad, the first thing the reader notices is a reprinting of the preface to *The Nigger of the "Narcissus."* While the ship's name is appropriately placed in quotation marks, no asterisk, footnote, or italics are deemed necessary for the other N word in the title (1756). The reader of "Heart of Darkness" must face this word every five or ten pages, with references to "dusty niggers," "an overfed young negro," "[a] quarrelsome band of footsore sulky niggers," "the fool-nigger" (21, 25, 32, 46), and other references to "niggers" and "savages," each presented in an apparently matter-of-fact tone without editorial comment or footnotes. The 1998 edition of *Merriam-Webster's Collegiate Dictionary*, by contrast, includes this note on usage: "*Nigger* [. . .] can be found in the works of such writers of the past as Joseph Conrad [. . .] but it now ranks as perhaps the most offensive and inflammatory racial slur in English. [. . . I]t is [. . .] a word expressive of racial hatred and bigotry."

The *Norton Anthology's* recent inclusion of Achebe's critique, along with his *Things Fall Apart*, provides instructors and students with greater opportunities for a discussion of the racial and colonial issues raised by Conrad's text. Reading the two novels together enables students to balance Conrad's Victorian European perspective on Africans with a more humanistic and three-dimensional one. In another sense, however, anything idyllic about the harmonious African precolonial society at the beginning of *Things Fall Apart* can only illustrate the life that was disrupted by the coming of the colonial powers. In "Heart of Darkness," we are already at the end of the process of social disintegration Achebe describes—things *have* fallen apart in the Belgian Congo for the natives of the region. Conrad's representations of dispirited Africans reduced to bestial labor and in thrall to the European ivory traders may, in fact, be more accurate and legitimate portrayals of Africans in that particular time and place than the proud athletic Okonkwo in Achebe's novel. One must not assume, as Achebe seems to do, that the African characters in "Heart of Darkness" are meant to represent all Africans rather than Africans in one place at one terrible moment in history.

It is here that the value of the Norton Critical Edition of "Heart of Darkness" can best be appreciated and employed. Students should read and discuss much of the "Backgrounds and Sources" section of the third edition before embarking on their voyage up the Congo with Marlow. The contemporary reports of the scenes of colonial atrocity Conrad and others witnessed, along with Conrad's own diary notes on what he saw and how he felt about it, contextualize Marlow's comments on the natives as arising out of, at worst, a colonizing bravado typical of the era put on for the benefit of others or to reassure himself, despite growing inner doubts, of his cultural superiority. At best, the racial epithets can be viewed as mere statements of fact concerning the debased condition of the Congolese people at the time, meant to evoke sympathy or pity at the wretchedness of their oppressed state. Even if one does view some of Marlow's descriptions of the natives as blatantly, undeniably racist, being provided with the context of Conrad's own intellectual and political journey can help one appreciate how Marlow's perceptions of the natives continues to evolve throughout the novel.

I would suggest starting with a look at Conrad's reflections on his schoolboy fascination with the blank spaces of unexplored and uncharted territories on maps of the world. Students will appreciate the childhood innocence in his admiration of explorers like Cook in the Pacific and Franklin in the Arctic, whose missions theoretically were motivated by scientific curiosity rather than greed. Students will see how his youthful sense of wonder, lust for adventure, and desire for the exotic contrasted with the mercenary and hypocritical outlooks of other Europeans in Africa during the period of colonization.

One could then acknowledge the ambiguity of the young Conrad's innocent motivation by looking at his description of his childhood fantasy image of Mungo Park, in which he is "lying on the ground in the shade [. . .] while [. . .] a charitable black-skinned woman is approaching him with a calabash full of pure cold water" ("Geography" [*Heart*] 146–47). This daydream suggests a desire on the part of the young Conrad to be attended to by dark-skinned native servants, a not altogether atypical dream for the petite bourgeoisie of Europe, many of whom joined the foreign service for just such amenities in the colonies, which would have been out of reach at home given the class hierarchies and limited opportunities of Europe.

Ironically, Conrad does come to experience the scene he dreamed about as a child. When he was deathly ill in the Congo in 1890, an "old negress" saved his life by bringing him water every day—even when, as he told Edward Garnett, "the white men never came near me" (Garnett, "Art" 196). If there is something racist in his schoolboy fantasy of being brought water by a native woman, his account to Garnett shows how much he's grown in his attitude. Clearly there is a newfound appreciation of the natives here. While in Conrad's childhood version they may have been dismissed as incidental menials or exotic contributions to the landscape, in the adult version the woman is a generous lifesaver, morally superior to the apathetic and self-serving white Europeans and physically superior to Conrad himself in his weakened condition. Condescension has turned to respect. The use of the archaic word "negress" in this context is therefore a good way to introduce the touchy subject of Conrad's language and give it both a historical and a personal context.

One could then point to the process of disillusionment Conrad experienced when the "white heart of Africa" ("Geography" [*Heart*] 147) turned out to be a heart of darkness. Clearly the adult Conrad recognizes and has transcended the foolishness of his schoolboy view of Africa as merely a place of adventure and exotic experience. In a memoir published more than twenty years after his Congo trip, he writes, "the sin of childish audacity was to be visited upon my mature head"(*Personal Record* 33). In a diary entry made during his 1890 trip, Conrad already has the maturity of perspective to dismiss the famed meeting of Stanley and Livingstone as an "unholy [. . .] prosaic newspaper 'stunt'" (*Last Essays* 25). Clearly, he has grown out of the naive spirit of adventure to consider the human costs of colonialism and to see the mission of Europeans in Africa as one of exploitation rather than exploration. He told Garnett later that he "was a perfect animal [. . . who] had reasoned and reflected hardly at all over the varieties of life he had encountered" prior to his Congo experience, where "human fatuity, baseness, and greed had swept away the generous illusions of his youth and had left him gazing into the heart of an immense darkness" (Garnett, "Art" 195).

Interestingly, Conrad remarks in a letter included in the Norton Critical Edition that he has read Rimbaud's poems. A contrast between Rimbaud's African adventures and Conrad's would prove instructive. Though their African journeys may have sprung from the common origins of a childhood desire for exotic adventure, Rimbaud—formidable intellect and writer that he was—whether because of his early death or lack of intellectual growth, never rose above a mere cynicism and despair at the banality and inhumanity of what he found in Africa to articulate the enlightened anticolonialist position that Conrad worked into masterpieces of literature that are still influential (cf. Fowlie 322–63).

It would then be helpful to discuss the equivocal position that writers like Conrad, Rudyard Kipling, and George Orwell found themselves in. Although their views and patterns of speech may have been conditioned by the age they belonged to, such writers often transcended the complacency and unproblematic support for the colonialist enterprise of Britain and other nations felt by the British and European masses back at home.

Their writings offer, in varying degrees and in different ways, critiques of the system of colonialism they themselves were involved in. One could point, for instance, to Kipling's implied critique of the British government's exploitation of soldiers sent to fight and die in colonial wars in his cynical depictions of the empire's soldiers in poems such as the 1892 "Widow at Windsor," in which a hapless bewildered soldier refers to himself and his comrades in arms as "poor beggars in red," as "O' Missis Victorier's sons" who are sent off to fight in "barbarious wars" (Abrams 1675). One could also look at the scathing critique of colonialism in Orwell's first novel *Burmese Days*, written in 1934 following his miserable service in the British Imperial Police in Burma in the 1920s, or at some of his anticolonialist journalism such as the famous "Shooting an Elephant" (2228) to show how his experience as a colonizer led to his enlightened views on colonialism. Without acting as an apologist for such writers, one could then use writings like Conrad's letters and *Congo Diary* to show that firsthand experience of the effects of colonialism may be necessary to formulate a critical awareness of its impact and a subsequent condemnation of it.

Despite the controversy over Conrad's position on imperialism, certainly his sympathetic view of Roger Casement, who crusaded against Belgian atrocities in the Congo, points to a shared attitude of condemnation of colonial abuses. Conrad confessed in a letter to Unwin that "Heart of Darkness" was written to express "all my indignation at masquerading philanthropy" (*Collected Letters* 1: 294). He wrote in a letter to Arthur Symons, "I've always approached my task [of writing novels] in the spirit of love for mankind" (Symons, "Every Novel" 234). Yet could Conrad merely be attacking the hypocrisy of King Leopold of Belgium and government propagandists or attacking the excesses and abuses of the colonial administration while still accepting the larger idea of a civilizing mission for Europeans in Africa, a racist taking up of the "white man's burden," as his critics, like Edward Said, have claimed? He does write in a letter to William Blackwood that the novel he's writing is about "the criminality of inefficiency and pure selfishness when tackling the civilizing work of Africa" (*Collected Letters* 2: 139–40). This statement of purpose does seem to support the position of those who attack Conrad as ultimately sharing in the overall colonialist project and in the ideas of racial superiority that underlie such a project. Yet one must recognize Conrad's tendency toward intentional misrepresentation of his true political purposes. His 1920 "Author's Note" to his novel *The Secret Agent* seems to cater to the anti-Bolshevist sentiments of his post–Russian Revolution reading public in misstating the purposes of that novel, which were, in fact, largely sympathetic to radicals and socialists and rather hard on their attackers (see *Secret Agent* 3–8).

He could be more frank with his liberal friend Ford Madox Ford regarding his political leanings when critiquing governmental authorities than with his conservative friend John Galsworthy, from whom he carefully hid his true feelings about *The Secret Agent*. His letter to his publisher Blackwood may have been somewhat misleading, an attempt to downplay the controversial nature of the novel so as to ease the publisher's fears of a backlash from the government, critics, or reading public. Conrad's attempt, as a foreigner, to assimilate into a stodgy xenophobic Victorian British society may also account for his reluctance to be too explicit about his more radical anti-imperialist views in his commentaries on his work. He may have trusted intelligent readers to extract from his often elliptical and ironic novelistic prose an impassioned message condemning the inhumanity of Belgian colonization and of the European ivory trade in the Congo.

We see him writing to Casement that "the Congo State today" represents a moral regression for Europe, since what is happening is comparable to the inhumanity of the earlier "slave trade," and he pleads for Europe's conscience to awaken "to take up the cudgels for humanity, decency, and justice" (qtd. in Franklin, "Williams" 124).

If one accepts Conrad as an enlightened reformer and critic of colonialism, how does one then cope with the apparently racist images of Africans in the novel? Even in his letters and diary, he seems to offer negative images of African natives. In an 1890 diary entry, he writes of falling into a muddy puddle: "Beastly. The fault of the man that carried me" ("Congo Diary" [*Heart*] 162). No doubt his bearer was Congolese or an imported laborer from Zanzibar. Since the native was being used as a beast of burden, itself an ugly image of Conrad's own participation in colonial exploitation, the "beastly" comment could be taken as referring to the ineptitude of the bearer or to the bearer himself. Such a reading would be in accord with Achebe's critique of Conrad's alleged view of Africans as animalistic. Yet given the larger context of Conrad's misery and his growing anticolonial feelings, one could see the epithet "beastly" as a general comment on the unpleasant nature of the entire situation

Conrad found himself in and on the beastliness of an exploitative colonial system that has white Europeans carried like kings by natives through their own country.

He does say in a letter to his aunt that in the Congo, "Everything is repellent to me. Men and things, but men above all" (*Collected Letters* 1: 62), and he says in his diary that "my life amongst the people (white) around here cannot be very comfortable" ("Congo Diary" [*Heart*] 159). Both these statements suggest that Conrad's misanthropy was not simple racism but a growing sense of horror at man's inhumanity to man. One could also read racism into Conrad's diary description of African women he met in the Congo, whose "features [were] very Negroid and ugly" ("Congo Diary" 161), but his further description of them as albinos with "chalky white" skin "with pink blotches" and "red eyes" and "red hair" suggests perhaps less a general antipathy or loathing and more a critique of white Europeans' raping of African women, assuming these women derived their features from such unions or from the prostitution documented by George Washington Williams as being widespread in the Congo at the time ("Open Letter" 109). Williams also writes of the presence of a smallpox epidemic and other diseases, which may have disfigured the faces of these women, making them "ugly" ("Report upon the Congo-State" 92–93).

We are left with the problem of the many negative portrayals of Africans in the novel itself that prompted Achebe's original critique. Williams, by nature a sympathetic observer of the native African peoples he encountered on his own 1890 trip to the Congo, offers negative images of Africans in the region, images presumably free of any racist motives. He describes some natives as "diminutive in form, obsequious, deceitful, untrustworthy, unmanly, and unreliable [. . . living in] huts, poorly constructed of bad material [. . .] hapless victims of their own filth" (91). He describes others as "jaundiced [. . .] covered with the most revolting looking scars" (92). It may simply be a fact that Conrad was dispassionately describing what he saw. Marlow's negative reactions to the natives in "Heart of Darkness" may simply reflect the ugliness that pervaded the region at that time. This is far from saying that Africans are ugly by nature. Williams also encounters Africans in certain parts of the Congo whom he could describe as "the most splendid types of physical manhood I have seen in any land [. . .] brave, frank, and generous [. . .] eager [. . .] industrious and peaceable" (92). He diagnoses the problem as a demoralization of some of the peoples of the Congo, whose contact with Europeans has led to the poisonous effects of liquor, forced prostitution, forced back-breaking labor, disease, imprisonment, floggings, and the despoliation of the natural habitat. A letter writer who had visited the Congo the same time as Conrad, Casement, and Williams remarked, "The country is ruined [. . .] there is not an inhabited village left [. . .] a country formerly so rich [. . . is] today entirely ruined" (qtd. in Morel 40). Should we then blame Conrad for reporting on the ugliness of the Africa he has seen? If this were the only image of Africa and Africans that Western readers absorbed, Achebe would be right in attacking its partiality, yet could it not be that it was true enough of the Congo interior in 1890?

One is still left with the problem that Conrad seems to accuse Africans of a native depravity, according to some critics of the novel. Could this depravity be also simply rooted in the disturbing facts of the time and place Conrad found himself in? Williams describes personally witnessing cut-off human hands and human skulls on proud display by natives, as well as acts of human sacrifice and cannibalism and slaves of tribal chiefs being buried alive. If this is savagery, even given the ethnocentric eyes through which Conrad viewed such "unspeakable rites," must one not acknowledge it as such? Conrad at least tempers any such conclusions with a full admission of European depravity and even an awareness that though Kurtz may have been morally corrupted by his exposure to native customs, the natives have been equally corrupted by their exposure to European immorality.

As students proceed to read "Heart of Darkness," keeping these issues and perspectives in mind, their encounters with the seeming racial slurs of the text will be less traumatic and emotional, perhaps, and may produce more thoughtful and studied responses. Such a point in the learning process is not the time, however, to dismiss the value of personal emotional responses or to abandon debate over the questions they raise. I would suggest a class devoted to reader-response discussions, followed in subsequent classes by discussions of the novel from other perspectives, drawing on historical contexts and structural models, motif studies, feminist readings, and so forth. However, students should not be expected to become inured to the disturbing power of the N word. An understanding of the novel's higher purposes and the historical situation out of which it was bred may, nonetheless, channel feelings of anger into the ultimately positive experience of intellectual engagement with history, literature, and politics.

After our discussion of the novel itself, Achebe's and Singh's critiques can be brought in, along with the rebuttals contained in the Norton Critical Edition, as well as other cogent responses by Hunt Hawkins, Said, Cedric Watts, and others (see Hawkins, "Issue"; Said, "Intellectuals"; Watts, "Bloody Racist"; Sarvan; Blake; Brantlinger, *Rule*; Carey-Webb; Fleming; Kuesgen; London, "Reading"; and Hamner, "Colony"). It would be useful to insert into the discussion Montaigne's famous essay on cannibals (Wilkie 1999) to raise important questions about the sort of moral and cultural relativism toward such customs Singh expects us to take. Students can then decide for themselves, with perhaps a deeper reflection and broader awareness, whether Conrad indeed is a "bloody racist," an imperialist, or a radical critic of the colonialist enterprise.

A Choice of Nightmares:
Reading "Heart of Darkness"
through *Apocalypse Now*

Margot Norris

Perhaps the most difficult concept to convey to student readers of "Heart of Darkness" is the way the story functions as a process of conversion—a tale designed to enable the listener or the reader to experience the ethical choice that Marlow confronts in the heart of Africa and that he terms "a choice of nightmares" (62). Readers accustomed to think of ethical choices in terms of the simple binary of good and evil are obliged by the story to confront the possibility of having to choose between different kinds of evil. This choice becomes even more difficult when the worse evil belongs to one's own culture, to Western civilization, and when it outstrips and exceeds the cruelties we conventionally think of as primitive barbarism. Putting "Heart of Darkness" into dialogue with Francis Ford Coppola's 1979 film *Apocalypse Now* allows readers to find Conrad's exposé of Belgian and British imperialism relevant to United States military intervention in Southeast Asia two or three decades ago. Coppola inverts and reverses syllables in the name of Marlow to transform him into Willard. As Conrad's protagonist does nearly eighty years earlier, Willard makes a journey up a river, not into Africa but into Cambodia, to find a renegade named Kurtz. Like Marlow, Willard finds a Kurtz gone native and indulging in barbaric cruelties. Willard also recognizes, like Marlow, that Kurtz merely externalizes and makes visible the far greater barbarism, cruelty, and hypocrisy of the invading "civilized" nation.

This displacement of one historical context to another is, of course, inscribed into the frame narrative of "Heart of Darkness" itself, in its twice-told structure introduced by a jingoistic Englishman who rhapsodizes the glories of England's great explorations ("all the ships whose names are like jewels flashing in the night of time, from the *Golden Hind* returning with her round flanks full of treasure [. . .] to the *Erebus* and *Terror*, bound on other conquests [. . .]. The dreams of men, the seed of commonwealths, the germs of empires" [8]). This silent paean to the British Empire is punctured by the voice of Marlow, who reminds the men on board the ship *Nellie* anchored in the Thames River, that "this also [. . .] has been one of the dark places of the earth" (9). Marlow not only reminds his listeners that proud England was itself once a primitive land conquered by a civilized Roman empire but also employs a naturalistic rhetoric to describe that conquest's mundane, unromantic, and sordid character: "Sandbanks, marshes, forests, savages, precious little to eat fit for a civilised man [. . .]. Here and there a military camp lost in a wilderness like a needle in a bundle of hay—cold, fog, tempests, disease, exile, and death—death skulking in the air, in the water, in the bush. They must have been dying like flies here" (9–10).

Conrad sets up a paradigm of imperialism as historic displacement and repetition: civilized empires were themselves once primitive places conquered by
others. Although Marlow's story will expose Belgium's plunder of the African
Congo, the point of his story is clearly to deflate his companion's fantasies of
the illustrious and glorious founding of the British empire in conquest of the
Americas, India, and other lands. By using "Heart of Darkness" as a silent
intertext or hidden script, Coppola imports Conrad's lesson of displaced imperialism by alluding to both the American genocide of the native Indians (in the
US cavalry hat of Captain Kilgore and in the Playboy girls' costumes and danc-
ing play of "cowboys and Indians" during the USO show) and the history of
slavery (by the references to Abraham Lincoln during Willard's briefing in
army headquarters and by the presence of the African Americans among the
boat's crew). Although *Apocalypse Now* is set in the heart of the Vietnamese
and Cambodian jungles, Coppola seems to remind viewers that the United
States, too, was once "one of the dark places of the earth."

As Marlow tells the story of his steamship trip on the Congo River into the
heart of Africa to retrieve the renegade agent Kurtz, he demystifies the European mission in Africa with a series of images that suggest the venture's absurdity and destructiveness. His ship encounters a French man-of-war "firing into
a continent" at some hidden native encampment while its crew was "dying of
fever at the rate of three a day," and gives them their mail. "There was a touch
of insanity in the proceeding," Marlow remarks of the purposeless shooting
(17). Coppola repeats this scene when Willard's boat stops at the Dun Lo
Bridge, where a similarly incomprehensible and functionless shooting is in
progress and where the men don't even know who is in charge, let alone what
they are shooting at and fighting for. Coppola may have chosen a bridge rather
than a ship to make this point in order to allude to a famous World War II film
that uses the building and destruction of a bridge in the Malaysian jungle—
David Lean's Academy Award–winning *The Bridge on the River Kwai*—to
metaphorize the absurdity of war. Coppola also uses this scene to show a deliv-
ery of mail to a population that is in the process of dying. Willard's boat is
attacked while the men are reading their letters and listening to their tapes
from home, and the young African American Clean dies from the shots while
his mother's voice speaks her family's love to the boy.

As Marlow continues his journey down the river into the heart of Africa, he
encounters increasingly more disturbing scenes of suffering. However, Conrad
is careful to show that Marlow cannot consider himself an innocent witness or
outsider to these scenes: by joining the trading company, he has joined the
enterprise responsible for creating misery and inflicting cruelties on the
natives. To make this point, Conrad uses the powerful metaphor of bloody
shoes—a variant of the trope of having bloody hands—to indicate that one can
be guilty of violence without wielding the actual implement or committing the
actual act. Violence may be structural, institutional, and self-perpetuating, Conrad seems to suggest, by indicating that Marlow's journey follows the already

bloody tracks or footprints of predecessors—specifically, the Dutch Captain Fresleven, who was killed while menacing an African chieftain in a dispute over a couple of black hens. When, late in the journey, Marlow's shoes are literally filled with the blood of the dead helmsman killed by a spear at his feet, his disgust and horror remind us that his path into the African jungle is the European path of colonial violence, which his predecessors have already marked with bloody tracks. He has now stepped into their shoes. Coppola has no comparable metaphor for these bloody shoes, and a scene he had planned for the film, which was to be set on a French plantation to hark back to Vietnam's prior colonization as Indochina by the French, was edited out of the final cut.

However, Conrad recognizes that although it may be difficult to represent, or recognize, a colorless entity like a trading company as an agent of violence, oppression, and cruelty, this equation is precisely the point he must make if he is to convey to the reader that colonialism and imperialism take the strangely pallid, undramatic form of European companies plying their trade in undeveloped parts of the world in the nineteenth century. He therefore shows Marlow first acquiring this insight as he stands in a grove of death where native African workers are sick, dying, beaten, and marched in chain gangs. This is no scene of atrocity but just business as usual, and Marlow reflects that all this misery and suffering is produced by the trading company's dull bureaucrats, the colorless hollow men who wreak immense evil by the infernal conditions they create out of systematic corporate enterprises and ways of doing business they justify as civilized practice. Marlow reflects: "I've seen the devil of violence, and the devil of greed, and the devil of hot desire; but by all the stars these were strong, lusty, red-eyed devils that swayed and drove men—men, I tell you. But as I stood on this hillside I foresaw that in the blinding sunshine of that land I would become acquainted with a flabby, pretending, weak-eyed devil of a rapacious and pitiless folly" (19–20).

The way Conrad chooses to bring the trading company's cruelty home to the reader is by creating in the figure of Kurtz a double, an oppositional figure who is a product of the trading company but who dramatizes its cruelty in garish and macabre images designed to shock and repel both Marlow and the reader—while forcing us to recognize that Kurtz merely acts out in pathological form what the company does routinely. The "unsound method" (61) that the company imputes to Kurtz in his dealings with the natives is most shockingly dramatized by the heads and skulls of the enemies he has impaled on posts around his compound. While Conrad miniaturizes this shocking scene by having Marlow first see it through the lens of a telescope (57), Coppola makes the scenes of Kurtz's depravities more shocking still, by filling the screen of Willard's first view of Kurtz's compound with bodies hanging and dangling from trees like decaying fruit and with heads protruding from the ground like tubers. Both Conrad and Coppola make the figure of Kurtz charismatic—intelligent, poetic, eloquent, engaging, powerful—but with a shocking capacity for evil that in Coppola's film is epitomized when Kurtz tosses the severed head of

Chef into Willard's lap as though it were a cabbage. The figure of Kurtz is intended in both novella and film to be both more attractive and magnetic than the hollow men of the trading company and the army, respectively, and more repellent in its capacity and lust for violence. But the directness of Kurtz's violence, and his willingness to confront and own it as he looks into his soul to see "The horror! The horror!" (68), makes Marlow and Willard ally themselves with the nightmare of Kurtz rather than with the nightmare of the corporate colonial or military enterprise. The difference is that Kurtz is capable of a moment of self-recognition—the moment that Greek tragedy calls anagnorisis or that in existential philosophy is the ethical acceptance of responsibility for one's actions: "Did he live his life again in every detail of desire, temptation, and surrender during that supreme moment of complete knowledge?" (68). The internal journey into the heart of darkness requires looking into one's own soul and taking responsibility for what one has done. Seeing Kurtz confront his own darkness obliges Marlow and Willard to confront theirs and acknowledge that, as parties to a murderous enterprise, they are as guilty as Kurtz.

In "Heart of Darkness" Marlow does not kill his double, Kurtz, as does Willard in *Apocalypse Now*, but he does become his executor, as it were: the guardian of his papers, his reputation, and his memory in the heart of Kurtz's fiancée, the Intended. This task proves to be as painfully difficult as a snail moving along the edge of a straight razor and surviving, to borrow a metaphor from *Apocalypse Now*. Marlow refuses to cooperate with the trading company's demand for Kurtz's papers and information, but when he meets the Intended, he learns that she idolizes Kurtz. The Intended wants her interview with Marlow to corroborate her saintly image of Kurtz, and Marlow realizes with horror that she is asking him to perjure himself in order to preserve her illusions about the civilized nature of an ostensibly civilized man. The dialogue between Marlow and the Intended is suspenseful with ironies, as we are obliged to watch him try to elude her pressured need to have Kurtz's greatness and goodness affirmed:

> "And you admired him!" she said. "It was impossible to know him and not to admire him. Was it?"
>
> "He was a remarkable man," I said unsteadily. Then before the appealing fixity of her gaze that seemed to watch for more words on my lips, I went on, "It was impossible not to. . . ."
>
> "Love him," she finished eagerly, silencing me into an appalled dumbness. (73)

Eventually the Intended's passionate determination to learn everything she can from Marlow about Kurtz traps him into making a fatal confession: "'I heard his very last words. . . .' I stopped in a fright." To her plea, "Repeat them [. . .] I want—I want—something—something—to—to live with" (75), Marlow can only tell her the lie that Kurtz at the last uttered her name.

A small detail in the civilized Belgian room that contains Marlow's interview with the Intended provides a poignant symbol of the overlay of the best of civilization with the worst of civilized barbarism when Conrad revisits the metaphor of the "whited sepulchre"(13)—a biblical trope for hypocrisy, for a beautiful exterior hiding a corrupt interior—that Marlow had earlier used to describe the implied city of Brussels: "A grand piano stood massively in a corner with dark gleams on the flat surfaces like a sombre and polished sarcophagus" (72). The keys of the grand piano in the Intended's beautiful living room would have been made of ivory, the commodity for whose sake Kurtz's trading company plundered Africa and subjugated its native populations. The concerti and sonatas of Beethoven, Mozart, and Haydn would be produced from instruments figuratively steeped in the blood of African natives. Coppola uses more histrionic variants of the same motif in *Apocalypse Now*. When Colonel Kilgore's helicopters fly to Charlie's Point—a spit of land held by the Viet Cong whose fantastic surfing beaches Kilgore wants to take so his men can surf—he has his helicopters blare Wagner's "Ride of the Valkyries" in order to terrify the population below, which includes a grammar school full of children and their teachers. Great Western music becomes an instrument of terror and destruction, and Coppola here alludes to the perceived affinity for Wagner in the Third Reich and the way Nazi glorification and use of Wagnerian opera masked and perhaps justified the regime's barbarism against the Jews during World War II. Coppola uses a different metaphoric structure—centered on the image of a cow—to tie the bloody and barbaric end of Kurtz in his compound to the army's hypocritical attempts to sanitize its murderousness. At the beginning of the film, Willard is given his euphemistic orders to assassinate Kurtz ("terminate with extreme prejudice") while being served a civilized meal of roast beef at headquarters. At the end of the film, a horrific scene filming an actual slaughter of a live cow by the natives in Kurtz's compound reminds us that the beef we eat on a regular basis is, of course, also produced by the slaughter of live cows and that therefore we, too, however innocent of violence we like to think ourselves, are implicated in acts of violence in our simple daily living. Willard repeats the slaughter of the cow when he slaughters Kurtz in the same way— and the army's sanitary language for illicit murder is exposed as a barbaric lie.

Marlow's story of his river voyage into the heart of darkness becomes, by novella's end, a voyage into one's soul as an ethical center where one must confront responsibility not only for the acts one commits willfully but also for the effects of economic and political institutions to which one belongs and the benefits one receives from governmental policies and practices that may be exploitive or injurious. Conrad uses multiple strategies to produce this moral education in his novella—most notably the use of doubles to show how the seemingly benign and civilized enterprise of an organization or of an individual can be as guilty of producing oppression and cruelty as the malevolent practice of the monstrous individual. Just as Kurtz becomes the mirror of a trading company whose evil is immensely widespread and significant yet disavowed, so Marlow must recognize himself as implicated in the trading company's project. Using irony and insight, he is able to distance himself from his civilized colleagues and choose to ally himself with the nightmare that is at least more open and overt, less lying and hypocritical. Willard, of whom we learn that he has previously assassinated six people, must similarly acknowledge that Kurtz is only a monstrous version of himself and that Kurtz's murderous compound is only a miniature and histrionic version of the United States Army's spreading of death over Southeast Asia. Through Marlow's story, not only his listeners aboard the *Nellie* but also his British readers enjoying the benefits of empire in early-twentieth-century Europe are made to reflect on their symbolically bloody hands. It is easy for teachers and students alike to demonize colonial aggression as something that is committed by culturally and historically remote others—perhaps ancient Romans or Spanish conquistadors. But in devising a method of narrative doubling that makes the reader one of the listeners of Marlow's tale, Conrad teaches us how the act of reading can be an ethical experience of accepting responsibilities for activities in which one is implicated. Using the interplay between Conrad's and Coppola's works, we can update that lesson for ourselves and our students. By tracking with them the narrative devices of Conrad's "Heart of Darkness" that the filmmaker Coppola translates into the film *Apocalypse Now*, students can be led to understand and accept that even the democratic and civilized United States also has blood on its hands.

Teaching "The Secret Sharer"
at the United States Naval Academy

Mark D. Larabee

Future officers at the Naval Academy read "The Secret Sharer" with particular interest, finding this nautical coming-of-age tale a source of lively discussions about identity, community, ethics, psychology, classmate loyalty, and leadership. Our midshipmen share many of the same reactions to this story that general readers might have, such as wondering if Leggatt's presence is a figment of the captain's imagination. But as naval officers in training, they also debate more specialized concerns, such as the ethical implications of an authority figure harboring a fugitive or the advisability of the sailing maneuver at the end of the story. They can sympathize with the captain's need to prove his competence, knowing firsthand the difficulty of establishing oneself in a leadership role. And exactly what kind of captain, they ask, would dismiss the anchor watch, assume the watch himself alone—and then leave his post (a strict taboo) to get a cigar? For these readers the story offers a wide variety of appealing initial approaches.

Yet making the connection between literary studies and a naval officer's professional development can sometimes be a challenge for our largely technically minded student body. Because midshipmen will all someday travel to the most distant and exotic settings an author such as Conrad portrays, however, our students are especially attuned to descriptions of place. For that reason, I like to use the story's setting to introduce the important theme of perfection—a theme with large implications in an institution that makes the daily approach to perfection a mandatory goal. Most of our first-year students go on to technical majors and are constitutionally reluctant to engage in a self-reflective literary analysis, but they will comfortably debate more concrete issues such as the accuracy of topographical representations. Entering the story through place—or precision of setting—thus offers a safe first step toward the more slippery territory of personal engagement with deeper issues.

The opening scene of "The Secret Sharer," with its references to stillness, mystery, and isolation, establishes the mood of the story. But the narrator's careful explanation of what he sees amounts to something more than atmosphere. In fact, the start of the tale introduces three major narrative elements involving the landscape. First, the physical setting is something to be read; the landscape seems to contain a hidden message. Second, the narrator's description of the setting, and his struggle to read it, focuses on a ubiquitous opposition between perfection and the presence of flaws. Finally, the physical setting parallels the protagonist's internal landscape, full of the rocks and shoals of self-doubt and the contradictory currents of solitude and community. Through the narrator's analyzing, anguished reading of his surroundings, he effectively projects his own tensions onto the setting. The resolution of these tensions through the agency of Leggatt also plays itself out on the topographical surface of the story.

I like to begin with a close reading of the opening scene, assembling a list of topographical features and emphasizing what the narrator tries to do with those details. Starting with the story's first image, "lines of fishing-stakes," the narrator attempts to read the landscape, calling what he sees "a mysterious system" that is "incomprehensible" and "crazy of aspect." While this system of man-made objects resists the narrator's efforts to decode it, in the very next sentence he goes on to impose a system of meaning on the "group of barren islets" he sees in the other direction. To the narrator, these islands "[suggest] ruins of stone walls, towers, and blockhouses" (24). By describing the islands in this way (discerning a system where there logically can be none), the narrator apparently tries to compensate for his failure to read the system of the fishing stakes.

If the landscape offers itself as a text to be read, as the narrator implies, then the tale it tells has to do with the tension between wholeness and interruption—between perfection and flaws. In the narrator's description of his surroundings, he emphasizes the almost unreal, near-flawless geometry and color of the scene. The sea is "so still and stable" that it "look[s] solid"; the setting sun "[shines] smoothly, without that animated glitter which tells of an imperceptible ripple." Turning his eyes to another quarter of the horizon, the narrator sees "the straight line of the flat shore joined to the stable sea, edge to edge, with a perfect and unmarked closeness, in one levelled floor half brown, half blue under the enormous dome of the sky" (24). Yet flaws keep intruding into this vision of perfection, and the narrator struggles to contain the irregularities that frustrate his reduction of the landscape to pure geometrical forms.

He proceeds to relegate those islands (so noticeable and evocative just moments before) to "insignificance," the word he then applies to "two small clumps of trees" that mark the mouth of the Meinam River—itself "the only fault in the impeccable joint" between sea and sky. "[F]ar back on the inland level," he tells us, rests "a larger and loftier mass, the grove surrounding the great Paknam pagoda." But how, we may ask, can the "joint" be truly "impeccable" and of "a perfect and unmarked closeness" if it contains a "fault"? How can a shoreline that features "the great Paknam pagoda" be truly "flat"? The contradictions inherent in the narrator's language only deepen when he calls the pagoda "the only thing on which the eye could rest from the vain task of exploring the monotonous sweep of the horizon" (24–25). Surely a horizon that features such interesting fishing stakes, islands, and pagoda defies the characterization of "monotonous"; nevertheless, throughout this passage the narrator insists on making his surroundings as uniform, whole, and flawless as possible.

At this point, a blackboard sketch of the setting is a handy way to give students their bearings and dramatize the situation. One might either bring something prepared or have students give it a try. Both an aerial view and horizon perspective can help demonstrate the peculiarity of the narrator's depictions. Attempting an aerial-view sketch soon reveals an interesting surprise when we try to put each item of the landscape in its proper place. In reality, the coastline in this area runs generally from east to west, with the anchorage almost due south from the Meinam River mouth.[1] If the fishing stakes are on the narrator's right hand, the islets on his left, and the river apparently behind him (at least, he must turn his head to see the tug), then the setting sun—also seemingly on the narrator's left—would lie to the east! The description is not perfectly clear on these points. Nevertheless, this simple exercise graphically demonstrates how the narrator has managed to make completely plausible a landscape that on closer inspection does not entirely make sense; on another level, he has imposed an integrated vision on logical discontinuities.

Toward the end of the first paragraph and at the start of the second, a tension between solitude and community begins to parallel the tension between visual flawlessness and imperfection. As we have seen, in the narrator's description of the islands he invents stonemasons, as if to repopulate a scene from which the "nomad tribe of fishermen" has fled (24). Not only do those islands appear as "ruins" (abandoned habitations), but the pagoda suggests both the presence and absence of humanity: it symbolizes communal worship, yet the worshipers cannot be seen. The last glimpse of humanity, the tug that has brought the ship down the Meinam, disappears into the landscape "as though the impassive earth had swallowed her up without an effort, without a tremor." Finally, the narrator is "alone with [his] ship" and therefore able to contemplate the great test that lies before him, a test that can properly take place only "far from all human eyes, with only sky and sea for spectators and for judges" (25). After explaining that these two paragraphs set the stage for the action to follow and restating the major narrative elements present here (the deeper significance of physical setting, the tension between perfection and flaws, and the contrast between companionship and solitude), I like to divide the class into three groups to catalog the details of each element as they appear in the rest of the story. Initially, details such as those I have discussed so far tend to escape the notice of many of our students. But midshipmen, having been trained to apply a meticulous attention to detail in their professional roles, quickly respond to this strategy once they understand what to look for.

Students tracking physical setting will soon discover an acute narrative awareness of cryptic meanings in the landscape, indicated by words such as "mystery" and "accounting" for things. For example, after the narrator announces the presence of the *Sephora*, the chief mate joins him in attempting to decipher the landscape. The captain informs us how the chief mate "was trying to evolve a theory of the anchored ship," being the sort of person who "'liked to account to himself' for practically everything that came in his way" (26). The narrator makes the chief mate seem unusual in having an inquisitive turn of mind; yet this desire to find an explanation for everything is quite like the narrator's own eagerness to find meanings in the arrangement of fishing stakes and islands. According to Conrad, the physical setting offers a story and demands an explanation from every observer. As we see later, for example, the L-shaped construction of the captain's cabin assumes a crucial importance as a way to keep Leggatt, "[t]he mysterious arrival," hidden (33). In effect, the captain must keep others from reading the story that the landscape of his cabin might tell.

The group of students pursuing the tension between perfection and flaws will focus on several episodes marked by the key words "absolute," "incertitude," "exact," and, of course, "perfect." At the beginning of the tale the captain concludes his survey of the horizon with the sudden, disappointed recognition that beyond the islands lies "something which did away with the solemnity of perfect solitude." This "something," the mastheads of the *Sephora*, spoils the perfection of the physical setting (25). As if to regain his vision of perfection, the captain describes how, when he first boarded the ship in Bangkok, he visualized the cartographic progress of the voyage home. Here again, however, a spatial perfection—the completely known track home—gives way to the awareness of a flaw: his ignorance of "the novel responsibility of command" (27).

This cycle continues for another round when the narrator takes heart from reflecting that his knowledge of the sea and ships will allow him to overcome the challenges of his new responsibility. He bases his reasoning on yet another recasting of perfection, in the form of the "elemental moral beauty" of life at sea, with its "absolute straightforwardness" and "singleness of [. . .] purpose." This confidence in the moral integrity of shipboard life breaks down at the sight of the next flaw: the rope ladder left hanging over the side. "I became annoyed at this," he tells us, "for exactitude in small matters is the very soul of discipline" (28). Flaws quickly progress beyond the level of "small matters," however. The most fantastic example occurs when Leggatt appears in the water at the foot of the ladder, "complete but for the head" (29). Later, the narrator seems incomplete in a comparably unnerving way. As he puts it, he suffers from "the confused sensation of being in two places at once" and struggles to keep from losing his own head, metaphorically speaking (38).

The third group of students, tasked with finding moments of tension between solitude and community (key words: "alone," "communion," "communication," etc.) will likely return to the moment when the captain first notices the masts of the *Sephora* and feels both solitude and his communion with his ship ("a trusted friend") slip away (25). Significantly, at that instant the narrator also suffers from the "disturbing sounds" of his awakening crew—an ironic description, as feelings of communion are interrupted by the sounds of human companionship (25). This passage introduces the complex balancing act facing the narrator. Not only must he arrive at a private understanding of the vessel and its motions, but he needs to establish his authority and competency in the eyes of his crew, accommodate himself to a leader's lonely responsibility, and put on a captain's persona—a blend of fatherly familiarity and authoritarian aloofness. This multifaceted task is made more complicated because it is the narrator's first command and he does not enjoy the benefit of his predecessor's advice.

Leggatt's arrival gives the captain the catalyst he needs to reorder his internal landscape. As the narrator puts it, "[a] mysterious communication was established already between us two—in the face of that silent, darkened tropical sea" (30). The captain starts to build a connection between his inner and outer settings. Later, he complains of the "horrible manoeuvering" required to keep his double concealed, even as the ship works her laborious way down the Gulf of Siam—"tack for tack, in light winds and smooth water." The narrator's description of "this miserable juggling with the unavoidable" thus applies to both the ship's movements and his own (49).

A recapitulation of the relation between landscape and the three narrative elements I have outlined prepares the class for a discussion of the final scene, in which the story returns to a detailed analysis of the topography of the coastline. Here, Conrad uses key words and images we now recognize as shorthand for the central themes of the story. "Unknown to trade, to travel, almost to geography," as the narrator describes the islands along the Cambodian coast, "the manner of life they harbour is an unsolved secret. There must be villages—settlements of fishermen at least—on the largest of them, and some communication with the world is probably kept up by native craft. But all that forenoon [. . .] I saw no sign of man or canoe" (53). Now that the class has become sensitive to landscape's role as more than simply a backdrop for the story, even this short excerpt offers numerous points for discussion. Conrad's use of words such as "unknown," "geography," "secret," "fishermen," "communication," and "no sign" (of humanity) reconstructs the complex web of interrelations among solitude, community, topography, nature, and structure that fill the narrator's description at the beginning of the story. That there are unseen settlements and hidden communications echoes the narrator's awareness of his concealed relationship with Leggatt, for instance, while the "unsolved secret" points toward both the "mysterious system" of fishing stakes and the "hidden manner of life" the narrator has cultivated with his secret sharer.

As the ship draws nearer to the coast and the two men examine a chart of the area, we see how the landscape bears an uncanny similarity to that at the head of the gulf. Koh-ring features "two hills and a low point," corresponding to the "two small clumps of trees" marking the low point of the Meinam River mouth (53). Opposite Koh-ring "there is what looks like the mouth of a biggish river—with some town, no doubt, not far up": a description that could easily apply to the Meinam and Bangkok (53–54). The "towering" island (57) resembles "the mitre-shaped hill of the great pagoda" (25). And just as that hill "swallowed [. . .] up" the steam tug "without an effort, without a tremor," Koh-ring (like the "gate of Erebus") threatens to swallow up the narrator's ship "without a light, without a sound" (57). Both the return to explicit geographic description and the unmistakable parallels between the landscapes at the head of the gulf and at Koh-ring signal the crucial role that physical setting will play at the end of the story. Just as the narrator's preoccupation with meanings and imperfections makes his perception of the landscape a revelation of his internal topography, what ultimately happens in the physical world explains the changes the narrator has undergone and the final integration he achieves.

The captain's deft ship handling at the conclusion of the tale piques our students' interest. All midshipmen receive basic sailing training, and many are avid members of our sailing teams. Square-rigged sailing is unfamiliar to them, however, and some intervention is required to demonstrate just how anxious those moments would have been. At this juncture, a sketch of the narrator's maneuvers under the shadow of Koh-ring effectively illustrates the ship's peril.[2] The point I stress here is that success or failure depends on the narrator's ability to read the landscape as he searches for a clue in the water that will tell him if the ship has begun to make way. That he does maneuver the ship successfully thanks to the hat he gave Leggatt (which, ironically, is a flaw in the water as well as a reminder of community) marks a profound confluence of the three narrative elements I have discussed. Only a demonstration of competence can earn the crew's respect, and the narrator's calm, deliberate execution of the saving maneuver reaps the reward of the crew's "cheery cries." Meanwhile, the captain celebrates the "silent knowledge and mute affection" he has achieved: "the perfect communion of a seaman with his first command" (59). Leggatt's departure thus makes possible the integration of the narrator's external and internal landscapes, reconciling flaws and achieving perfection in both realms.

The real test of the voyage, as the narrator acknowledges near the beginning, consists of measuring "how far [. . . one is] faithful to that ideal conception of one's own personality every man sets up for himself secretly" (26). Ultimately, it is this notion of an internalized ideal and the constant measurement of one's fitness that bring home to our students the impact of the final scene. Every day, midshipmen at the Naval Academy are exhorted to perfect themselves mentally, morally, and physically. But our students are not alone in feeling the pressure to improve, and the critical self-assessment common among college-aged readers offers the instructor a useful way to relate this story to students' lives.

A close reading that emphasizes the fictional element of setting might at first seem to the student like more of the kind of dry literary analysis that all too often distances the work from the real world. As we have seen in this particular tale, however, physical and psychological settings interact to reveal how a British captain in a distant sea a century ago is not such an alien creature: he and today's students share some of the same needs. If our goals as instructors include cultivating our students' self-awareness while demonstrating how art and life intersect, then this particular approach offers signal advantages along just those lines. In a world in which traditional hermeneutics often seems obsolete, the time-honored union of *res et verba* may not be so outdated after all. For both teachers and students engaged in forging links between the outer and inner landscapes of ordinary human experience, Conrad casts an illuminating beam over the waters of every reader's "silent, darkened tropical sea."

NOTES

I would like to thank Brian Richardson, Robert Madison, and John and Suzanne Wooten for their encouragement and advice.

[1]Any atlas will provide the general outlines of the vicinity, although a more detailed depiction appears on such nineteenth-century British Admiralty charts as *China Sea: Gulf of Siam, Sheet II, Koh Ta Kut to Cape Liant*. For a modern, more easily accessible chart of this area, one might try the United States Defense Mapping Agency's *Laem Chabang to Mae Nam Chao Phraya*. The nearest islets actually lie to the southeast of the anchorage—almost twenty miles away and over the horizon.

[2]In this instance, I find it better to provide the drawing myself; the illustration by Paul F. Foye, Bruce Harkness, and Nathan L. Marvin in "The Sailing Maneuver in 'The Secret Sharer'" works very well (122).

Teaching "Heart of Darkness" in a Western Civilization or Humanities Core Course

William M. Hagen

Originally modeled on a two-year Humanities Program at Davidson College, the Western Civilization Program at Oklahoma Baptist University is sequenced into three semesters during the freshman and sophomore years and required of most students. The fall and spring sophomore sections are led by teams of faculty members from the history and English departments. What we teach is neither strictly history with literature nor literary study with contexts but a blend structured by themes, movements, epochs, and ideologies—nearer to social or intellectual history than anything else. How well a text or event fits the program structure may count for more than does its place in the canon or its political significance. Yearly workshops and negotiations renew faculty commitment to the syllabus, reflected in the annual editions of an ancilla of readings, time lines, and unit essays.

Goethe's *Faust*, Leo Tolstoy's "The Death of Ivan Ilych," Joseph Conrad's "Heart of Darkness," and Erich Maria Remarque's *All Quiet on the Western Front* have long been anchor texts of the spring semester. Conrad's novella is situated in the middle of the second unit, entitled "The Bourgeois Century: Apogee and Crisis." A history colleague once quipped, "This is the unit where everything gets smashed up." Indeed, it follows a unit that sets up a somewhat optimistic, expansive Western outlook, coming out of the American and French Revolutions into industrialism, classical liberalism, and Romanticism. The second unit begins with European wars of unification, the United States Civil War, and ends with World War I. Other pieces of literature in the unit include, in order, Tolstoy's story, Stephen Crane's *Maggie, a Girl of the Streets*, Eugene O'Neill's *The Hairy Ape*, Kate Chopin's *The Awakening*, Fyodor Dostoevsky's "The Grand Inquisitor," and Remarque's novel. The list displays the chronological displacement that occurs for the sake of the themes. The naturalistic and expressionistic literary techniques of Crane and O'Neill become secondary to their representing industrial alienation and entrapment as a challenge to classical liberalism. Conrad's novel connects two threads in the unit: imperialism and the new consciousness of human nature asserted by such figures as Sigmund Freud, Friedrich Nietzsche, Henri Bergson, and Dostoevsky. Their views challenge Enlightenment assumptions of reason, conscience, and their cultivation in Europe, representing one explanation of how imperialism can create such horrors as Conrad found in King Leopold's Congo. We study "Heart of Darkness" for approximately three class periods, after which the unit moves directly to World War I and Remarque, where young men must lose all the high culture of Europe and become animals if they are to survive and an older generation of parents and patriots is unable to comprehend the reality of what is happening on the front, much as Kurtz's Intended cannot comprehend what is happening in Africa.

A typical essay exam question for the unit might begin as follows:

> During the late nineteenth and early twentieth centuries, European culture seemed to reach new heights. Material prosperity continued unabated for many, as the result of scientific and technological achievements, and European nations spread their culture around the world through colonies and trade. This prosperity and power led many in the middle class to believe that their faith in reason and progress was fully justified. However, some thinkers, including Marx, Dostoevsky, Nietzsche, Bergson, Freud, and Conrad, continued the countercultural tradition started by the Romantics and raised serious questions about whether such a faith was justified, indeed whether human beings and their enterprises were really rational. A sense of disillusionment spread into popular consciousness as a result of World War I, a process chronicled by Remarque in his novel.

Given its complexity for undergraduates, this portion of the essay exam question might be handed out early. The question that follows the introduction would direct students to explore this disillusionment, its origins and manifestations, through the history, the thinkers, and the works of literature.

The Audience and the Middle Class

A study of "Heart of Darkness," emphasizing the new consciousness, might begin with the group of listeners. An unnamed narrator defines the characteristic outlook of sailors, oblivious to the distinctions of a foreign land, preferring stories with obvious moral lessons. The internal audience, united by the sea, seems to exemplify European pretensions to reason, a pride based on common sense and attainment. English sailors have reason for some national and imperial pride too, having prevailed against other navies, conveying those who bear the "torch and the sword," the "sacred fire" of culture into "uncivilized" lands (8). The particular group listening to Marlow contains, as well, several examples of middle-class success: a lawyer, an accountant, a director of companies.

After setting up the group of auditors and carefully noting the unnamed narrator's comments about Marlow's singularity as a sailor and a teller—setting up the question of how Marlow is different—the instructor can come back to this group at those points when Marlow breaks the story to complain about how difficult it is for him to articulate such an experience to his listeners. The group in the story, in a sense, stands in for the student readers, even down to the sighs, the impatience with the manner of telling, the apparent "Absurd!" uttered at one point, which prompts one of the book's most famous passages regarding middle-class incomprehension of others' conditions or experiences:

> Here you all are each moored with two good addresses like a hulk with two anchors [. . .] excellent appetites, and temperature normal—hear you—normal from year's end to year's end. (48)

> [A page later, Marlow sharpens the attack.] You can't understand? How could you—with solid pavement under your feet, surrounded by kind neighbours ready to cheer you or to fall on you, stepping delicately between the butcher and the policeman, in the holy terror of scandal and gallows and lunatic asylums [. . .]. (49)

We hope students connect such remarks to two other texts that hector the middle-class reader, Ralph Waldo Emerson's "Self-Reliance" and Rebecca Harding Davis's exhortative *Life in the Iron Mills*. But quite apart from that feature, Marlow's characterization of the limitations of middle-class common sense echoes many other texts from this unit and the one preceding: Tocqueville's awareness of how majority opinions in a democracy can fix themselves into tyrannical social conventions, Emerson's sense of society as a conspiracy to keep one from becoming an unconventional individual, Davis's popular account of the great gulf of understanding and communication between industrial workers and the middle class, Melville's more particular analysis of a gulf between a well-meaning legal copyist and his perverse employee ("Bartleby, the Scrivener"), Tolstoy's story of a life mislived in conforming to middle-class standards, and the Grand Inquisitor's insistence that most people desire ordered security over individual freedom.

It is with this idea that we can take up the nineteenth-century male characterization of European women as well. By this point in the semester, the students will have studied some feminist documents and read Chopin's *The Awakening*. They should be familiar with the ideology of separate spheres against which reformers fought in the nineteenth century: the sense that women are best suited and society best served when they stay in their sphere: nurturing, beautifying, and idealizing the best in society, while men strive and build in the political and commercial realms. Marlow's bemused view of the idealistic aunt who secured his position, representing him as one of a new breed of secular missionaries, advising him to wear woolens in the Congo, is of a piece with his view of Kurtz's Intended, who enshrines Kurtz in her memory. Like the privileged Mildred in O'Neill's *Hairy Ape*, who faints when confronted by working-class profanity in a ship's stokehold, neither the aunt nor the Intended could stand one touch of the reality Marlow has experienced. But he asserts that the idealism of such women is necessary for middle-class males to carry on. This assumption opens one way to understand his statements about imperial conquest, the necessity of a redeeming idea, even if only a "devotion to efficiency," something that one can "bow down before, and offer a sacrifice to" (10). Middle-class Europeans, both men and women, are necessarily blind to certain realities.

What keeps the listeners listening? ("And why should we read on?" some students say.) Ironically enough, they seem to listen because of their kinship with Marlow as a sailor and finally as a sensible fellow who affirms something like conventional morality, even while doubting its foundation. His attention to duty, his appreciation of others' attention to duty (the accountant, the native helmsman), his management of the little steamer, even his confession that watching for snags saved him from losing his equilibrium—all are elements that reasonably reflective members of his class can understand. We have no evidence at the end that any of the listeners, except possibly the unnamed sailor, has comprehended more. Even the few words from him—the final vision of sky, river, and darkness could be read as a lingering mood. The Director, however, is attentive to nautical matters: "We have lost the first of the ebb" (76).

Of course, the exotic story holds them too, like the snake (river) that fascinates the younger Marlow (12). They can certainly understand going to such a place for the challenge, a place that will inscribe the blankness in a restless young man. Going to sea, a blank place of its own, has had an appeal for this group. They may understand, too, the dangers presented by extremities: the heat; the muddle of working undisciplined and irrational natives; the temptations presented by one's isolation, power, and distance from mother country. Marlow's listeners may even understand Kurtz, from a distance; they probably read Marlow's resistance to Kurtz as reassurance that rational middle-class morality and English resolve can hold one true. The apostle of Kurtz who was once a seaman, the "harlequin," might give them pause, though the fact that he was a Russian might comfortably marginalize his behavior for these English. But Marlow's own musings on the prehistoric jungle, his fascination with Kurtz, his choice of him as a lesser nightmare, and the corresponding rejection of the Manager's judgment that Kurtz's enormities were "unsound" or bad for business (61) would likely reinforce their view of Marlow as different.

The Moral Pattern and the New Consciousness

To get students into the problematic aspects of Marlow's tale, we mention the plot's kinship with other epic journeys. Using a chart based on one in John Barth's *Chimera,* we refer to a pattern that students have encountered in a number of texts from previous semesters: *The Odyssey, The Aeneid, The Divine Comedy, Paradise Lost,* and *Candide,* to name the most obvious. Some of us might mention Jung's idea that such plots are part of a racial unconscious, making Marlow's sense of journeying back in time take on both a biological and psychological aspect. Reinforced is the theme of a moral testing of the self. Obviously absent from Conrad's version, however, are the cosmic forces that traditionally give the struggle its ultimate significance. The story lacks even Voltaire's impertinent questioning, in *Candide*, of a beneficent, rational providence.

It is useful to ask students to scour "Heart of Darkness" for religious language. They will find an abundance: exclamations invoking the heavens or abhorring devils, references to company men as pilgrims, references to faith, to Mephistopheles, to evil . . . Kurtz had "kicked himself loose" or "kicked the very earth to pieces" in a kind of despair; "his intelligence was perfectly clear [. . .]. But his soul was mad" (65). Reference to traditional views of sin can help students understand the choice of Kurtz as a lesser nightmare. In choosing, Marlow does not worship the man, as the natives had. As I have argued elsewhere (Hagen 294), Marlow makes a choice based on solid medieval (Dantean) grounds: sins of unrestrained appetite are less serious than sins that involve one's reason. Those of apparently sound mind who embrace, without compunction, a success ethic, those such as the Manager whose ultimate judgment of Kurtz is that he used "unsound methods," ruining the region for further exploitation—such technocrats represent the greater evil for Marlow. If one supposes that a mad Kurtz might have eaten human flesh, one could even summon support for Marlow's choice from "On Cannibals," where Montaigne finds the custom of eating an enemy's flesh in tribal cultures less reprehensible than Europeans' practice of torturing and dismembering one another in the name of religion. Preparing the way for such a choice, too, is the grim irony of a presumably irrational cannibal crew showing more restraint, given their hunger, than their supposedly civilized white passengers, the "pilgrims" who so enjoy shooting into the crowd of villagers when they depart (42–43, 66–67).

Students will notice the disjuncture of religious language from traditional belief. Witness Marlow's reluctance to give a name to the crimes or sins Kurtz may have committed and the striking understatements that the man merely "lacked restraint" or that there was "something wanting in him" (57). Marlow's reticence could be read as not so different from the Manager's "unsound methods." The world is not a battlefield of opposed, transcendental ultimates, it seems: the devils are flabby and local, the futility is all too human; Mephistopheles is no Satan but merely a hollow man, made of papier-mâché (29). Even Kurtz, with his will to exterminate (51), his souvenir heads, his desire to possess the earth (59), and his uttered "The horror!" (68), is not beyond the reach of this world. Marlow can turn him from possibly ordering a massacre of the Company expedition by setting before him his reputation, the false conception of himself held by others. In such a context, it is wishful to interpret Kurtz's horror as a glimpse of eternal fires, though some might argue for an equally absolute void. Marlow raises earthly possibilities—some realization of self (68), of the heart of humanity (66), of the wilderness pressing humanity into service. Likewise, Marlow's "darkness" is of this planet, the prehistoric jungle, the primitive human beings in the jungle, the civilized human beings transformed by the jungle. And, through Kurtz, the darkness is in the very soul of humanity, civilized or not.

Just as Mephistopheles is reduced to an amoral aristocratic rake by Goethe, just as Melville's lawyer struggles with an unyielding scrivener whom he finally identifies with humanity, just as Ivan Ilych struggles with a finally undiagnosed pain or dissolution in himself and then is able to find a terminal peace by forgiving his self-absorbed family, so do Marlow and Kurtz seem to live in a world in which human-based codes or their denial may have no sanction in divine or infernal imperatives, no first cause in supernatural grace or malice.

Once having acknowledged what J. Hillis Miller termed a "disappearance of God" from Western culture (*Disappearance*), rather than turn Conrad's novella into an allegory of biological or materialist (imperialist) determinism, we revisit the noted lack of restraint in Kurtz, Marlow's observation that seemed so disappointing as a moral judgment. If the jungle has patted Kurtz on the head and if it affects Marlow too, their difference seems to be something internal, at least according to Marlow. A simple-minded Freudian approach might assert that Kurtz has an inadequately developed superego or ego, except that Kurtz is presented as preeminently and assertively civilized, the best that Europe can produce. We seem pushed toward the later, darker Freud, of *Civilization and Its Discontents*, written after the Great War.

Many of the same texts that help establish a desacralized world also call into question Enlightenment assumptions about innate reason or common sense. Goethe begins his masterpiece with a great disgust at what rational attainment in the traditional disciplines can offer by way of fulfillment or happiness. Tolstoy, Melville, and especially Dostoevsky (in "Notes from Underground") call attention to the dead ends of rational consciousness; to the tendency of human beings to act against their own self-interest; to their tendency to act on the basis of instincts, imaginative sympathy, and even spite. The restless, striving will of *Faust* finds its ground in a universe of ceaseless contention, referred to by Schopenhauer, both of which are referred to by Nietzsche in his assertion of a world as will. His conception of the overman, instinctively acting, unfettered by rational and Christian standards, suggests the possibility of a Kurtz, although the man himself seems a victim of obsessions when he comes into view. At the point where he must live in the gaze of Europeans again, where he recalls their construction of him, a touch of herd conscience seems to wring the final cry from him. But, to turn Freudian again, one can account for his lack of restraint by a lack of restrainers, the neighbors that Marlow says monitor middle-class behavior. Free of this superego watch group, the forbidden urges repressed into the unconscious can return; as the document Suppression of Savage Customs reveals (50), civilizing or secular missionary activities are but incomplete sublimations of irrational desires. Most pessimistically, one could read Marlow as concluding that all ideals are idols, worshiped but having no power in and of themselves—a sort of lie—unless something else is inside, a restraint that is not learned or that has become instinctive.

Having threaded the story this far, we stand back and remind ourselves how far we have come; how like a dream this Bergsonian unrolling of Marlow's experience is; and how difficult it is to communicate when each self evolves through its own private journey, apprehending only fitfully the journeys of others. Having done that, we can do little more than urge "Heart of Darkness" as a central document of modern Western consciousness.

Teaching "Heart of Darkness" in a Seminar on Modernism and Postmodernism

Philip M. Weinstein

For a seminar that begins by probing the limits of Western realism, there are few better starting dates and texts than "Heart of Darkness" (1899). Likewise, some weeks later, there are few better ways of probing the limits of the Western modernism Conrad helps to launch than by juxtaposing the novella against certain salient postmodern and postcolonial novels. The double-credit seminar on twentieth-century fiction that I teach at Swarthmore thus starts with Conrad and moves through E. M. Forster and William Faulkner (kindred modern masters). Turning then to six contemporary writers—Chinua Achebe, Gabriel García-Márquez, Toni Morrison, Leslie Marmon Silko, Louise Erdrich, and Salman Rushdie—we are able to analyze postmodern and postcolonial practice as different attempts to say good-bye to both realist and modernist confines.

How does the darkness coiled in Conrad's novella serve to introduce the dark heart of modernism? We approach this question by exploring how several fictional elements that stabilize realism—coherent voice, established place, progressive time, and developmental theme—here become destabilized. Taking over a narrative that began in the third person, Marlow ranges unpredictably among narration of former events, meditation on them, and conversation with his present companions on the *Nellie*. His disembodied voice injects into the narrative a host of fragmented phrases of others—the Brussels "doctor," the chief accountant, the Manager, the harlequin, Kurtz—all of whom emerge as momentary, spectral (rendered by quotes within quotes), detached from their frame of reference, their words lassoed by Marlow's and knotted into a skein of cryptic, portentous utterances. Multicultural long before the term was invented, "Heart of Darkness" fleetingly cites its motley, half-obscured cast of characters, producing an uncentered field of speech acts profoundly unlike the definiteness of verbal interchange in Austen, Dickens, Eliot, or Hardy.

Just as the vocal field loses its clarity in Conrad's text, so the deployment of time and space becomes slippery. Students must work overtime to align specific utterances within a shifting time frame (sometimes on the *Nellie*, more often earlier—but exactly when?—in the Congo). Likewise, the spatial frame keeps shifting location: Brussels (the "whited sepulchre" [13]), crossing the Atlantic, the outer station, the journey up the Congo, the Inner Station, the return to the coast, then to Europe, all these settings interspersed unpredictably with the foregrounded one of the *Nellie* on the Thames. In seeking to cope with these narrative dislocations, students notice, uneasily, the distressful things happening to dislocated characters in the narrative itself. With respect to both reader and characters, Conrad is as intent on stripping thought and behavior from the fabric of familiar sequence that orients them as his Victorian predecessors are intent on supplying and repairing that fabric.

Thus estranged from readerly expectations, "Heart of Darkness" registers its most memorable effects. Drawing examples from a single page (19), we note a ship "firing into a continent," a "boiler wallowing in the grass," a cliff "not in the way of anything" yet undergoing an "objectless blasting." The scene of purposive activity that normalizes realist fiction here becomes casually outrageous. The realist subject who typically enacts his identity through focused activity— his shaping impact on objects or others—becomes stymied, turns dysfunctional. Work itself, the grounding project of the bourgeois subject, the transformation of matter into a mirror of the subject's resources, registers as absurd when removed from customary Western settings. Nothing in these African settings sustains the imposition of Western empire without turning bizarre, not even language itself: "Rebels! What would be the next definition I was to hear. There had been enemies, criminals, workers—and these were—rebels" (58). This dynamic of definitions out of place, radically inadequate to the behavior they would characterize, is not confined to the Belgians: it inhabits/inhibits Marlow's narrative as well. "Do you see the story? Do you see anything?," Marlow implores his friends on the *Nellie*, knowing that all language—his included—is parochial, limited to a local sphere of efficacy, incapable of conveying that which is other (30).

Having analyzed the story's dislocations as a refusal of the orientations that make realism satisfyingly legible, the seminar then begins to unpack the story's canonical standing, the fact that it has served so long as a favorite of the anthologies. We see that, in saying good-bye to the fundamental business of realist fiction—the depiction of viable social norms, subject quests that are achievable, intentions ("My Intended") that can be realized—"Heart of Darkness" reconfigures the novelistic landscape. What emerges in the wake of such collapse is "a choice of nightmares" (62), a fiction centered on crisis, alienation, and the question of authenticity. In a word, the lawless depths embodied in Kurtz, the fidelity to those depths embodied in Marlow. This is *the* text that twentieth-century Anglo-American readers have turned to as witness to individual fortitude when confronting the radical collapse of the social. It is the text in which, for over fifty years, the West has taken most satisfaction in reading the elusive measure of its losses, the failure of its support systems. That such satisfaction was never innocent, that the acknowledgment of loss might all along have acted to conceal power, is the burden of a postcolonial critique of the book that other essays in this volume amply provide. My point is only that a literature of modernist heroism centering on the courage to confront impotence arises, not accidentally, in the most powerful nations on earth—a collocation this seminar goes on to explore in the equally canonized work of Forster and Faulkner.

For the next three weeks we pursue the modernist paradigm of collapse launched by "Heart of Darkness." Forster's *A Passage to India* and Faulkner's

Light in August and *Absalom, Absalom!* show, powerfully, the inability of one set of cultural convictions to make sense of another culture's beliefs and behaviors. *Passage* is drawn, as though magnetically, to the all-arresting scene in the Marabar caves: the scene in which liberal goodwill fails to rise to the otherness of the other, and crisis erupts. As in Conrad, the subject is unable to measure the object—no one British (including Forster's delegated narrator) can see India's unplotted vastness and responsibly map it. The interpretive maps the British do draw on are pure ideology (England's shorthand colonial narrative for managing the Indian, reducing him to caricature), and Forster's colonials read Aziz as rapist no less insistently than Conrad's "pilgrims" read the native as savage. Adela's tormenting echo echoes Marlow's stammer: "Do you see the story? Do you see anything?" To which Forster's plot supplies the dismal answer: the British see only their own obsessions. The two cultures cannot meet—there is no passage in *Passage*—and even Mrs. Moore's capacious religion becomes, under the alienating pressure of Muslim-Hindu India, "poor little talkative Christianity" (166), a parochial set of shrill utterances with no grasp on the real itself. As in "Heart of Darkness," the real cannot be said. Language reduces to either a dominant culture's boast of mastery or (by way of narrative blockage, confusion) the stammering confession of limited, parochial understanding.

Conrad's African natives, Forster's Indian natives: these othered and abused figures reemerge as Faulkner's formerly enslaved blacks. The white-authored language that would speak them everywhere confesses (through the narrative recalcitrance of Faulkner's novels, through their circuitous flights and inversions) the incapacity of such language to say black otherness. *Light in August* and *Absalom, Absalom!* relentlessly give their reader effects before causes, reactions before actions. Not knowing, not being able to judge, is a full-time enterprise for students reading Faulkner, just as pre-knowing, pre-judging is the irresistible behavior of the white community he describes. Inspired by Conrad, Faulkner forges a rhetoric whose destabilizing moves rebuke premature decision, warn of the impossibility of "getting it right." The encounters Faulkner stages, like those in Conrad, issue not into resolution but deeper crisis. No social schemas are available in either writer's work—as they are unavailable more largely in the deracinated literature of modernism—for engaging the other on terms that might genuinely access that other. Again as with Conrad, this dilemma is made manifest through the resistances embodied in narrative form itself: the very withholding of clarification eloquently testifies to the exhaustion of general interpretive norms. When Henry James praised Conrad as "absolutely alone as a votary of the way to do a thing that shall make it undergo most doing" ("The New Novel" 331), he identified modernism's larger investment in the "ungivenness," the cultural bias, that attends all local acts of understanding and that mandates such rigorous "doing."

The intricacy of cultural impasse, the collapse of social norms capable of adjudicating the trouble, the incapacity of words to escape their parochial provenance: if these elements join together to deepen the power of modernist interrogation, at the same time they severely limit the canvases they enable. Shaped to deliver the drama of failed mastery (intent on rebuking realist over-confidence), modernist fictions are good at registering nightmare but poor at registering dreams. Intent on crisis and arrest, they are poorer yet at narrating breakthrough and motion. And they are poorest of all at conveying unalienated images of social cohesion. The second half of our syllabus attends to postcolonial and postmodern attempts to say good-bye to modernist undoing. Put otherwise, a good deal of this more recent literature is interested in states of experience kept out of the modernist canvas or permitted only in the form of parody. Other cultures (especially minoritized cultures) have all along managed to imagine positively—rather than oppositionally—relations between the individual and the social, the individual and the natural, the real and the desired. Enter, now, Achebe, García-Márquez, Morrison, Silko, Erdrich, and Rushdie.

We study these later developments in three phases. The first phase begins with Achebe, less as Conrad's critic than as an African writer who registers the social in ways wholly foreign to the foregoing Western modernists. In Achebe's fiction the social appears as the enabling framework for all individual unfolding. Not the territory where Conrad locates collapse, where Forster locates stereotyping, where Faulkner locates racism—all territories built of convention, ideology, and prejudice, all relentlessly superficial—Achebe's social is both singular and plural, surface and depth. As John Mbiti puts it in *African Religions and Philosophy*, "Whatever happens to the individual happens to the whole group, and whatever happens to the whole group happens to the individual. The individual can only say: 'I am, because we are; and since we are, therefore I am'" (108–09). Such a saying is unthinkable in the Western modernist literature of alienation, where the group is by definition predictable, conventional, myopic, superficial: boring. Modernist quest flees the group like the plague. What is authenticity but that (fantasized) achievement of an interiority uniquely one's own, owing nothing to group norms? The week during which we read *Things Fall Apart* (and a good deal of commentary on African cultures) emerges as pedagogically our most strenuous, for the students' first take on Achebe is invariably disappointment. Where is the drama? they ask. Trained by a lifetime of reading realist literature and at least several weeks of modernist literature, they are looking for—and not finding—individual wavering and recovery, profound psychology, intricate plotting: in a word, private depth. What I try to get them to see is that, once one probes the notion of private depth, one is able to look afresh at the notion of social surface. When, a few weeks later, we go on to read Silko's *Ceremony*, students are better positioned to recognize something of that novel's achievement: its way of launching its protagonist (Tayo) as a figure oddly (unfamiliarly) of a piece with the landscape, cut out of kindred cloth, sharing his sentience with all that biologically and geologically surrounds him. This Native American belief in an identificatory cosmos—

human life in unsentimental, continuous, nonantagonistic relation to natural life—allows Silko pervasively to reconceive the figure/ground opposition that modernism (and realism before it) must assume in order to produce novels at all.

Phase 2 of the period after modernism centers on magic realism and is launched by *One Hundred Years of Solitude*. Making sense of García Márquez is almost as pedagogically strenuous as making sense of Achebe, not because the students fail to respond to the text but because they lack an interpretive framework for what they admire. With the help of a few essays on magic realism, they begin to see that García Márquez is writing—by way of images that neither realism nor modernism can permit itself—a literature of unscientific (non-Newtonian) possibility. His text draws on Latin American folklore (as well as Western mythology) to produce a rhetoric of unbound human motion and emotion. Possessing little psychological depth, his multigenerational Buendías are supremely at home in their culture; the "solitude" they suffer from is generic, not personally tailored. Surrounded by butterflies, rising into the heavens, suffering insomnia plagues, making love and war on an Olympian scale, they transcend (as in Achebe's and Silko's work) the oppositional figure/ground assumption that yields the questing individual of Western realism and modernism. In addition, reading *One Hundred Years of Solitude* between Faulkner and Morrison allows students to see that when Morrison revises Faulknerian materials, she has the example of García Márquez to spur her imagination. Pilate and the flying Solomon in *Song of Solomon*, Beloved returned from the dead—indeed from the abyss of the Middle Passage—in *Beloved*: these figures are nourished by a range of folkloric traditions that envisage the human trajectory as larger than realism can say and requiring for articulation the more ambitious idiom of romance. As Morrison put it in *Playing in the Dark*, this form "offered writers not less but more; not a narrow ahistorical canvas but a wide historical one; not escape but entanglement" (37).

The final text we read, for the third phase of the period after modernism, does indeed give us entanglement on an unprecedented scale: *The Satanic Verses*. Here again García Márquez is the guide, but when Rushdie practices magic realism, we get not the seamless wonder of *One Hundred Years of Solitude* but rather the almost inconceivable hybridity and discontinuity of the contemporary migrant's boundary-crossing experience. Metamorphic as no sober work of realism can afford to be, *The Satanic Verses* registers a textual universe that, in the words of one of Rushdie's own essays, "is radioactive with history [. . . full of] terrible unquiet fuss" ("Outside the Whale" 100, 101). Sustained common sense, familiar sequences, a focus on individual depth and desire, and the plot moves that might follow from these: such staple attributes of realism get no respect in a novel in which only the surprising has a chance of catching up with the anything but realistic realities of media-saturated, power-stratified postcolonial life. To take only a single instance of Rushdie's procedures, when Chamcha (one of the two main protagonists) is transmogrified into a hairy, horny goat, he implores a fellow victim, "But how do they do it?" The other responds, "They describe us [. . .]. They have the power of description, and we succumb to the pictures they construct" (168). If we ask why this representational dynamic is unthinkable in realism and modernism, we begin to recognize Western culture's privileging (ever since the Enlightenment) of the subject who shapes others, not postcolonialism's focus on those on the receiving end of colonial power, who are (literally, in Rushdie's conceit) bent out of shape by that power. Nothing short of prodigious, then, is the way the seminar's last novel escapes the limits of modernism as it reconfigures, yet again and almost a century later, that crucial encounter with the other that Conrad was able so memorably to articulate, only by escaping the limits of realism.

Teaching "Heart of Darkness" across Disciplinary Boundary Lines

Barry Stampfl

Often I hesitate even to put "Heart of Darkness" on the reading list, in part because it is so frequently assigned. Most of my students have dealt with the story in a classroom setting more than once by the time they get to me. Sometimes there are muted groans when the title is spotted on the syllabus. I wouldn't want to overreact to that response, but, then again, I have plenty of reason to acknowledge my bias in favor of Conrad's gloomy, cryptic, and controversial novella. The truth is that the story rocked my world when I first read it as a sophomore in college. Later on, in graduate school and thereafter, whatever critical chops I have come to possess were developed in crucial ways in the effort of fathoming that magically sinister first impression. Thus I am caught between wanting to share with students an experience that has been particularly meaningful to me and wishing to spare them a brush with yet another professorial overcommitment. With some regularity, the yeas have it, and I find myself teaching "Heart of Darkness." Then my challenge is precisely to facilitate my students' own responses to the text—that is, not to dictate conclusions.

To this purpose, I have found it strategic to draw on considerations that tend to push the interpretation of Conrad's novella beyond disciplinary boundary lines. Now I have phrased this general description with some care in order to avoid saying that I pursue interdisciplinarity. For, if being interdisciplinary implies an integration of materials and methods from distinct disciplinary domains—as Julie Klein, for one, plausibly has suggested—the college English class probably has too much on its mind in the way of promoting higher literacy skills to do justice to this difficult aspiration. The emphasis in literature classes quite properly remains on literary studies: the question of questions, as I teach "Heart of Darkness" anyway, is, What is the work telling us? The richly variegated tradition of "Heart of Darkness" interpretation shows us, of course, how tellingly materials from other disciplines can affect our answers to this question. Indeed, this body of criticism amply and persistently has testified to the powerful centrifugal force of Conrad's story, which, with its combination of mimetic-realistic assumptions and symbolic resonances, has ever displayed a strong tendency to bolt the domain of the literary, narrowly conceived. In this brief essay, then, I confine myself to mentioning only three disciplinary border regions into which the interpretation of "Heart of Darkness" readily and profitably can be understood to overspill.

The first is the often noted intersection of literature and history secured by the recognition that Conrad's story constitutes a kind of report on current events, that is, an exposé of scandalous conditions existing in King Leopold's Free Congo State in the last decade of the nineteenth century. While the importance of this approach in and of itself can scarcely be overestimated, its impact, I think, may be extended and clarified in the light of a second trans-disciplinary emphasis: the contemplating of the work under the rubric of trauma. Though psychological-psychoanalytic approaches to "Heart of Darkness" have multiplied like rabbits over the decades, the emphasis on trauma potentially adds something new by drawing on a clinical literature that recently has assumed unprecedented prominence. Finally, as a kind of antidote both to the approach through history and to the approach through trauma, I describe a writing assignment I have developed in an effort to bridge the specifically intradisciplinary gap that divides literature classes from courses in creative writing and rhetoric.

That "Heart of Darkness," first published in 1899, plausibly may be read as a fictionalized account of Conrad's visit to Africa in 1890, is a position that has much to recommend it. Conrad himself affirmed that the story "is experience [. . .] pushed a little (and only very little) beyond the actual facts of the case" (*Heart* [Kimbrough] 4), and his biographers have confirmed that he based it "very closely on personal experience, and that most of his characters can be traced to actual people" (Hawkins, "Conrad's *Heart*" 207). Classroom materials supporting the suggestion that "Heart of Darkness" is a hybrid species of jour-nalism—comparable, perhaps, to today's docudrama—are readily available. (In this reading, of course, Kurtz figures as the quintessential composite charac-ter.) Many of the casebooks that have been published on the text handily sum-marize the political-historical background out of which the work emerges. However, where time permits, a recent study by Adam Hochschild, *King Leopold's Ghost* (1998), might well be assigned; in any case it can be recom-mended as extra reading to interested students, in order to bring out more fully the great human interest of this background. The tale that Hochschild recounts, with its contrasting elements of treachery and greed, on one hand, and of the birth of that crusading indignation that gave rise to the modern human rights movement, on the other, itself partakes of hybridity, combining novelistic appeal and historical documentation.

While many aspects of the Scramble for Africa during the late nineteenth century are pertinent to the interpretation of "Heart of Darkness," to me what seems most crucial for our students to grasp is the enormity of the violations committed. By "enormity," I refer to dimensions both moral and quantitative: the mind-blowing extremity of individual cases of victimization and also the imagination-boggling scope of these victimizations. A sufficiently determined instructor might attempt to convey the extremity of these events by providing students with reprints of photographs that, shortly after the turn of the century, were instrumental in the turning of international public opinion against King Leopold. (I admit that I have never mustered the resolution to take this step.) A recurring motif in these photos—many of which were taken by Alice Seeley Harris, the wife of a Baptist missionary—is the dismemberment of the hands and feet of children, who were mutilated as punishment for a village's failure to meet rubber production quotas. As shocking as these pictures are, they arguably are no more so than our best estimates of the number of Africans who died during the period of which we speak—estimates that uniformly horrify even as they express a considerable range of opinion. Hunt Hawkins goes for the low ball: "Between 1885 and 1908, in order to effect his policy of forced labor, Leopold killed an estimated three million people" (215). Leroi Jones ups the ante, referring to "the five to eight million Africans killed in the Congo" (Tal 30). Hochschild, delving into the methods by means of which such estimates are reached and citing the work especially of Jan Vansina, "perhaps the greatest living ethnographer of Congo basin people," comes up with a higher figure yet. "[D]uring the Leopold period and its immediate aftermath," he states, "the population of the territory dropped by approximately ten million people" (233).

The intensity of the photographic records and the astronomical scale of the death counts serve to disclose that the historical background out of which "Heart of Darkness" emerges is comparable to the worst large-scale killings of the twentieth century, including the Holocaust, our paradigmatic case of mass murder. Thus, we arrive at the second of the border regions to which contemplation of this work readily conduces: the study of trauma, itself a burgeoning multidisciplinary enterprise. Clearly, the history that breathes through "Heart of Darkness" is traumatic, meaning that it tends to elude apprehension, interpretation, and communication. My own decision not to show the pictures of the mutilated children perhaps is symptomatic of this elusiveness, insofar as the obscenity of these images—in other words, what makes them effective as signs of atrocity—seems to overwhelm the plan of employing them merely as a pedagogical tool. Along the same lines, the objectivity with which statistical summaries of massacre in the Congo roll so very many individual existences into a number too gigantic to relate to everyday life may, after all, conceal as much as it reveals. My attempts to convey to students something of the enormity of the historical circumstances with which Conrad and his earliest readers were confronted may be implicated in "the central problem facing any historical approach to understanding *Heart of Darkness*, the problem that the story itself calls into question whether literature, or any kind of writing, for that matter, can represent history" (Hawkins, "Conrad's *Heart*" 208).

Theories of trauma speak to this "central problem" of the (in)communicability of history by defining traumatic experience as a breakdown of habitual cognitive processing under the pressure of extreme events. Cathy Caruth influentially has elaborated the definition of posttraumatic stress disorder to highlight the fact that at its core is the nonassimilation of the traumatic impression: "The pathology consists [. . .] solely in *the structure of its experience* or reception: the event is not assimilated or experienced fully at the time, but only belatedly, in its repeated *possession* of the one who experiences it. To be traumatized is precisely to be possessed by an image or event" (4). Geoffrey Hartman unpacks some of the paradoxical implications of this emphasis:

> Any general description or modeling of trauma [. . .] risks being figurative itself, to the point of mythic [ph]antasmagoria. Something "falls" into the psyche, or causes it to "split." There is an original inner catastrophe whereby / in which an experience that is not experienced (and so, apparently, not "real") has an exceptional presence—is inscribed with a force proportional to the mediations punctured or evaded.   (537)

The perspectives opened by Caruth and Hartman provide a theoretical framework for understanding "Heart of Darkness" as an attempt to bear witness to "the exceptional presence" of a cognitive disruption.

Though Caruth and Hartman are exemplary for isolating the paradoxical mystery of "an experience that is not experienced," to lead a class of undergraduates into a discussion of the psychological dynamic underlying Conrad's novella I find Ronnie Janoff-Bulman's *Shattered Assumptions* to be most useful. The relative accessibility of Janoff-Bulman's analysis permits students to build on their familiarity with the concept of trauma as they have imbibed it from popular culture and thus readily to rethink and reevaluate traumatic experiences that they personally may have undergone. Obviously, the making of such personal connections can have a wonderfully vitalizing effect on class discussion. At the same time, it is important to appreciate that Janoff-Bulman's theory of trauma goes well beyond the discourse of television talk shows, carrying real weight in academic psychology. Thus, Susan L. Reviere suggests that Janoff-Bulman's adaptation of "schema theory" to the study of trauma "may provide a bridge between dynamic conceptualizations of traumatic memory and the relationship of these conceptualizations to cognitive processes" (27).

Schema theory postulates that we acquire from earliest childhood a conceptual system that generally enables us to function effectively (Janoff-Bulman 5). This system is a set of internal representations that provides us with expectations about the world and about ourselves. Especially important to Janoff-Bulman's understanding of these constructs is the idea that they are arranged hierarchically, "with our most fundamental assumptions being those that are most abstract and general, as well as most pervasive in their applicability" (5). The three assumptions that she finds to be both most fundamental and most germane to the study of trauma assert that:

> The world is benevolent.
> The world is meaningful.
> The self is worthy.   (6)

The objection that the belief system outlined in terms of these three assumptions is too naively optimistic to be credited by most adults is met by Janoff-Bulman's reference to the hierarchical nature of our presuppositional networks. As a fundamental set of beliefs, the benevolence and meaningfulness of the world and the worthiness of the self are ordinarily impervious to testing. Although easily perceiving that great suffering often is meted out to many, individuals persist in believing that horrible things will not happen to them personally.

With the onslaught of the traumatic experience, these assumptions suddenly are subjected to overwhelming attack. Traumatic experiences compel belief in a cruel and capricious world or in an unworthy self and thereby leave victims enmeshed in anxiety and depression. The suddenness of the downgrading of world and self is crucial to this devastating effect. The fundamental assumptions have been discredited in a moment, while the emotionally untenable nature of the dark views that rush to replace them "makes routine, automatic, secure, self-confident activity impossible" (61). Consequently, recovery from trauma means a reconfiguring of schematic beliefs to the end that traumatic stimuli can be integrated into habitual cognitive processing.

The optic provided by Janoff-Bulman brings into focus Marlow's central conflict as a trauma survivor caught between the imperative to bear witness to overwhelming events and the impossibility of recapturing and communicating them. Neither Marlow nor his audience aboard the *Nellie* are able to assimilate recognitions that are wildly incongruent with the fundamental assumptions Janoff-Bulman describes, especially as these inform the mind-set of professional British men deeply implicated in ideologies of colonialism. At the same time, Marlow must try "to carry the tale of horror back to the halls of 'normalcy'" (Tal 120). Thus, the approach to "Heart of Darkness" through history and the theory of trauma points to the distinction between Marlow, the primary narrator, and Conrad, the implied author who hovers at some degree of remoteness. Conrad, the trauma survivor in real time, takes pains to present Marlow as an unreliable narrator in order to stage a collision between cognition and the real, in which the failure of cognition itself becomes evocative of indescribable events. The contradictions and lacunae of the story make sense when we consider them as part and parcel of a distinctly posttraumatic aesthetic organized in terms of an obsessive desire to give expression to the inexpressible.

Setting forth this interpretation in the context of a college literature class, however, I am more concerned to engage the students in the complexities of Conrad's story than I am to convince them that my reading is right.

I turn to the writing assignment that I have been tweaking for some time, the essay of creative response. Without lapsing into an anything-goes permissiveness, this assignment drastically expands the scope of what may be said in an interpretive essay.

The prompt for this assignment invites students to identify a problem in a literary text and then write a creative supplement to the text that explores this problem. The essay is divided into three parts.

First, students are directed to write an introduction that identifies a particular problem and explains its significance. The problem is usually a contradiction, inconsistency, or absence that is not easily recuperated to authorial intent. In "Heart of Darkness," Marlow's formal assertion of an unspecified "idea" that redeems the project of conquering the world (10) seems to be contradicted by the text's subsequent evocation of mass murder in the Congo. Another related problem might be Conrad's decision not to explore the psychological interiority of Africans. Yet another might be the silence of the female characters. In prewriting discussions and workshop exercises, I support my students' efforts to develop convincing, thoughtful, and nuanced discussions of problems that are pertinent to the novella's turbulent critical history.

Second, in the body of the essay, students produce an imaginative supplement to the literary text. They may add to the text or revise it. Since this supplementing is an essay of creative response, I do not set limits on the form of the interventions that might be made. Epistolary responses are always popular, as are sequels and prequels. Occasionally I receive TV scripts, song lyrics, and fairy tales.

Third, students briefly explain the effect of the interventions they have made. What has been gained, and what has been lost?

This writing assignment, though its description seems slight in relation to the discussion that preceded it, nonetheless may represent the most pedagogically significant of the transdisciplinary extensions I am recommending here. As narcissism dotes on small differences, the barriers that divide literary studies from classes in rhetoric and writing, including creative writing, may well figure as an irresistible provocation to those inclined to traverse disciplinary boundary lines. The essay of creative response allows students to build on approaches to "Heart of Darkness" through history or trauma, or to set out in another direction altogether. It supplies an occasion for an engagement with Conrad's text that in some ways is deliciously unfettered, although ultimately still answerable to traditional standards of academic interpretation.

Teaching "Heart of Darkness" in a Creative Writing Class

Janet Burroway

In the typical fiction workshop the only text is the student story. But both students and faculty members increasingly seek in the creative writing curriculum a course designed as a practicum, in which writer-students and writer-teacher analyze, in order to master them, the techniques of published fiction. The matter of such a course is not far divorced from literary analysis, but the emphasis shifts—significantly, it must be said, in the direction of intentional fallacy—from "What does the story do or say?" to "What problem did the writer face here?" and "Why does the author choose this technique?" and "What can I learn or steal?"

For such purposes, some writers are better than others, and even the best writers are not equally useful. Ernest Hemingway and Henry James, for example, are relatively easy for talented students to imitate—and imitation can be an energizing exercise—but they are not good models, precisely because the imitables reside in superficialities of style. Joseph Conrad, however, offers an immensely varied school of techniques, and "Heart of Darkness," particularly in the manipulation of point of view, can be used to help students grok some fundamentals otherwise dimly understood.

My students are familiar with the idea that every writer will eventually—and implicitly—manipulate point of view by answering the questions Who speaks? To whom? In what form? At what distance? With what limitations? The point of view may be cast, for example, in the first, second, or third person, as an omniscient author or a central or peripheral narrator. The text may be addressed to the traditional reader or to another character, in the form of a traditional story or any number of variations from monologue, report, or oratory to diary, letter, or stream of consciousness. The narrative stance may include distance in space or time, or it may create the illusion of immediate action. The diction may be formal or intimate. The narrator may be totally or partially trustworthy in any number of areas to do with moral, intellectual, or other capacity. All these elements will inform the point of view and hence our experience of the story.

The author's choice of point of view will be largely instinctive, a matter of a feel for the voice, as a poet works with a feel for rhythm. But just as a poet, when the rhythm goes wrong, had better be able to scan the feet and recognize that a stress is missing here or that this spondee needs to be a trochee, so the fiction writer had better know, when point of view goes wrong, how to finesse diction, person, distance, and connotation in order to adjust the effect (or affect).

Conrad's scheme in "Heart of Darkness" calls for a narration within a narration, a complex feat. One narrator must provide a frame for the second, whose story must appear to be a monologue. Both are white males of the same profession; both have little physical presence, each being mainly a voice. They must credibly present the voices of working sailors, even old salts, but they also, especially the one speaking aloud, must rise without losing that character to all the heightened language of literary eloquence at the author's command.

It is usual to signal to the reader in the first few sentences the degree of knowledge or omniscience the author is going to assume (the point-of-view contract). It is also quite usual in the limited omniscient voice to introduce a point-of-view character first from the outside, objectively, and then move to the character's thoughts, thus establishing the author's right to both exterior and interior. Narrators usually begin with a reference to "I" or "me" and establish a voice at once. They may describe from the outside only what they see or might somehow know as a limited human being. Conrad departs radically from these expectations, and it is worth examining his opening contract in detail.

Students are often surprised that the first sentence of "Heart of Darkness" does not suggest a narrator at all, and certainly not a sailor sitting in the boat he describes; it sets the scene in the familiar diction of an author both external and authoritative: "The *Nellie*, a cruising yawl, swung to her anchor without a flutter of the sails and was at rest" (7). The second sentence is also technically external, but the voice becomes more colloquial, and the idioms introduce a note of character: "The flood *had made*, the wind was nearly calm, and being *bound down* the river *the only thing for it* was to *come to* and wait for *the turn of the tide*" (7; italics mine).

Now the voice is that of a practical man of the sea, and if the story remained in the third person, it would partake of stylistic contagion, in which the narrative voice catches the idiom of the character being described. But the second paragraph reveals that this story is being told in the first person: "The Sea-reach of the Thames stretched before us like the beginning of an interminable waterway" (7)—though even here the first-person plural holds us at a little distance still, while the "interminable" acts as the first rhetorical permission for all those *inscrutables*, *immeasureables*, and *immensity*s to come. So in these three sentences Conrad has, in addition to setting the scene, established his authorial right to objectivity, colloquial idiom, narrator interpretation, and eloquence. (Students might at this early point in the discussion be asked to write a paragraph of fiction establishing several divergent authorial rights.)

The narrator of "Heart of Darkness" does not, as would be usual by this time, diminish the distance between himself and the reader. His only first-person singular is offered in the throwaway "as I have already said somewhere" (7) that announces him as a practiced storyteller (Marlow, by contrast, will begin many paragraphs with an "I"), while he identifies the other listeners by their (rather institutional) professions as the Director of Companies, the Lawyer and the Accountant, naming only Marlow.

Once the narrator has "evoked the great spirit of the past" in his panoply of historical heroes (and the ships "whose names are like jewels flashing in the night"), Marlow is introduced in his own voice: "And this also has been one of the dark places of the earth" (8, 9). This pronouncement, rather high-minded for a sailor, has been prepared by the narrator's interior speculations and in turn prepares us for the portentous latitude Marlow will take in speech.

From the technical standpoint the contrast between the two voices is now established. The outer narrator speaks to the convention of the reader from the convention of a narrator of a story. Marlow, however, speaks to other characters as a narrator of a spoken monologue. Marlow's tale must have the recurrent if not constant illusion of the speaking voice, but at the same time Conrad has the luxury of an external interpreter to make points that it would be hard to convey through the manipulation of the single viewpoint.

Some of this interpretation amounts to literary criticism of Marlow's style, including the famous contrast between the cracked nut and the misty halo (9). More interesting is the tangle of viewpoints at the beginning of Marlow's tale proper. "I don't want to bother you much with what happened to me personally," Marlow begins, and the narrator-as-critic intervenes to observe that Marlow is like many tale tellers "who seem unaware of what their audience would best like to hear." (As a literary judgment, this remark may be seen as prescient of our confessional times.) The conclusion of Marlow's sentence, however, contradicts its introduction and makes a promise to the reader that the narrator's perception will be honored: "yet to understand the effect of it on *me* [. . .]" (11; my italics).

This is a good place in a practicum to discuss the dictum of Rust Hills (in *Writing in General and the Short Story in Particular*) that the point-of-view character must be the one moved or changed by the action (142). This principle is one of the most difficult and most important to convey to young writers, who can be saved many hours of pallid character-writing if they understand it. Marlow announces himself as a peripheral narrator (a technique not confined to Conrad) and denies that he means to tell his own story—but this statement is of course disingenuous. We can scarcely be moved by Kurtz's experience, which we do not share, but only by Marlow's experience of Kurtz. Marlow is our eyes; he filters and interprets for us, so to the extent that the story is successful, we will be moved as he is moved. Ultimately Marlow will drop the modest pretense and acknowledge that we are thoroughly involved in *his* story: "If anybody had ever struggled with a soul I am the man" (65). But he will continue to offer disingenuous modesty, especially as to his powers of articulation, and this modesty is one of the techniques by which Conrad will earn him his eloquence.

The case of the outer narrator is more complex. Why isn't he subject to Hills's law? Because the distancing devices mentioned above keep us from identifying with him? Because his romantic view of sea history contrasts unfavorably with Marlow's harder and more imaginative view of the Thames as a wilderness? Because the story is handed off to Marlow before we become interested in the first narrator? Such questions will lead into a discussion of the more difficult of the point-of-view elements: From what distance (and what kind of distance? rhetorical, emotional, spatial, temporal?) do these narrators tell their tales? What failures of intellect, emotion, experience affect the reliability of each narrator? How does the author present irony by or against the speaker in order to direct our judgment?

Of great practical use to young writers is Conrad's manipulation of distance between the two narrators—which is to say, between the boat on the Thames and the drama in Africa. It is always a fiction writer's problem to give the past tense the immediacy of the present, and in this case we have two pasts. Also, Marlow needs to tell the story with a detail and literary intricacy that stretch the bounds of monologue. As it is, the account contains patent absurdities: that the narrator can reproduce what he remembers Marlow said that he (Marlow) remembered that he overheard the Manager and his uncle say, and so forth. (Students may at this point want to discuss the degree of suspension of disbelief we are willing to allow in fiction, by contrast with that allowable in literary nonfiction or memoir.)

For most of the novel we are in the Africa of Marlow's sojourn there. In these scenes we often lose the sense of a recital. Marlow becomes for a time the convention of author telling the story to the convention of reader, until it suits Conrad's purpose to foreground again the boat on the Thames and "bounce the reader" into accepting his flexible point of view (Forster, *Aspects* 78).

Conrad reminds us of the frame setting with several techniques that also establish Marlow's character and earn his reliability. Marlow asks questions, including frequent rhetorical questions; he declares himself incapable of articulating something or other; he criticizes himself; he repeats himself, breaks off, starts over, dislocates syntax to indicate agitation. In each case we are reminded that he has an audience, and that his story is spoken aloud. With surprising rarity, the first narrator directly returns to make an observation and reset the scene. Usually these passages are introduced by having Marlow stop speaking. The first return of the narrator exhibits most of these techniques:

> "Do you see him? Do you see the story? Do you see anything? It seems to me that I am trying to tell you a dream—making a vain attempt [. . .]"
>
> He was silent for a while.
>
> ". . . No, it is impossible; it is impossible to convey the life-sensation of any given epoch of one's existence—that which makes its truth, its meaning—its subtle and penetrating essence. It is impossible. We live, as we dream—alone. . . ."
>
> He paused again as if reflecting, then added:
>
> "Of course in this you fellows see more than I could then. You see me, whom you know. . . ."
>
> It had become so pitch dark that we listeners could hardly see one another. For a long time already he, sitting apart, had been no more to us than a voice. (30)

Such techniques are used repeatedly and are a means of transition between greater and lesser awareness of the scene on the Thames (see also 38, 48–50,

60, 73). For young writers their study can foster an awareness of such manipulation of distance—spatial, temporal, and psychic—and this awareness can help them in managing the more frequent authorial need of transition between present action and flashback.

A related issue is, How does Conrad establish Marlow's reliability despite Marlow's melodrama and overstatement? Devices similar to (in some cases the same as) those already mentioned posit for Marlow a voice at once colloquial and exalted. He juxtaposes as a matter of habit a heightened concept with one that deflates, that is trivial or mean. This contrast undercuts his oratorical sonority, develops his ironic worldview, and at the same time promotes a sense of extemporaneous speech and of internal struggle. Sometimes Marlow accomplishes this juxtaposition in a quick paradox, as in "this papier-mâché Mephistopheles," sometimes in the form of a mock-heroic: "Moreover I respected the fellow. Yes. I respected his collars" (29, 21). Often it is the intrusion of a jarring word: "a dying vibration of one immense jabber" or of a throw-away phrase: "an unfathomable enigma, a mystery greater—when I thought of it—than the curious, inexplicable note of desperate grief" (48, 43).

Marlow's self-put-downs are a (common literary) device to forestall our own objections and therefore make us trust him, as when he begins to worry his Continental relations for a job: "I wouldn't have believed it of myself, but then—you see—I felt somehow I must get there by hook or by crook" (12). Likewise his protestations of incapacity buy him the right to his eloquence: "a smile—not a smile—I remember it, but I can't explain"—after which of course he explains very well: "It came at the end of his speeches like a seal applied on the words to make the meaning of the commonest phrase appear absolutely inscrutable" (24).

Marlow's—and Conrad's—metaphors partake of this same habit of undercutting contrast, and students will eagerly seek out the hundreds of qualifying effects of light on dark, haze on sun, gleam on fog, dark on glow. They can also learn much about the nuances inherent in the frame of reference from which a metaphor is built. Conrad manipulates comparison between the natural and the manufactured world to achieve his deflationary effects, as when "our eyes were no more use to us than if we had been buried miles deep in a heap of cotton-wool" or when the "white fog, very warm and clammy [. . .] lifted, as a shutter lifts" (44, 41). But the deflation can also be achieved the other way around, by comparing the larger object or emotion to the smaller natural phenomenon: "the little begrimed steamboat like a sluggish beetle crawling," "some weird incantation [. . .] as the humming of bees comes out of a hive," or "mangroves that seemed to writhe at us in the extremity of an impotent despair" (37, 63, 17).

Once such passages and techniques have been analyzed in the practicum, I assign an exercise in which the students practice, using their own subject matter and choice of idiom, what they have learned. Here are a few exercises that might come out of the discussion outlined:

Write a passage in which a narrator introduces a speaker who recounts the dialogue of a third. Characterize all three. Do so partly through metaphors taken from the frame of reference of each.

Write a monologue that is a simple narrative of an event, but establish the presence and the character of the audience (the *you*) through questions, including rhetorical questions.

David Daiches observes that Conrad used the English language in a way no Englishman would dare, without any evidence of the restraint Marlow so praises in "Heart of Darkness" (1156). Dare to write a monologue using at least three of the following words unironically: *inscrutable, immeasurable, immensity, unfathomable, inconceivable, impenetrable, incomprehensible, innumerable, unspeakable, intolerable, inexorable, unextinguishable, invisible.* You might also try to slip in a few of these: *luminous, brooding, gloom, diaphanous, enigma, rapacious, pitiless, primeval, mystery, benevolence, bloodthirsty, vile, imbecile, abomination, extremity, horror, universal genius.*

If (as is likely) the resulting speaker seems unreliable, try rewriting the monologue by interspersing the overstatement with deflating idioms, images, or metaphors. Does the character become more believable in the judgments expressed?

Write a monologue in two strongly contrasting styles, playing the two styles off each other—the rhetoric of chivalric heartbreak from a computer geek, trash talk full of classical allusion, and so forth.

Have a narrator set a scene in such a way as to undermine our confidence in the narrator's judgment. Then let the narrator introduce and pass judgment on a second character we are therefore inclined to trust more.

Luminous Spaces:
Teaching "Heart of Darkness"
through Film

Mark Osteen

"Heart of Darkness" is a highly cinematic text. The frame narrator, operating somewhat as a "camera functions in film" (Cahir 181–82), depicts the *Nellie* resting in a "luminous space" full of "gaudy and radiant" mist, ready-made for a set of establishing helicopter and crane shots (Conrad, *Heart* [Kimbrough] 7, 8). As darkness falls, a director would bring us to the spotlit scene of narration through ever-closer lap dissolves, in the manner of the opening of *Citizen Kane*. Marlow's narration, with its striking images of violence, ritual, and mystery, seems equally poised to be filmed. Despite these camera-ready features, "Heart of Darkness" has proven to be a difficult nut to crack: several planned film versions were never produced, others were scuttled in preproduction, and still others encountered difficulties grave enough to sink most films.[1]

Its unfilmability notwithstanding, the various screenplays and completed film versions of Conrad's novella can be superb pedagogical instruments. When brought into the classroom along with the novella, these adaptations can illuminate a difficult text, help students comprehend how literary and cinematic texts are constructed, and enable them to think in fresh ways about point of view, style, characterization, and theme. Perhaps most importantly, since every adaptation is an interpretation, attentive film viewing may prompt advanced students to recognize their own interpretive practices and biases. Such self-awareness is, of course, very much in the spirit of "Heart of Darkness," a text that is in many ways about interpretation. In this essay I discuss three important film versions of Conrad's work—one well known, the others less so—and suggest that failed adaptations sometimes work better in the classroom than successful ones, precisely because they underscore the problems of interpreting such a text.

One warning: before moving to the individual film versions, one should give students prescreening questions, so as to slough off the habit of passive viewing they will have cultivated over the years. Of course, they should finish reading the text before watching any of the films.

Unproduced Screenplays

Citizen Kurtz

The first attempt to film "Heart of Darkness" was Orson Welles's aborted 1939 project for RKO (he had earlier produced a radio version for his Mercury Theater).[2] For film students, this fact alone should invite them to link Kurtz with later Wellesian characters such as Charles Foster Kane or *Touch of Evil*'s corrupt sheriff Hank Quinlan (indeed, *Touch* is a kind of bordertown version of "Heart" with Charlton Heston as Marlow and Quinlan's underlings playing Kurtz's "savage" minions). As Robert Carringer notes, Welles repeatedly returned to the "dramatic situation of the morally transcendent hero, excessive and compulsively self-destructive, who is an object of veneration and awe to a lesser man" (3). As if replicating Kurtz's hubris (and showing an astute grasp of the text's psychological undertones), Welles had planned to play both him and Marlow. After mentioning Welles's plan to students, an instructor can ask what hidden parts of the text would be exposed if the same actor were to play both roles. The parallels between "Heart" and Welles's finished films can also yield some fruitful exercises. For example, one might ask a group to watch *Touch of Evil* and give a presentation in which they compare it in theme, visual style, and characterization with "Heart of Darkness." One might then consider why such figures remain compelling and examine precursors for Kurtz and Kane in Greek drama or in novels such as *Frankenstein*.

To update the story, Welles incorporated references to European fascism and told journalists that "the picture is, frankly, an attack on the Nazi system" (qtd. in Brady 212). Using these alterations, one might ask students to think of other historical or contemporary parallels to Kurtz (*Apocalypse Now* offers an obvious analogue). The very good *Great Books* program on "Heart" produced by the Learning Channel declares that Conrad's skeptical vision of human corruption presages some of the horrors of the twentieth century ("*Heart*"). I have students watch this documentary before the second day of discussion and ask them to test this assertion. If you had to update the story, I ask, where would you set it, and what would the premise be?

Welles made some other questionable but potentially illuminating changes in the story. For example, Kurtz's Intended (named Elsa) accompanies Marlow up the river, and Marlow falls in love with her (Rosenbaum 32; Welles reused the boat journey—and the name Elsa—in his 1948 film *The Lady from Shanghai*). In class we discuss whether the presence of Kurtz's Intended compromises the relationship between Marlow and Kurtz and whether it adds anything (Elsa departs before Marlow's climactic encounter with Kurtz). Welles had also hoped to use 3,000 black actors as extras and planned to highlight the interracial relationship between Kurtz and his African mistress. As Guerric DeBona notes, such a relationship would have been "shockingly unorthodox" for the time (18; one merely has to watch *Gone with the Wind*, released the same year, to glimpse Hollywood's treatment of race in 1939); of course, the Production Code Administration, headed by the reactionary Joseph Breen, stipulated that there be no hint of such miscegenation. With these facts in mind, one may introduce the vexed question of Conrad's (and Marlow's) racism, assigning Chinua Achebe's famous attack, along with the responses by Frances Singh and C. P. Sarvan (all reprinted in Kimbrough's Norton Critical Edition).

Clearly these aspects of Welles's film would have unsettled contemporary viewers. But the most unorthodox feature of the film was its radical treatment of point of view. In an effort to capture the flavor of Marlow's narration, Welles had planned to use a subjective camera almost exclusively in the film, with Marlow as the camera eye. The only Hollywood film that employs this technique extensively is Robert Montgomery's adaptation of Raymond Chandler's *Lady in the Lake*, in which the subjective camera often interferes with the narrative. Whether it would have worked in the filmed *Heart of Darkness* is difficult to determine, and in later years Welles himself was skeptical about it (Rosenbaum 31). To help viewers adjust to this radical technique, Welles's script begins with an introduction in which he addresses the audience in voice-over, while the camera becomes, in turn, a bird in a cage, a prisoner about to be electrocuted, and a golfer. The voice-over declares, *"You're not going to see this picture—this picture is going to happen to you"* (Welles, "Sequence" 26; italics his). At the end of the introduction, the camera turns on a motion picture theater full of movie cameras facing the "screen." A black screen then fades in; on one side of the screen appears a human eye, followed by an equals sign and a capital *I*. The camera eye, in other words, is identical with the first-person narrator—and hence with each audience member's eye. Welles's pedagogical method thus seeks to dramatize Conrad's famous statement that the primary task of art is "to make you hear, to make you feel—it is, before all, to make you *see*" (*Heart* [Kimbrough] 225; preface to *The Nigger of the "Narcissus"*).

Jonathan Rosenbaum notes that Welles's introduction ingeniously demonstrates "the playful and gimmicky aspects of the technique *before* the story begins, thus clearing the way for its subsequent use as a serious narrative device." Thenceforward, Rosenbaum claims, the camera would become "neutral" (31). But it is more likely that the technique would have constantly drawn attention to itself, as Marlow does during the breaks in the written text. Indeed, Robert Spadoni argues that the technique would have "demonstrated the paradox that a narrative consisting principally of point-of-view shots effectively blocks viewer identification" (80). I submit that Welles's subjective camera would simultaneously block *and* engage the viewer's observational faculties. By continually reminding viewers of the nature of the medium, it would create a split reaction like the one that readers experience as we both accompany Marlow on his journey and maintain a slightly ironic distance from him, recognizing his struggle not only with Kurtz but with language itself. If we become the narrative I, nonetheless our eye is not merely a camera eye, because we both watch the action and watch the observer.

These issues are fertile ground for classroom discussion and research papers, especially in upper-division courses for literature or film majors. One might first have some students watch *Lady in the Lake* and present examples of the advantages and disadvantages of the extended use of a subjective camera. One might also ask them to imagine or, in a class with more advanced students, write one scene using this technique. One might then employ these exercises to discuss the merits of Welles's plan. Would his approach capture Marlow's point of view? How do other films depict first-person point of view? To what degree does Marlow operate as a camera eye? One might also wish to contrast Welles's experiment with the way that Francis Ford Coppola and Nicolas Roeg show point of view in their versions of the story.

But even more than by sight, Welles's version is "guided and controlled by sound" (Rosenbaum 29)—not surprisingly, since Welles made his reputation in radio. In the opening sequence, for example, snatches of jazz music, voice-over, tom-toms, and bell buoys all foreshadow Marlow's experiences.[3] But silence in radio is just dead air, so Welles felt compelled to fill the text's evocative silences with narration (Spadoni 88). Nevertheless, his version conveys the eloquence of the man who appears to Marlow primarily as a voice (Conrad, *Heart* [Kimbrough] 60, 67). At the end of Welles's script, as in Conrad's text, Marlow tells Elsa that he heard Kurtz's "very last words," and we too hear Kurtz softly uttering them. Marlow narrates: "The dusk was repeating them around us, like the first whisper of a rising wind. *Kurtz's voice:* The horror! The horror!" (qtd. in DeBona 28–29; cf. Conrad, *Heart* [Kimbrough] 75). Analyzing Welles's use of sound (along with pertinent articles from *Conrad on Film* [Moore]) not only helps students recognize the brilliance of Conrad's manipulation of sound and silence but also prepares them for the aural montages in Roeg's and Coppola's films.

Assigning Welles's introduction and excerpts from his script opens several productive avenues for discussion, papers, and presentations and also enables students to assess later filmmakers' solutions to the problems of point of view, narration, and sound in their adaptations of "Heart of Darkness."

Dark Country

A second unproduced screenplay of "Heart of Darkness" sheds a different light on the difficulties of adaptation. In 1988 the Conrad scholar Adam Gillon finished a screenplay entitled "Dark Country," excerpts of which are reprinted in his book *Joseph Conrad: Comparative Essays* ("Excerpts"). Like Welles, he places the Intended on the boat with Marlow, here an American named William Reston. Gillon aimed to create a stronger woman, one "able to face the truth about her lover and herself" ("Adapting" 176). This change raises questions about the sexism of the text: is the Intended a real woman? What does Marlow's attitude about women reveal about Conrad's? About the sexism of the time?

To deepen Marlow's character, Gillon gives him a dark secret, importing from *Lord Jim* the protagonist's abandonment of a ship filled with passengers. Early in the film Reston recalls his trial, at which he is told he should crawl "into the darkest hole on this earth, to hide your shame" (Gillon, "Excerpts" 233). This alteration provides an additional explanation for Marlow's desire to go to the Congo and explains his fascination with Kurtz (here named Jason) as part of a compelling need for self-redemption. Gillon also supplies an added element to the Marlow-Kurtz relationship when he gives Reston a dream in which Jason turns into Reston's father (267). These changes can be a springboard for questions about Marlow's motivation in the novella: To what degree is Marlow trying to prove something to himself or others? What kind of person is driven to explore? What are the obligations of empire or authority? Can such explorations be noble or moral? Is the relationship between Marlow and Kurtz in any sense a father-son relationship?

The remainder of Gillon's screenplay, however, reveals how even well-intentioned and well-informed projects can founder. It rather ludicrously turns Kurtz into a devil worshiper and presents a scene in which the Intended (named Cathy) is prepared for sacrifice and placed nude on a pyre. In case we miss the psychological overtones in the Marlow-Kurtz relationship, the Russian harlequin man is named Siggy Freund. In general, the screenplay over-explains, as when Freund tells Reston, "I think you're looking for the Jason element in yourself. [. . .] It's the readiness [. . .] to go all the way. [. . .] It's the absence of all restraint. . . . Total freedom" (250). For some reason Gillon also replaces Kurtz's enigmatic final words with "I know the power of evil . . . yes . . . yes . . . the glory of darkness" (265). One can all too easily imagine Vincent Price intoning these words in a grade-B horror film from the 1950s.

Yet despite—or because of—its failings, Gillon's screenplay can be a useful teaching aid, especially when paired with other film versions. By drawing attention to these questionable choices, one may engage students in discussing the effects of understatement and ask them if (or where) Marlow himself exaggerates or overexplains. How does Conrad invite readers to use their imaginations to picture the jungle, Kurtz's appearance, his "unsound" methods (61)? Gillon's interpretation invites students to advance their own: what is the nature of Kurtz's evil? What do his last words mean? To what degree is there a Kurtz in Marlow?

Completed Films

Coppola's Nightmare

That most Wellesian of contemporary American directors, Francis Ford Coppola, also nearly failed to bring forth his 1979 film (structured on "Heart of Darkness") *Apocalypse Now*. Since *Apocalypse Now* is treated elsewhere in this volume, I refrain from discussing it in detail here. But I would urge anyone teaching the Coppola film to couple it with the documentary *Hearts of Darkness: A Filmmaker's Apocalypse*, which is not only an illuminating chronicle of the director's near-Kurtzian arrogance and monumental courage but also a primer on how movies are made (hence, I often teach "Heart of Darkness" and its screen versions early in film adaptation courses). The documentary suggests how deeply "Heart of Darkness" has infiltrated popular culture. It also points to parallels between Coppola and figures in his films such as Don Corleone in *The Godfather* and the automaker in *Tucker: The Man and His Dream*. As Coppola says in the documentary, "a film director is one of the last few dictatorial posts left in the world." Thus, juxtaposing *Hearts of Darkness* with *Apocalypse Now* and Welles's unproduced script can lead to fruitful discussions of the role of the Promethean overreacher in twentieth-century culture. Coppola's statement might also spur comparisons between his ambitions and those of the American military. Indeed, one striking feature of the documentary is its revelation of how ambition led Coppola to replicate the American experience in Vietnam and the colonialist enterprise of bringing the money and technology of advanced capitalism into a less developed region. Coppola seems to grasp this historical parallel, stating in one sequence that "My film is not about Vietnam. It *is* Vietnam."

He might just as easily have said, "My film is not about 'Heart of Darkness'; it *is* heart of darkness": as Eleanor Coppola's voice-over declares in the documentary, the director confronted his own heart of darkness while making the film. A fateful series of events nearly sank the production: Martin Sheen had a heart attack, a typhoon ruined sets, Marlon Brando showed up unprepared and overweight, Dennis Hopper couldn't remember his lines, Coppola ran out of money, and so on. It is remarkable that *Apocalypse Now* was completed at all. One can easily picture a Marlow-like studio employee venturing to the Philippines to bring back Coppola, whose methods had become "unsound" and who had established his own private kingdom in the jungle. Indeed, for Coppola as for other filmmakers who wrestled with Conrad's text, Marlow's journey came to represent their own struggle to bring the text to the screen: "Heart of Darkness" became a metaphor for filmmaking itself. As Thomas Elsaesser and Michael Wedel note, "to 'become Kurtz,' and thus to put oneself in the center of one's own fiction, is to realize a primary fantasy that has also become one of Hollywood's most essential public relations strategies" (153).

Roeg's Gallery

Coppola's flawed masterpiece continues to overshadow the most recent film version of "Heart of Darkness," a modest treatment directed by the English maverick Nicolas Roeg (written by Benedict Fitzgerald) for Turner Network Television in 1993.[4] More conventional in structure and more faithful to the text than Coppola's film, Roeg's version exhibits flaws of its own. Seymour Chatman argues that Roeg overemphasizes Conrad's critique of imperialism at the expense of his psychological and moral penetration (208–09), and the film's frequent shots of elephant hide and tusks certainly stress the theme of greed and exploitation. Some viewers may prefer this streamlining to Coppola's grandiosity. In any case, Roeg's film can be a fine teaching tool.

The film effectively depicts Marlow's alienation, also enhanced by the narrative frame in which his listeners, believing he is hoarding away valuable documents that Kurtz left, are hostile to him. In contrast to the other Europeans—a gallery of greedy grotesques—Tim Roth is a substantial Marlow whose disillusionment is graphically (albeit obviously) embodied by his white linen suit, which gradually becomes soiled and rumpled as he moves toward the Inner Station. A fine way to begin discussion of this film version is thus to focus on Marlow: how, for example, does this film depict his path toward self-knowledge and his rising horror? I usually ask why it is important that Marlow is a captain and what a captain's responsibilities are. Then I suggest that he is our narrative captain as well and ask if the Marlow characters in the film versions are equally reliable. What elements of his character does each version emphasize or underplay? These questions should also alert students to the visual aspects of each narrative. Are there visual parallels between him and Kurtz?

Using flickering light effects, innovative camera angles (a mix of hand-held shots and extremely high or low angles), an eerie soundtrack (thunder, heavy breathing, drums, disembodied moaning), and numerous montage sequences, Roeg creates a menacing mise en scène. The film's use of aural and visual montage should encourage discussion of Conrad's and Marlow's famous fixation on the inscrutability of Africa and its people. An instructor might ask students to name a couple of ways that Roeg attempts to capture the style of the novella and its atmosphere of confusion and foreboding. One might also ask them to list and classify the various sounds in the film. How many derive from the environment? From Marlow's consciousness? Can we make this distinction in the novel as well? Why or why not?

Roeg's film fleshes out Marlow's relationship with his African helmsman, here named Mfumu. After Mfumu is speared, his blood remains on Marlow's face throughout the scenes with Kurtz, incarnating Marlow's irrevocable tainting by the imperialist depredations he discovers. This African character also provides another prime opportunity to raise the question of race: despite his supposed friendship with Marlow, Mfumu remains an enigma in the film. Is he derisive or merely brusque? Does he really care about Marlow or his mission or is he just going along for the reward? The portrayal of Mfumu thus permits one to introduce the issue of racial stereotyping—one of Conrad's worst sins, according to Achebe—and furnishes evidence for both sides of the question of Marlow's (and Conrad's and Roeg's) alleged racial bias.

Striking images of John Malkovich's Kurtz, surrounded by tusks, effectively illustrate the text's implication that he has been consumed by ivory. But in general Marlow's encounter with Kurtz in this film seems anticlimactic. One problem is Malkovich, who, though suitably skeletal, is curiously self-regarding, as if he is more interested in being John Malkovich than in inhabiting Conrad's Promethean character. Another weakness—one that plagues all adaptations of "Heart of Darkness"—is the dialogue. A few of Kurtz's lines are taken directly from the text, but many more are transformed and, as in Gillon's screenplay, err on the side of explicitness, as when Kurtz intones, "It is dangerous to tear away the layers of thought and look into the abyss." More effective than Malkovich's acting is Roth's traumatized, empty face as he watches Kurtz's followers throw dust on Kurtz's corpse. An effective final montage combines fire, a dying pilgrim named Heche, the accountant's servant woman, the European pilgrims, a map of Africa, Mfumu, and point of view shots of the jungle—all to evoke Marlow's horror and fear.

In his last words Kurtz tells Marlow that "there is no more empty nor detestable creature in nature than a man who runs away from his demon. No faith, no fear. . . . The horror, the horror." As Chatman points out, Malkovich utters these lines "meditatively," as a "philosophical question" rather than "a tormented plaint" (207). That Kurtz's words suggest meditation rather than declaration is a defensible interpretation. Indeed, Malkovich's reading can provide the pretext for a brief assignment. One can begin by asking whether his approach to the scene works and move from that to a writing assignment on the meaning of "the horror." Is it a tentative appraisal? A self-description? A philosophical judgment? A pronouncement on imperialism? An exhausted lament? How does Marlow interpret it in the film? Does his interpretation correspond to your understanding of its meaning(s) in the text?

At the end of the film, we occupy Marlow's point of view as the Intended stares directly at the camera, standing stock-still as if becoming Kurtz's painting. Marlow reassures her, "His last words gave me your name": the implication remains that her name is related to "the horror." Then, as Marlow concludes his narrative, Roeg cuts from an overhead shot of Marlow to his departing listeners and then to his ravaged face, as he hears Kurtz repeat in voice-over his warning about a man who runs from his demon. We cut to a close-up of an elephant's eye and hear the elephant trumpet. Although this ending is effective, it exposes a significant problem in virtually all cinematic adaptations: the difficulty of capturing a character's inner world. Juxtaposing the more conventional methods of this film—voice-over, close-ups, selected subjective shots, a blend of nondiegetic and diegetic sounds—with Welles's proposed experimental strategies can thus highlight not only the strengths and limitations of each adaptation but also the differences between literature and cinema.

In general, the best way to use this adaptation is to compare it with the others. I almost always require both Roeg's version and Coppola's, along with *Hearts of Darkness*, in order to force students to think about the choices each director makes and the ramifications of these choices. Of course, the great danger in using film versions in class is that the images will become imprinted on students' minds and usurp their experience of reading the text. Certainly the power of *Apocalypse Now* lingers, and some of my students have also become confused about whether certain lines are from the novella or from Roeg's film. But because these adaptations offer such a range of interpretive choices, of successes and failures, they can be used not only to stimulate papers and discussions and to illuminate the text's inscrutabilities but also to reveal the power and uniqueness of Conrad's narrative. For, just as readers eventually bow to its magnificently rich ambiguities, so filmmakers who grapple with "Heart of Darkness" inevitably face the limitations of their abilities and of their medium.

NOTES

[1]This list does not include two American television productions from the 1950s described by Moore (234).

[2]For a thorough history of this aborted production, see Carringer; Rosenbaum. For sketches of the production design, see Carringer 4–7. These sketches are also displayed,

along with a brief discussion of Welles's project, in the documentary *Hearts of Darkness* (Bahr, Hickenlooper, and Coppola).

[3]Most other adaptations of "Heart of Darkness" also employ sound effectively. As Elsaesser and Wedel note, *Apocalypse Now* presents such brilliant and complex aural montages (helicopter noises, music, silence, echoes, etc.) that Coppola invented a new title, "sound designer," to describe Walter Murch's indispensable contributions to the film (160–61, 169–70).

[4]Roeg established his reputation with films such as *Walkabout* (1971)—an evocative tale about two children lost in the Australian outback and their encounter with a young aborigine—which resembles "Heart of Darkness" and suggests why Roeg was attracted to the project.

APPENDIX

Assignments and Topics for Discussion: Orson Welles's *Heart of Darkness*

1. Read the extant excerpts from Welles's screenplay. How does the introduction seek to create effects similar to those in the narrative frame? Does it succeed? How would viewers respond to the use of subjective camera?
2. Write one scene using Welles's characters and subjective camera and read it to the class. Have other students comment on it and revise it for production.
3. Watch *Lady in the Lake*. How well does the subjective camera technique work? What are its advantages and disadvantages as a storytelling device? As a way of identifying with the narrator? To what degree does it involve us or distance us from the story?
4. How do other films capture first-person point of view? What techniques do Coppola and Roeg use in their film versions? What are the differences between cinematic and literary points of view?
5. What effects would have been produced by placing the Intended on the boat with Marlow and having them develop a relationship? How would it change the nature and intention of Marlow's final lie? Of his relationship with Kurtz?
6. What other characters in Welles's films resemble Kurtz? How do they differ from him? If you were to make a film of "Heart of Darkness," to whom would you compare him? Are there any current films or contemporary novels that use similar plots or characters?

Assignments and Topics for Discussion: *Dark Country*

1. Read Gillon's screenplay and choose one scene to enact with partners. Then discuss with the class your selection, how successful you feel the scene is in dramatizing Conrad's text, and the choices you made in performing it.
2. Discuss Gillon's additions and omissions. What is gained or lost in making Kurtz a worshiper of Satan? In having the Intended accompany Reston-Marlow and portraying her as a sacrificial victim?
3. Compare and contrast Kurtz's death scene in Welles's and Gillon's screenplays. Which is better? Why?
4. How appropriate are Welles's and Gillon's shifts in setting?

NOTES ON CONTRIBUTORS

Janet Burroway, Robert O. Lawton Distinguished Professor of English at Florida State University, is the author of plays; poetry; children's books; and seven novels, most recently *Cutting Stone*. Her textbook, *Writing Fiction*, now in its fifth edition, is used at more than three hundred colleges and universities across the United States.

Marianne DeKoven, professor of English at Rutgers University, New Brunswick, is the author of *A Different Language: Gertrude Stein's Experimental Writing* and *Rich and Strange: Gender, History, Modernism*. She is the editor of *Feminist Locations: Global and Local, Theory and Practice* and is completing a study entitled "Utopia Limited: The Sixties and the Emergence of the Postmodern."

Mark A. Eaton, assistant professor of English at Azusa Pacific University, teaches American literature, postcolonial literature, and film studies. He is currently at work on a book titled "Critical Mass: The Literary Uses of Mass Culture in Modern America."

Avrom Fleishman, professor emeritus of English at Johns Hopkins University, is the author of nine books of literary, film, and cultural criticism, including *Conrad's Politics: Community and Anarchy in the Fiction of Joseph Conrad* and, most recently, *New Class Culture: How an Emerging Class Is Transforming America's Culture*.

William M. Hagen teaches the course Western Civilization and English at Oklahoma Baptist University. He has published extensively in the area of film adaptation, including an article on "Heart of Darkness" and *Apocalypse Now*, reprinted in the Norton Critical Edition of "Heart of Darkness."

Hunt Hawkins is professor and chair of English at Florida State University. His essays on Conrad have appeared in *PMLA*, *Journal of Modern Literature*, *South Atlantic Review*, *Conradiana*, *Conradian*, *Polish Review*, and *Joseph Conrad: Essays for the Eighties*. He has served as president of the Joseph Conrad Society of America and editor of *Joseph Conrad Today*.

Carola M. Kaplan, professor of English at California State University, Pomona, is the coeditor of *Seeing Double: Revisioning Edwardian and Modernist Literature* and the author of numerous essays on Conrad's fiction. She is currently completing a book titled "Silence, Exile, and Cunning: Moving across Cultures in Joseph Conrad, E. M. Forster, T. E. Lawrence, and Christopher Isherwood."

Mark D. Larabee was senior instructor of English at the United States Naval Academy while preparing this essay. A naval officer with fifteen years of service, he is currently the executive officer of a Pacific fleet cruiser. He has published articles on Conrad's eastern fiction in *Studies in the Novel* and *CEA Critic*.

John A. McClure teaches English at Rutgers University, New Brunswick. He is the author of *Kipling and Conrad: The Colonial Fiction* and *Late Imperial Romance*. He is at work on a study of postsecular impulses in contemporary American fiction.

Joseph F. Militello, assistant professor of English at Oklahoma State University, is the author of an essay on Eliot's *Waste Land*. He is presently at work on a book that explores the relation between aesthetics and politics in modernism.

Padmini Mongia, professor of English at Franklin and Marshall College, teaches courses on late-nineteenth-century British literature, contemporary postcolonial literature and theory, and Indian literature in English. She has published articles on Conrad and is currently at work on a book examining contemporary Indian fiction.

Margot Norris is professor of English and comparative literature at the University of California, Irvine. She has authored two books on James Joyce; a book on the turn away from anthropocentrism in the late nineteenth and early twentieth century, *Beasts of the Modern Imagination: Darwin, Nietzsche, Kafka, Ernst, and Lawrence*; and a book on warfare from World War I to the Persian Gulf War, *Writing War in the Twentieth Century*.

Mark Osteen, professor of English and director of film studies at Loyola College, is the author of *The Economy of* Ulysses: *Making Both Ends Meet* and *American Magic and Dread: Don DeLillo's Dialogue with Culture*. He is the editor of the Viking Critical Library edition of DeLillo's *White Noise* and the coeditor of *The New Economic Criticism*.

Brian Richardson, associate professor of English at the University of Maryland, is the author of *Unlikely Stories: Causality and the Nature of Modern Narrative* and the editor of *Narrative Dynamics: Essays on Plot, Time, Closure, and Frames*. He is presently at work on a book on modernism and the reader.

Daniel Schwarz, professor of English and Stephen H. Weiss Presidential Fellow at Cornell University, is the author of three books on Conrad, including the recent *Rereading Conrad*, and the editor of the Bedford Case Studies in Contemporary Criticism edition of Conrad's "The Secret Sharer." He is also the author of nine books on subjects ranging from Holocaust narratives and the relation between modern literature and modern art to studies of James Joyce, Wallace Stevens, and Benjamin Disraeli's fiction.

Brian W. Shaffer, associate professor of English and associate dean of academic affairs at Rhodes College, is the author of *The Blinding Torch: Modern British Fiction and the Discourse of Civilization* and *Understanding Kazuo Ishiguro*. His essays on Conrad have appeared in *PMLA, ELH, Conradiana*, and *A Joseph Conrad Companion*.

Barry Stampfl is associate professor of English and comparative literature at San Diego State University, Imperial Valley. His essays have appeared in *Criticism, Modern Fiction Studies*, and *Henry James Review*.

Ray Stevens, professor emeritus of English at McDaniel College and president of the Mencken Society, is editing *Last Essays* for the Cambridge University Press edition of Conrad's works and has published essays on Conrad in *Journal of Modern Literature, English Literature in Transition, Conradiana*, and other journals.

Philip M. Weinstein, Alexander Griswold Cummins Professor of English at Swarthmore College and president of the William Faulkner Society, is the author of four books, most recently *What Else but Love? The Ordeal of Race in Faulkner and Morrison*. He is completing a book on modernism entitled "Unknowing: The Work of Modernist Fiction."

Andrea White, associate professor of English at California State University, Dominguez Hills, has written *Joseph Conrad and the Adventure Tradition: Constructing and Deconstructing the Imperial Subject* as well as many essays and review articles on Conrad, among these "Conrad and Imperialism" for the *Cambridge Companion to Joseph Conrad.*

Jeffrey J. Williams teaches at the University of Missouri, Columbia. He is the author of *Theory and the Novel: Narrative Reflexivity in the British Tradition*, the editor of *PC Wars: Politics and Theory in the Academy* and *The Institution of Literature*, and an editor of the *Norton Anthology of Theory and Criticism.*

SURVEY PARTICIPANTS

Paul Armstrong, *State University of New York, Stony Brook*
Patrick Brantlinger, *Indiana University, Bloomington*
Monika Brown, *University of North Carolina, Pembroke*
Sinkwan Cheng, *University of California, Irvine*
Jonathan Druker, *Wichita State University*
Mark A. Eaton, *Azusa Pacific University*
Avrom Fleishman, *Johns Hopkins University*
Chris Foss, *Texas Christian University*
William M. Hagen, *Oklahoma Baptist University*
Bruce Harkness, *Kent State University, Kent*
Douglas Ivison, *University of Montreal*
Carola M. Kaplan, *California State Polytechnic University*
R. B. Kershner, *University of Florida*
Susan Lanoff, *Harvard University*
Mark D. Larabee, *United States Naval Academy*
David Laubach, *Kutztown University*
Clifford Manlove, *Penn State University, McKeesport*
Irene Martyniuk, *Fitchburg State College*
John A. McClure, *Rutgers University, New Brunswick*
Joseph F. Militello, *Mississipi Valley State University*
Andrew Mozina, *Washington University*
Peter Nazareth, *University of Iowa*
Margot Norris, *University of California, Irvine*
Mark Osteen, *Loyola College in Maryland*
John Peters, *University of Wisconsin, Superior*
Mavis Reimer, *University of Winnipeg*
Brian Richardson, *University of Maryland, College Park*
Edward Rielly, *Saint Joseph's College of Maine*
Daniel Schwarz, *Cornell University*
Barry Stampfl, *San Diego State University*
Ray Stevens, *McDaniel College*
David Tutein, *Northeastern University*
Andrea White, *California State University, Dominguez Hills*
Jeffrey J. Williams, *University of Missouri, Columbia*

WORKS CITED

Abrams, M. H., ed. *The Norton Anthology of English Literature*. 6th ed. Vol. 2. New York: Norton, 1993.

Achebe, Chinua. *Hopes and Impediments*. London: Heinemann, 1988.

———. "An Image of Africa: Racism in Conrad's *Heart of Darkness*." Conrad, *Heart* [Kimbrough] 251–62.

———. *Things Fall Apart*. New York: Anchor, 1994.

Adelman, Gary. *"Heart of Darkness": Search for the Unconscious*. Boston: Twayne, 1987.

Adorno, Theodor. *Aesthetic Theory*. 1970. Trans. C. Lenhardt. New York: Routledge, 1984.

Ahmad, Aijaz. *In Theory: Classes, Nations, Literatures*. London: Verso, 1992.

Alighieri, Dante. *The Divine Comedy*. Trans. H. R. Huse. New York: Harcourt, 1954.

Allen, Jerry. *The Sea Years of Joseph Conrad*. London: Methuen, 1967.

Ambrosini, Richard. *Conrad's Fiction as Critical Discourse*. Cambridge: Cambridge UP, 1991.

Ancilla: Western Civilization: History and Literature. 21st ed. Vol. 2. Shawnee: Oklahoma Baptist U, 2001.

Arac, Jonathan. Huckleberry Finn *as Idol and Target: The Functions of Criticism in Our Time*. Madison: U of Wisconsin P, 1997.

Arendt, Hannah. *The Origins of Totalitarianism*. San Diego: Harcourt, 1973.

Armstrong, Paul. *The Challenge of Bewilderment*. Ithaca: Cornell UP, 1987.

———. "*Heart of Darkness* and the Epistemology of Cultural Differences." Fincham and Hooper 21–41.

Ascherson, Neal. *The King Incorporated*. London: Allen, 1963.

Ash, Beth Sharon. *Writing In Between: Modernity and the Psychosocial Dilemma in the Novels of Joseph Conrad*. New York: St. Martin's, 1999.

Bahr, Fax, with George Hickenlooper and Eleanor Coppola, dirs. *Hearts of Darkness: A Filmmaker's Apocalypse*. ZM/Zoetrope, 1991.

Baines, Jocelyn. *Joseph Conrad: A Critical Biography*. New York: McGraw, 1960.

Bakhtin, Mikhail. *The Dialogic Imagination*. Austin: U of Texas P, 1981.

Ballantyne, Robert Michael. *Black Ivory: A Tale of Adventure among the Slavers of East Africa*. 1873. Chicago: Afro-Am, 1969.

———. *The Coral Island*. London: Nesbit, 1913.

———. *Ungava: A Tale of Esquimau Land*. 1857. London: Nelson, 1895.

Barnett, Louise K. " 'The Whole Circle of the Horizon': The Circumscribed Universe of 'The Secret Sharer.' " *Studies in the Humanities* 8.2 (1981): 5–9.

Barth, John. *Chimera*. Greenwich: Fawcett, 1972.

Batchelor, John. *The Life of Joseph Conrad*. Oxford: Blackwell, 1994.

Benson, Carl. "Conrad's Two Stories of Initiation." *PMLA* 69 (1954): 46–56.

Berman, Jan, ed. *Imperial Monkey Business: Racial Supremacy in Social Darwinist Theory and Colonial Practice.* Amsterdam: Vrije UP, 1990.

Berthoud, Jacques. *Joseph Conrad: The Major Phase.* Cambridge: Cambridge UP, 1978.

Billy, Theodore. *A Wilderness of Words: Closure and Disclosure in Conrad's Short Fiction.* Lubbock: Texas Tech UP, 1997.

Blackburn, William, ed. *Letters to William Blackwood and David S. Meldrum.* Durham: Duke UP, 1958.

"Black Ivory." Def. 3. *The Shorter Oxford English Dictionary.* Rev. 3rd ed. 1968.

Blake, Susan L. "Racism and the Classics: Teaching *Heart of Darkness.*" *College Language Association Journal* 25 (1982): 396–404.

Bloom, Allan. *The Closing of the American Mind.* New York: Simon, 1987.

Bloom, Harold, ed. *Joseph Conrad's "Heart of Darkness."* New York: Chelsea, 1987.

Bonney, William. *Thorns and Arabesques.* Baltimore: Johns Hopkins UP, 1980.

Bradbrook, M. C. *Joseph Conrad. England's Polish Genius.* Cambridge: Cambridge UP, 1941.

Brady, Frank. *Citizen Welles.* New York: Doubleday-Anchor, 1990.

Brantlinger, Patrick. *Crusoe's Footprints: Cultural Studies in Britain and America.* New York: Routledge, 1990.

———. "*Heart of Darkness*: Anti-Imperialism, Racism, or Impressionism?" Conrad, *Heart* [Murfin] 277–98.

———. *Rule of Darkness: British Literature and Imperialism, 1830–1914.* Ithaca: Cornell UP, 1988.

Bride, James H., dir. and prod. *Joseph Conrad: "Heart of Darkness.* Bride Media Intl., 1998.

Brooks, Peter. *Reading for the Plot.* New York: Knopf, 1984.

Brown, Michael B. *The Economics of Imperialism.* Harmondsworth: Penguin, 1974.

Burden, Robert. *"Heart of Darkness": An Introduction to the Variety of Criticism.* London: Macmillan, 1991.

Burgess, C. F. *The Fellowship of the Craft: Conrad on Ships and Seamen and the Sea.* Port Washington: Kennikat, 1976.

Butler, Judith. *Bodies That Matter: On the Discursive Limits of "Sex."* New York: Routledge, 1993.

———. *Gender Trouble: Feminism and the Subversion of Identity.* New York: Routledge, 1990.

Cahir, Linda Costanzo. "Narratological Parallels in Joseph Conrad's *Heart of Darkness* and Francis Ford Coppola's *Apocalypse Now.*" *Literature/Film Quarterly* 20 (1992): 181–87.

Carey-Webb, Allen. "*Heart of Darkness, Tarzan,* and the 'Third World': Canons and Encounters in World Literature, English 109." *College Literature* 9 (1982): 111–31.

Carringer, Robert L. *The Making of Citizen Kane.* 1985. Rev. ed. Berkeley: U of California P, 1996.

Caruth, Cathy, ed. *Trauma: Explorations in Memory*. Baltimore: Johns Hopkins UP, 1995.

Caserio, Robert. *Plot, Story, and the Novel*. Princeton: Princeton UP, 1979.

Chatman, Seymour. "$2^1/_2$ Film Versions of *Heart of Darkness*." Moore 207–23.

Chopin, Kate. *The Awakening*. New York: Bantam, 1992.

"Christmas Books for Boys." *Illustrated London News* 14 Dec. 1901: 929.

Clifford, James. "On Ethnographic Self-Fashioning: Conrad and Malinowski." *Reconstructing Individualism*. Ed. Thomas C. Heller et al. Stanford: Stanford UP, 1986. 140–62.

——. *The Predicament of Culture: Twentieth-Century Ethnography, Literature, and Art*. Cambridge: Harvard UP, 1988.

Coetzee, J. M. *Foe*. New York: Penguin, 1988.

Collins, Harold R. "Kurtz, the Cannibals, and the Second-Rate Helmsman." *Western Humanities Review* 9 (1954): 299–310.

Conrad, Borys. *My Father: Joseph Conrad*. New York: Coward, 1970.

Conrad, Jessie. *Joseph Conrad and His Circle*. London: Jarrolds, 1935.

——. *Joseph Conrad As I Knew Him*. London: Heinemann, 1926.

Conrad, John. *Joseph Conrad, Times Remembered*. Cambridge: Cambridge UP, 1981.

Conrad, Joseph. *Almayer's Folly: A Story of an Eastern River*. Cambridge: Cambridge UP, 1994.

——. "Amy Foster." *Typhoon and Other Stories*. Harmondsworth: Penguin, 1992. 135–62.

——. "Author's Note." *'Twixt Land and Sea*. London: Penguin, 1978. 3–5.

——. *The Collected Letters of Joseph Conrad*. Ed. Frederick R. Karl and Laurence Davies. 5 vols. Cambridge: Cambridge UP, 1983–96.

——. "The Congo Diary." Conrad, *Heart* [Kimbrough] 159–66.

——. "Congo Diary." Ms. Harvard U Houghton Lib.

——. "Geography and Some Explorers." Conrad, *Heart* [Kimbrough] 143–47.

——. "Geography and Some Explorers." Conrad, *Last Essays* 1–17.

——. "The Heart of Darkness." *Blackwood's Edinburgh Magazine* 100 (1899): 193–220; 101 (1899): 479–502; 102 (1899): 634–57.

——. *Heart of Darkness*. CD-ROM. Sandy: Quiet Vision, 1999.

——. *Heart of Darkness*. Ed. Robert Kimbrough. 3rd ed. New York: Norton, 1988.

——. *Heart of Darkness*. Ed. Ross C. Murfin. 2nd ed. Boston: Bedford–St. Martin's, 1996.

——. *"Heart of Darkness" with "The Congo Diary"*. Ed. Robert Hampson. New York: Penguin, 1995.

——. *Last Essays*. Ed. Richard Curle. Garden City: Doubleday, 1926.

——. *Letters of Joseph Conrad to Marguerite Poradowska, 1890–1920*. Ed. John A. Lee and Paul J. Sturm. New Haven: Yale UP, 1940.

——. *Lettres françaises*. Ed. G. Jean-Aubry. Paris: Gallimard, 1930.

——. *Lord Jim*. Ed. Thomas Moser. 2nd ed. New York: Norton, 1996.

——. *The Mirror of the Sea*. New York: Harper, 1906.

——. *Notes on Life and Letters*. Garden City: Doubleday, 1921.

——. "An Outpost of Progress." Conrad, *Tales* 86–117.

——. *A Personal Record*. New York: Doubleday, 1912.

——. *The Secret Agent*. Garden City: Doubleday, 1953.

——. *The Secret Sharer*. CD-ROM. Sandy: Quiet Vision, 1999.

——. "The Secret Sharer." *Harper's Magazine* 121 (1910): 349–59, 530–41.

——. *The Secret Sharer*. Ed. Daniel R. Schwarz. Boston: Bedford–St. Martin's, 1997.

——. *The Shadow-Line*. Garden City: Doubleday, 1917.

——. *Tales of Unrest*. Garden City: Doubleday, 1926.

——. "Up-river Book." Ms. Harvard U Houghton Lib.

——. *"Youth" and Two Other Stories*. Garden City: Doubleday, 1926.

Conroy, Mark. *Modernism and Authority*. Baltimore: Johns Hopkins UP, 1985.

Coppola, Francis Ford, dir. *Apocalypse Now*. Omni Zoetrope, 1979.

——, dir. *Tucker: The Man and His Dream*. Zoetrope, 1988.

Cox, C. B. *Joseph Conrad: The Modern Imagination*. Totowa: Rowman, 1974.

Cox, Jeffrey N., and Larry J. Reynolds. "Introduction: The Historicist Enterprise." *New Historical Literary Study: Essays on Reproducing Texts, Representing History*. Ed. Cox and Reynolds. Princeton: Princeton UP, 1993. 3–38.

Crane, Stephen. *Maggie, a Girl of the Streets*. New York: Dover, 1990.

Crankshaw, Edward. *Joseph Conrad*. London: Lane, 1936.

Curle, Richard, ed. *Conrad to a Friend: 150 Selected Letters from Joseph Conrad to Richard Curle*. London: Low, 1928.

——. *The Last Twelve Years of Joseph Conrad*. Garden City: Doubleday, 1928.

Daiches, David. *A Critical History of English Literature*. London: Arrow-Random, 1994.

Daleski, H. M. *Joseph Conrad: The Way of Dispossession*. New York: Holmes, 1977.

Darras, Jacques. *Joseph Conrad and the West: Signs of Empire*. Totowa: Barnes, 1982.

Davis, Rebecca Harding. *Life in the Iron Mills*. Ancilla 68–93.

Dawson, Anthony B. "In the Pink: Self and Empire in 'The Secret Sharer.'" *Conradiana* 22 (1990): 185–96.

Dazey, Mary Ann. "Shared Secret or Secret Sharing in Joseph Conrad's 'The Secret Sharer.'" *Conradiana* 18.3 (1986): 201–03.

Dean, Leonard F., ed. *Joseph Conrad's "Heart of Darkness": Backgrounds and Criticisms*. Englewood Cliffs: Prentice, 1960.

DeBona, Guerric. "Into Africa: Orson Welles and *Heart of Darkness*." *Cinema Journal* 33.3 (1994): 16–34.

DeKoven, Marianne. *Rich and Strange: Gender, History, Modernism*. Princeton: Princeton UP, 1991.

Denby, David. *Great Books*. New York: Simon, 1996.

——. "Jungle Fever." *New Yorker* 6 Nov. 1995: 118–29.

Diamond, Jared. *Guns, Germs, and Steel*. New York: Norton, 1997.

DiYanni, Robert. *Literature*. New York: Random, 1986.

Dostoevsky, Fyodor. Notes from Underground *and* The Grand Inquisitor. Trans. Ralph E. Matlaw. New York: Dutton, 1960.

Dryden, Linda. *Joseph Conrad and the Imperial Romance*. Basingstoke: Macmillan, 1999.

———. "*An Outcast of the Islands*: Echoes of Romance and Adventure." *The Conradian* 20.1–2 (1995): 138–68.

D'Souza, Dinesh. *Illiberal Education: The Politics of Race and Sex on Campus*. New York: Free, 1991.

Eagleton, Terry. *Criticism and Ideology*. Atlantic Highlands: Humanities, 1976.

———. *Literary Theory*. Minneapolis: U of Minnesota P, 1983.

Eby, Cecil Degrotte. *The Road to Armaggedon: The Martial Spirit in English Popular Literature, 1870–1914*. Durham: Duke UP, 1987.

Ehrenreich, Barbara, and John Ehrenreich. "The Professional-Managerial Class." *Between Labor and Capital*. Ed. Pat Walker. Boston: South End, 1979. 5–45.

Ehrsam, Theodore G. *A Bibliography of Joseph Conrad*. Metuchen: Scarecrow, 1969.

Eliot, T. S. *The Complete Poems and Plays: 1909–1950*. New York: Harcourt, 1952.

Elsaesser, Thomas, and Michael Wedel. "The Hollow Heart of Hollywood: *Apocalypse Now* and the New Sound Space." Moore 151–74.

Emerson, Barbara. *Leopold II of the Belgians*. New York: St. Martin's, 1979.

Emerson, Ralph Waldo. *Selected Writings*. New York: New Amer. Lib., 1965.

Encyclopaedia Britannica. 9th ed. Chicago: Warner, 1896.

Erdinast-Vulcan, Daphna. *Joseph Conrad and the Modern Temper*. Oxford: Clarendon, 1991.

———. *The Strange Short Fiction of Joseph Conrad*. New York: Oxford UP, 1999.

Erdrich, Louise. *Love Medicine*. New York: Harper, 1987.

Evans, Robert O. "Conrad's Underworld." *Modern Fiction Studies* 2 (1956): 56–62.

Facknitz, Mark A. R. "Cryptic Allusions and the Moral of the Story: The Case of Joseph Conrad's 'The Secret Sharer.'" *Journal of Narrative Technique* 17.1 (1987): 115–30.

Faulkner, Peter. *Modernism*. London: Methuen, 1977.

Faulkner, William. *Absalom, Absalom!* New York: Vintage Intl., 1990.

———. *Light in August*. New York: Vintage Intl., 1990.

———. *The Sound and the Fury*. New York: Vintage, 1954.

"Fiction." Defs. 3 and 4a. *The American Heritage Dictionary*. 2nd college ed. 1982.

Fieldhouse, D. K. *The Colonial Empires*. New York: Dell, 1965.

———. *Economics and Empire*. London: Weidenfeld, 1973.

Fincham, Gail, and Myrtle Hooper, eds. *Under Postcolonial Eyes: Joseph Conrad after Empire*. Rondebosch, So. Afr.: UCT, 1996.

Firchow, Peter Edgerly. *Envisioning Africa: Racism and Imperialism in Conrad's "Heart of Darkness."* Lexington: UP of Kentucky, 2000.

Fleishman, Avrom. *Conrad's Politics*. Baltimore: Johns Hopkins UP, 1967.

Fleming, Bruce. "Brothers under the Skin: Achebe on *Heart of Darkness.*" *College Literature* 19–20 (1992–93): 90–100.

Fogel, Aaron. *Coercion to Speak: Conrad's Poetics of Dialogue.* Cambridge: Harvard UP, 1985.

Ford, Ford Madox. *Joseph Conrad: A Personal Remembrance.* London: Duckworth, 1924.

Forster, E. M. *Aspects of the Novel.* New York: Harcourt, 1956.

———. *A Passage to India.* New York: Harcourt, 1965.

Foster, John B., Jr. *Heirs to Dionysus.* Princeton: Princeton UP, 1981.

Fothergill, Anthony. *Heart of Darkness.* Milton Keynes, Eng.: Open UP, 1989.

Fowlie, Wallace. *Rimbaud.* Chicago: U of Chicago P, 1966.

Foye, Paul F., Bruce Harkness, and Nathan L. Marvin. "The Sailing Maneuver in 'The Secret Sharer.'" *Journal of Modern Literature* 2 (1971): 119–23.

Franklin, John Hope. *George Washington Williams: A Biography.* Chicago: U of Chicago P, 1985.

———. "Williams Ignored." Conrad, *Heart* [Kimbrough] 120–25.

Freud, Sigmund. *Civilization and Its Discontents.* New York: Norton, 1989.

———. "From the History of an Infantile Neurosis." 1918. Freud, *Standard Edition* 17: 1–122.

———. "Leonardo Da Vinci and a Memory of His Childhood." 1910. Freud, *Standard Edition* 11: 63–137.

———. *The Standard Edition of the Complete Psychological Works.* Ed. and trans. James Strachey. 24 vols. London: Hogarth, 1957–74.

Gann, L. H., and Peter Duignan. *The Rulers of Belgian Africa, 1884–1914.* Princeton: Princeton UP, 1979.

García Márquez, Gabriel. *One Hundred Years of Solitude.* New York: Harper-Perennial, 1998.

Gardiner, Robert, ed. *Sail's Last Century: The Merchant Sailing Ship, 1830–1930.* Annapolis: Naval Inst., 1993.

Garnett, Edward. "Art Drawn from Memory." Conrad, *Heart* [Kimbrough] 195–96.

———, ed. *Letters from Joseph Conrad, 1895–1924.* Indianapolis: Bobbs, 1928.

Gee, John A., and Paul J. Sturm, eds. *Letters of Joseph Conrad to Marguerite Poradowska, 1890–1920.* New Haven: Yale UP, 1940.

Gekoski, R. A. *Conrad: The Moral World of the Novelist.* New York: Barnes, 1978.

Gilbert, Sandra, and Susan Gubar. *No Man's Land.* New Haven: Yale UP, 1987.

Gillon, Adam. "Adapting Conrad to Film: A Scholar's Odyssey to Screenwriting." Brebach 145–82.

———. *Conrad and Shakespeare.* New York: Astra, 1976.

———. *The Eternal Solitary.* New York: Bookman Assocs., 1960.

———. "Excerpts from *Dark Country.*" *Joseph Conrad: Comparative Essays.* Ed. Raymond Brebach. Lubbock: Texas Tech UP, 1994. 231–68.

Glenn, Ian. "Conrad's *Heart of Darkness.*" *Literature and History* 13 (1987): 238–56.

Goethe, Johann Wolfgang von. *Faust.* Part 1. Trans. Randall Jarrell. New York: Farrar, 1976.

GoGwilt, Christopher. *The Invention of the West*. Stanford: Stanford UP, 1995.

Gone with the Wind. Selznick-MGM, 1939.

Goonetilleke, D. C. R. A. *Developing Countries in British Fiction*. London: Macmillan, 1977.

———. Introduction. *Heart of Darkness*. By Joseph Conrad. 2nd ed. Ontario: Broadview Lit. Texts. 1999. 9–47.

———. *Joseph Conrad: Beyond Culture and Background*. New York: St. Martin's, 1991.

Gordan, John D. *Joseph Conrad: The Making of a Novelist*. Cambridge: Harvard UP, 1940.

Graff, Gerald. "Teach the Conflicts." *South Atlantic Quarterly* 89 (1990): 51–67.

Graham, Kenneth. *Indirections of the Novel*. New York: Cambridge UP, 1988.

Graver, Lawrence. *Conrad's Short Fiction*. Berkeley: U of California P, 1969.

Great Britain. Admiralty. *China Sea: Gulf of Siam, Sheet II, Koh Ta Kut to Cape Liant (Chart No. 2720)*. London: Hydrographic Office, 1860. Large corrections up to 1880, small corrections up to 1908.

Green, Martin. *Dreams of Adventure, Deeds of Empire*. New York: Basic, 1979.

Greenblatt, Stephen. *Learning to Curse: Essays in Early Modern Culture*. New York: Routledge, 1990.

———. *Shakespearean Negotiations*. Berkeley: U of California P, 1988.

Griffith, John W. *Joseph Conrad and the Anthropological Dilemma*. Oxford: Clarendon, 1995.

Gross, Seymour L. "A Further Note on the Function of the Frame in 'Heart of Darkness.'" *Modern Fiction Studies* 3 (1957): 167–70.

Guerard, Albert J. *Conrad the Novelist*. Cambridge: Harvard UP, 1958.

———. Introduction. *"Heart of Darkness" and "The Secret Sharer."* By Joseph Conrad. New York: New Amer. Lib., 1978. 7–15.

Guetti, James. *The Limits of Metaphor*. Ithaca: Cornell UP, 1967.

Gurko, Leo. *Joseph Conrad: Giant in Exile*. New York: Macmillan, 1962.

Hagen, William M. *"Heart of Darkness* and the Process of *Apocalypse Now."* Conrad, *Heart* [Kimbrough] 293–301.

Haggard, H. Rider. *Allan Quartermain*. Mattituck: Ameron, 1983.

———. *King Solomon's Mines*. Barre: Imprint Soc., 1970.

———. *She: A History of Adventure*. London: Collins, 1969.

Hammond, Dorothy, and Alta Jablow. *The Myth of Africa*. New York: Lib. of Social Science, 1977.

Hamner, Robert. "Colony, Nationhood and Beyond: Third World Writers and Critics Contend with Joseph Conrad." *World Literature Written in English* 23 (1984): 108–66.

———, ed. *Joseph Conrad: Third World Perspectives*. Washington: Three Continents, 1990.

Hampson, Robert. *Cross-Cultural Encounters in Joseph Conrad's Fiction*. New York: Palgrave, 2000.

———. *Joseph Conrad: Betrayal and Identity*. New York: St. Martin's, 1992.

Harkness, Bruce, ed. *Conrad's "Heart of Darkness" and the Critics.* Belmont: Wadsworth, 1960.

——, ed. *"The Secret Sharer" and the Critics.* Belmont: Wadsworth, 1962.

Harpham, Geoffrey Galt. *One of Us: The Mastery of Joseph Conrad.* Chicago: U of Chicago P, 1996.

Hartman, Geoffrey. "On Traumatic Knowledge and Literary Studies." *New Literary History* 26 (1995): 537–63.

Hawkins, Hunt. "Conrad's Critique of Imperialism in *Heart of Darkness*." *PMLA* 94 (1979): 286–99.

——. "Conrad's *Heart of Darkness*: Politics and History." *Conradiana* 24 (1992): 207–17.

——. "The Issue of Racism in *Heart of Darkness*." *Conradiana* 14 (1982): 163–71.

——. "Joseph Conrad and Mark Twain on the Congo Free State." Diss. Stanford U, 1976.

——. "Joseph Conrad, Roger Casement, and the Congo Reform Movement." *Journal of Modern Literature* 9.1 (1981–82): 65–80.

Hawthorn, Jeremy. *Joseph Conrad: Language and Fictional Self-Consciousness.* Lincoln: U of Nebraska P, 1979.

Hay, Eloise Knapp. *The Political Novels of Joseph Conrad.* Chicago: U of Chicago P, 1963.

Headrick, Daniel R. *The Tools of Empire.* New York: Oxford UP, 1981.

"Heart of Darkness": Great Books. By Dale Minor. Narr. Donald Sutherland. Learning Channel, 1999.

Hegel, G. W. F. *The Philosophy of History.* Trans. J. Sibree. New York: Prometheus, 1990.

Henricksen, Bruce. *Nomadic Voices: Conrad and the Subject of Narrative.* Chicago: U of Illinois P, 1992.

Henty, G. A. *In Times of Peril: A Tale of India.* London: Griffeth, 1881.

——. *Under Drake's Flag: A Tale of the Spanish Main.* New York: Burt, 1883.

——. *With Clive in India.* London: Blackie, n.d.

——. *With Moore at Corunna.* London: Latimer, 1959.

Hertz, Neil. "Freud and the Sandman." *Textual Strategies: Perspectives in Post-structuralist Criticism.* Ed. with an introd. by Josué V. Harari. Ithaca: Cornell UP, 1979. 296–321.

Hervouet, Yves. *The French Face of Joseph Conrad.* Cambridge: Cambridge UP, 1991.

Hewitt, Douglass. *Conrad: A Reassessment.* Philadelphia: Dufour, 1952.

Hills, Rust. *Writing in General and the Short Story in Particular.* Boston: Houghton, 1987.

Hobsbawm, Eric. *The Age of Empire.* New York: Pantheon, 1987.

Hochschild, Adam. *King Leopold's Ghost: A Story of Greed, Terror, and Heroism in Colonial Africa.* Boston: Houghton, 1998.

Hodges, Robert. "Deep Fellowship: Homosexuality and Male Bonding in the Life and Fiction of Joseph Conrad." *Journal of Homosexuality* 4 (1979): 379–87.

Homer. *The Odyssey.* Trans. Robert Fitzgerald. New York: Farrar, 1963.

Howarth, Stephen. *Historic Sail.* London: Greenhill, 2000.

Howe, Susanne. *Novels of Empire.* New York: Columbia UP, 1949.

Hunter, Alan. *Joseph Conrad and the Ethics of Darwinism.* London: Croom Helm, 1983.

Hurwitz, Howard L. "PC Crowd Bans *Huckleberry Finn* Because Mark Twain Used 'N' Word." *Human Events* 51.35 (1995): 19.

Irigaray, Luce. *Speculum of the Other Woman.* Trans. Gillian C. Gill. Ithaca: Cornell UP, 1985.

Iser, Wolfgang. *The Act of Reading: A Theory of Aesthetic Response.* Baltimore: Johns Hopkins UP, 1978.

Jackson, Tony. *The Subject of Modernism.* Ann Arbor: U of Michigan P, 1994.

James, Henry. "The New Novel." *Selected Literary Criticism: Henry James.* Ed. Morris Shapira. New York: McGraw, 1965. 311–42.

———. *The Turn of the Screw. The Turn of the Screw and Other Short Novels.* New York: New Amer. Lib., 1962. 291–403.

Jameson, Fredric. *The Political Unconscious: Narrative as a Socially Symbolic Act.* Ithaca: Cornell UP, 1981.

JanMohamed, Abdul R. "The Economy of Manichean Allegory: The Function of Racial Difference in Colonialist Literature." *"Race," Writing, and Difference.* Ed. Henry Louis Gates, Jr. Chicago: U of Chicago P, 1986. 78–106.

Janoff-Bulman, Ronnie. *Shattered Assumptions: Towards a New Psychology of Trauma.* New York: Free, 1992.

Jean-Aubry, G. *Joseph Conrad in the Congo.* Boston: Little, 1926.

———. *Joseph Conrad: Life and Letters.* Garden City: Doubleday, 1927.

———. *The Sea Dreamer: A Definitive Biography of Joseph Conrad.* London: Allen, 1957.

Johnson, Barbara, and Marjorie Garber. "Secret Sharing: Reading Conrad Psychoanalytically." *College English* 49 (1987): 628–40.

Johnson, Bruce. *Conrad's Models of Mind.* Minneapolis: U of Minnesota P, 1971.

Johnson, Terence. "The Professions in Class Structure." Scase 93–110.

Jones, John F., ed. *A Study Guide to Joseph Conrad's "Heart of Darkness."* Audiocassette. Time Warner Audio Books, 1995.

Jones, Susan. *Conrad and Women.* Oxford: Clarendon, 1999.

Joyce, James. *Ulysses.* New York: Vintage, 1961.

Jung, C. G. *The Essential Jung.* Ed. Anthony Storr. Princeton: Princeton UP, 1983.

Kaplan, Carola M. "Colonizers, Cannibals, and the Horror of Good Intentions in Joseph Conrad's *Heart of Darkness.*" *Studies in Short Fiction* 34 (1997): 323–33.

Karl, Frederick R. "Introduction to the *Danse Macabre: Conrad's 'Heart of Darkness.'*" Conrad, *Heart* [Murfin] 123–38.

———. *Joseph Conrad: The Three Lives.* New York: Farrar, 1979.

———. *A Reader's Guide to Joseph Conrad.* New York: Noonday, 1960.

Keating, George T. *A Conrad Memorial Library.* Garden City: Doubleday, 1929.

Kiernan, V. G. *From Conquest to Collapse: European Empires, 1815–1960.* New York: Pantheon, 1982.

———. *The Lords of Human Kind.* Harmondsworth: Penguin, 1972.

Kingsley, Charles. *Westward Ho!* New York: Macmillan, 1886.

Kipling, Rudyard. *Kim.* Harmondsworth: Penguin, 1987.

Kirschener, Paul. *Conrad: The Psychologist as Artist.* Edinburgh: Oliver, 1968.

Klein, Julie Thompson. *Interdisciplinarity: History, Theory, and Practice.* Detroit: Wayne State UP, 1991.

Knowles, Owen. *An Annotated Critical Bibliography of Joseph Conrad.* London: Harvester, 1992.

———. *A Conrad Chronology.* London: Macmillan, 1989.

———. "Conrad's Life." Stape 1–24.

Knowles, Owen, and Gene Moore, eds. *The Oxford Reader's Companion to Conrad.* New York: Oxford UP, 2000.

Kuesgen, Reinhardt. "Conrad and Achebe: Aspects of the Novel." *World Literature Written in English* 24 (1984): 27–33.

Lacan, Jacques. *Ecrits: A Selection.* 1966. Trans. Alan Sheridan. New York: Norton, 1977.

———. *Feminine Sexuality: Jacques Lacan and the Ecole Freudienne.* Ed. Juliet Mitchell and Jacqueline Rose. Trans. Rose. New York: Norton, 1982.

Laing, R. D. *The Divided Self: An Existential Study in Sanity and Madness.* Baltimore: Penguin, 1965.

Langbaum, Robert. *The Modern Spirit.* London: Chatto, 1970.

Larson, Magali Sarfatti. *The Rise of Professionalism: A Sociological Analysis.* Berkeley: U of California P, 1977.

Laszlo, Veres. *The Story of Sail.* Annapolis: Naval Inst., 1999.

Lawton, Jonathan, dir. *Cannibal Women in the Avocado Jungle of Death.* Amer-Guacamole Films, 1988.

Lean, David, dir. *The Bridge on the River Kwai.* Columbia Pictures, 1957.

Leavis F. R. *The Great Tradition: George Eliot, Henry James, Joseph Conrad.* New York: New York UP, 1948.

Lee, Robert F. *Conrad's Colonialism.* The Hague: Mouton, 1969.

Leiter, Louis H. "Echo Structures: Conrad's 'The Secret Sharer.'" *Twentieth Century Literature* 6 (1960): 169–75. Rpt. in Harkness, "*Sharer*" 133–50.

Lester, John. *Conrad's Religion.* New York: St. Martin's, 1988.

Levenson, Michael. *A Genealogy of Modernism.* Cambridge: Cambridge UP, 1984.

———. "The Value of Facts in the *Heart of Darkness.*" Conrad, *Heart* [Kimbrough] 391–405.

Lewis, David Levering. *The Race to Fashoda.* New York: Weidenfeld, 1987.

Lindquist, Sven. *Exterminate All the Brutes.* New York: Norton, 1996.

Lohf, Kenneth A., and Eugene P. Sheehy. *Joseph Conrad at Mid-Century: Editions and Studies, 1895–1955.* Minneapolis: U of Minnesota P, 1957.

London, Bette. *The Appropriated Voice*. Ann Arbor: U of Michigan P, 1990.

———. "Reading Race and Gender in Conrad's Dark Continent." *Criticism* 31 (1989): 235–52.

Lothe, Jakob. *Conrad's Narrative Method*. Oxford: Clarendon, 1989.

Lubbock, Basil. *The Log of the Cutty Sark*. Glasgow: Brown, 1924.

Macdonald, Keith M. *The Sociology of the Professions*. London: Sage, 1995.

MacGregor, David R. *Fast Sailing Ships: Their Design and Construction, 1775–1875*. Newfoundland: Haessner, 1973.

———. *Merchant Sailing Ships, 1850–1875: Hey Day of Sail*. London: Conway Maritime, 1984.

MacKenzie, John M. *Propaganda and Empire: The Manipulations of British Public Opinion, 1880–1960*. Manchester: Manchester UP, 1984.

Mahood, Molly. *The Colonial Encounter*. London: Collings, 1977.

Marchal, Jules. *L'état libre du Congo: Paradis perdu. L'histoire du Congo, 1876–1900*. 2 vols. Burgloon, Belg.: Bellings, 1996.

———. *E. D. Morel contre Leopold II: L'histoire du Congo, 1900–1910*. 2 vols. Paris: L'Harmattan, 1996.

Mbiti, John. *African Religions and Philosophy*. London: Heinemann, 1969.

McClure, John. *Kipling and Conrad: The Colonial Fiction*. Cambridge: Harvard UP, 1981.

———. *Late Imperial Romance*. London: Verso, 1994.

McCutchan, Philip. *Tall Ships: The Golden Age of Sail*. New York: Crown, 1976.

McLynn, Frank. *Hearts of Darkness: The European Exploration of Africa*. London: Hutchinson, 1992.

Meisel, Perry. *The Myth of the Modern*. New Haven: Yale UP, 1987.

Melville, Herman. *"Bartleby" and Benito Cereno*. New York: Dover, 1990.

———. *Moby-Dick; or, The Whale*. Ed. Harrison Hayford and Hershel Parker. Norton Critical Ed. New York: Norton, 1967.

Merriam-Webster's Collegiate Dictionary. 10th ed. 1998.

Meyer, Bernard C. *Joseph Conrad: A Psychoanalytic Biography*. Princeton: Princeton UP, 1967.

Miller, Christopher. *Blank Darkness: Africanist Discourse in French*. Chicago: U of Chicago P, 1985.

Miller, J. Hillis. *The Disappearance of God: Five Nineteenth-Century Writers*. New York: Schocken, 1965.

———. "*Heart of Darkness* Revisited." Conrad, *Heart* [Murfin] 206–20.

———. *Poets of Reality*. Cambridge: Belknap–Harvard UP, 1966.

———. "Sharing Secrets." Conrad, *Secret Sharer* 232–52.

Milton, John. *Paradise Lost*. 1674 ed. Electronic Lit. Foundation. 1999. 6 Aug. 2002 <http://elf.chaoscafe.com/milton/>

Mongia, Padmini. "The Rescue: Conrad, Achebe, and the Critics." *Conradiana* 33.2 (2001): 153–63. Rpt. in *Conrad in Africa*. Ed. Attie de Lange and Gail Fincham, with Wieslaw Krajka. Boulder: Social Science Monographs; Lublin: Maria Curie-Sklodowska U; New York: Columbia UP, forthcoming.

"La monnaie." *Le Congo illustré* 1 (1892): 34–35.

Montaigne, Michel de. "On Cannibals." *Essays*. Harmondsworth: Penguin, 1958. 105–19.

Montgomery, Robert, dir. *Lady in the Lake*. MGM, 1947.

Montrose, Louis A. "Professing the Renaissance: The Poetics and Politics of Culture." Veeser, *Historicism* 15–36.

Moore, Gene M., ed. *Conrad on Film*. Cambridge: Cambridge UP, 1997.

Morel, Edmund D. *Red Rubber*. Manchester, 1906.

Morf, Gustav. *The Polish Heritage of Joseph Conrad*. London: Low, 1930.

Morris, Jan. *The Spectacle of Empire*. London: Faber, 1982.

Morrison, Toni. *Beloved*. New York: NAL-Penguin, 1987.

——. *Playing in the Dark: Whiteness and the Literary Imagination*. New York: Random, 1993.

——. *Song of Solomon*. New York: NAL-Penguin, 1987.

Morzinski, Mary. *The Linguistic Influence of Polish on Joseph Conrad's Style*. New York: Columbia UP, 1994.

Moser, Thomas C. *Joseph Conrad: Achievement and Decline*. Cambridge: Harvard UP, 1957.

Moses, Michael. *The Novel and the Globalization of Culture*. New York: Oxford UP, 1995.

Mudie, Rosemary. *The History of the Sailing Ship*. New York: Arco, 1975.

Murfin, Ross, ed. *Conrad Revisited: Essays for the Eighties*. Tuscaloosa: U of Alabama P, 1985.

Murphy, Michael. "'The Secret Sharer': Conrad's Turn of the Winch." *Conradiana* 18.3 (1996): 193–200.

Nadelhaft, Ruth. *Joseph Conrad*. Atlantic Highlands: Humanities Intl., 1991.

Najder, Zdzislaw, ed. *"Congo Diary" and Other Uncollected Pieces*. By Joseph Conrad. Garden City: Doubleday, 1978.

——. *Conrad in Perspective*. Cambridge: Cambridge UP, 1997.

——, ed. *Conrad's Polish Background: Letters to and from Polish Friends*. London: Oxford UP, 1964.

——. *Joseph Conrad: A Chronicle*. New Brunswick: Rutgers UP, 1983.

Nelson, Samuel H. *Colonialism in the Congo Basin, 1880–1940*. Athens: Ohio U Center for Intl. Studies, 1994.

Nettles, Elsa. *James and Conrad*. Athens: U of Georgia P, 1977.

Nietzsche, Friedrich. *The Portable Nietzsche*. Trans. Walter Kaufman. New York: Viking, 1954.

North, Michael. *The Dialect of Modernism*. New York: Oxford UP, 1994.

O'Hanlon, Redmond. *Joseph Conrad and Charles Darwin*. Atlantic Highlands: Humanities, 1984.

O'Hara, J. D. "Unlearned Lessons in 'The Secret Sharer.'" *College English* 27 (1965): 444–50.

Ondaatje, Michael. *The English Patient*. New York: Vintage, 1996.

O'Neill, Eugene. *The Hairy Ape. Four Plays by Eugene O'Neill.* New York: Signet, 1998. 245–308.

Orr, Leonard, and Ted Billy, eds. *A Joseph Conrad Companion.* Westport: Greenwood, 1999.

Paccaud, Josiane. "Under the Other's Eyes: Conrad's 'The Secret Sharer.'" *The Conradian* 12.1 (1987): 59–73.

Packenham, Thomas. *The Scramble for Africa.* New York: Random, 1991.

Palmer, John A. *Joseph Conrad's Fiction.* Ithaca: Cornell UP, 1968.

Panagupoulos, Nic. *The Fiction of Joseph Conrad: The Influence of Schopenhauer and Nietzsche.* New York: Lang, 1998.

Parry, Benita. *Conrad and Imperialism: Ideological Boundaries and Visionary Frontiers.* London: Macmillan, 1983.

Parry, Noel, and José Parry. "Social Closure and Collective Social Mobility." Scase 111–21.

Pecora, Vincent. *Self and Form in Modern Narrative.* Baltimore: Johns Hopkins UP, 1989.

Phelan, James. "Reading Secrets." Conrad, *Secret Sharer* 128–44.

Phillips, Gene D. *Conrad and Cinema: The Art of Adaptation.* New York: Lang, 1995.

Porter, Bernard. *Critics of Empire: British Radical Attitudes to Colonialism in Africa, 1895–1914.* New York: St. Martin's, 1968.

Powell, John. *Rhapsodie Negre for Piano and Orchestra.* Los Angeles Philharmonic. Cond. Calvin Simmons. New World Records, 1992.

Pratt, Mary Louise. *Toward a Speech-Act Theory of Literary Discourse.* Bloomington: Indiana UP, 1977.

Purdy, Dwight. *Conrad's Bible.* Norman: U of Oklahoma P, 1984.

Quick, Jonathan. *Modern Fiction and the Art of Subversion.* New York: Lang, 1999.

Rabinowitz, Peter. *Before Reading: Narrative Conventions and the Politics of Interpretation.* Ithaca: Cornell UP, 1987.

Raskin, Jonah. *The Mythology of Imperialism.* New York: Random, 1971.

Raval, Suresh. *The Art of Failure: Conrad's Fiction.* Boston: Allen, 1986.

Ray, Martin, ed. *Joseph Conrad: Interviews and Recollections.* Iowa City: U of Iowa P, 1990.

Remarque, Erich Maria. *All Quiet on the Western Front.* Trans. A. W. Wheen. New York: Fawcett, 1929.

Retinger, J. H. *Conrad and His Contemporaries.* London: Minerva, 1941.

Reviere, Susan L. *Memory of Childhood Trauma: A Clinician's Guide to the Literature.* New York: Guilford, 1996.

Rhys, Jean. *Wide Sargasso Sea.* New York: Norton, 1982.

Richardson, Brian. "Construing Conrad's 'The Secret Sharer': Suppressed Narratives, Subaltern Reception, and the Act of Interpretation." *Studies in the Novel* 33 (2001): 306–21.

Ridley, Hugh. *Images of Imperial Rule.* New York: St. Martin's, 1983.

Robbins, Bruce. *Secular Vocations: Intellectuals, Professionalism, Culture.* New York: Verso, 1993.

Roberts, Andrew M., ed. *Conrad and Gender.* Atlanta: Rodopi, 1993.

———. *Conrad and Masculinity.* New York: St. Martin's, 2000.

Roberts, Edgar A. *Literature.* Englewood Cliffs: Prentice, 1995.

Robinson, Ronald, and John Gallagher, *Africa and the Victorians: The Climax of Imperialism.* Garden City: Doubleday, 1961.

Roeg, Nicolas, dir. *Heart of Darkness.* Turner, 1994.

Rosenbaum, Jonathan. "The Voice and the Eye: A Commentary on the *Heart of Darkness* Script." *Film Comment* 8.4 (1972): 27–32.

Rosenfield, Claire. *Paradise of Snakes: An Archetypal Analysis of Conrad's Political Novels.* Chicago: U of Chicago P, 1967.

Roussel, Royal. *The Metaphysics of Darkness.* Baltimore: Johns Hopkins UP, 1971.

Ruppel, Richard. "*Heart of Darkness* and the Popular Exotic Story of the 1890's." *Conradiana* 21 (1989): 3–14.

Rushdie, Salman. "Outside the Whale." *Imaginary Homelands: Essays and Criticism, 1981–1991.* London: Granta, 1991. 87–101.

———. *The Satanic Verses.* New York: Viking, 1989.

Ryf, Robert. *Joseph Conrad.* New York: Columbia UP, 1970.

Said, Edward. *Culture and Imperialism.* New York: Vintage, 1994.

———. "Intellectuals in the Post-colonial World." *Salmagundi* 70–71 (1986): 44–64.

———. *Joseph Conrad and the Fiction of Autobiography.* Cambridge: Harvard UP, 1966.

———. *Orientalism.* New York: Vintage, 1979.

Salih, Tayeb. *Season of Migration to the North.* Washington: Three Continents, 1985.

Samarin, William J. *The Black Man's Burden.* Boulder: Westview, 1989.

Sandison, Alan. *The Wheel of Empire.* New York: St. Martin's, 1967.

Sarvan, C. P. "Racism and the *Heart of Darkness.*" Conrad, *Heart* [Kimbrough] 280–85.

Saveson, John. *Joseph Conrad: The Making of a Moralist.* Amsterdam: Rodopi, 1972.

Scase, Richard, ed. *Industrial Society: Class, Cleavage, and Control.* New York: St. Martin's, 1977.

Schopenhauer, Arthur. *The Essential Schopenhauer.* New York: Barnes, 1962.

Schwarz, Daniel. *Conrad:* Almayer's Folly *to* Under Western Eyes. Ithaca: Cornell UP, 1980.

———. *Conrad: The Later Fiction.* London: Macmillan, 1982.

———. "'The Secret Sharer' as an Act of Memory." Conrad, *Secret Sharer* 95–111.

Secor, Robert. *Joseph Conrad and American Writers.* Westport: Greenwood, 1985.

Sedgwick, Eve Kosofsky. *Between Men: English Literature and Male Homosocial Desire.* New York: Columbia UP, 1985.

———. *Epistemology of the Closet.* Berkeley: U of California P, 1990.

Semmel, Bernard. *Imperialism and Social Reform.* Cambridge: Harvard UP, 1960.

———. *The Liberal Ideal and the Demons of Empire: Theories of Imperialism from Adam Smith to Lenin.* Baltimore: Johns Hopkins UP, 1993.

Senn, Werner. *Conrad's Narrative Voice.* Bern: Francke, 1980.

Shaffer, Brian W. *The Blinding Torch: Modern British Fiction and the Discourse of Civilization*. Amherst: U of Massachusetts P, 1993.

——. "'Rebarbarizing Civilization': Conrad's African Fiction and Spencerian Sociology." *PMLA* 108 (1993): 45–58.

Shakespeare, William. Sonnet 130. *The Oxford Shakespeare*. Ed. W. J. Craig. Online ed. May 2000. 5 Feb. 2002 <http://www.bartleby.com/70/50130.html>.

Shelley, Mary. *Frankenstein; or, The Modern Prometheus*. Harmondsworth: Penguin, 1985.

Sherry, Norman. *Conrad and His World*. London: Thames, 1972.

——. *Conrad's Eastern World*. Cambridge: Cambridge UP, 1966.

——. *Conrad's Western World*. Cambridge: Cambridge UP, 1971.

——, ed. *Conrad: The Critical Heritage*. London: Routledge, 1973.

Shetty, Sandhya. "*Heart of Darkness*: Out of Africa Some New Thing Rarely Comes." *Journal of Modern Literature* 15 (1989): 461–74.

Showalter, Elaine. *Sexual Anarchy*. New York: Penguin, 1991.

Silko, Leslie Marmon. *Ceremony*. Harmondsworth: Penguin, 1986.

Singh, Frances B. "The Colonialistic Bias of *Heart of Darkness*." Conrad, *Heart* [Kimbrough] 268–80.

Slade, Ruth. *King Leopold's Congo*. London: Oxford UP, 1962.

Smith, Johanna M. "'Too Beautiful Altogether': Ideologies of Gender and Empire in *Heart of Darkness*." Conrad, *Heart* [Murfin] 169–84.

Smith, Walter E. *Joseph Conrad: A Bibliographical Catalogue of His Major First Editions*. N.p., 1978.

Spadoni, Robert. "The Seeing Ear: The Presence of Radio in Welles's *Heart of Darkness*." Moore 78–92.

Spender, Stephen. *The Struggle of the Modern*. Berkeley: U of California P, 1963.

Spittles, Brian. *Joseph Conrad: Text and Context*. Basingstoke, Eng.: Macmillan, 1992.

Stallman, Robert W. "Conrad and 'The Secret Sharer.'" *The Art of Joseph Conrad: A Critical Symposium*. East Lansing: Michigan State UP, 1960. 275–88. Rpt. in Harkness. "*Sharer*" 94–109.

Stanley, Henry M. *In Darkest Africa*. 2 vols. New York: Scribner's, 1890.

Stanley and Africa: Also the Travels, Adventures, and Discoveries of Captain John H. Speke, Captain Richard F. Burton, Captain James W. Grant, Sir Samuel and Lady Baker, and Other Distinguished Explorers. London: Scott, n.d.

Stape, J. H., ed. *The Cambridge Companion to Joseph Conrad*. Cambridge: Cambridge UP, 1996.

Stein, Gertrude. *The Autobiography of Alice B. Toklas*. 1906. *Selected Writings of Gertrude Stein*. Ed. Carl Van Vechten. New York: Random, 1934. 1–237.

Stewart, Garrett. "Lying as Dying in *Heart of Darkness*." Conrad, *Heart* [Kimbrough] 358–74.

Stewart, J. I. M. *Joseph Conrad*. New York: Dodd, 1968.

Symons, Arthur. "Every Novel Contains Autobiography." Conrad, *Heart* [Kimbrough] 234–35.

———. *Notes on Joseph Conrad; with Some Unpublished Letters*. London: Myers, 1925.

Tal, Kalí. *Worlds of Hurt: Reading the Literatures of Trauma*. Cambridge: Cambridge UP, 1996.

Teets, Bruce E. *Joseph Conrad: An Annotated Bibliography*. New York: Garland, 1990.

Teets, Bruce E., and Helmut E. Gerber. *Joseph Conrad: An Annotated Bibliography of Writings about Him*. Dekalb: Northern Illinois UP, 1971.

Thomas, Brook. "Preserving and Keeping Order by Killing Time in *Heart of Darkness*." Conrad, *Heart* [Murfin] 239–57.

Thorburn, David. *Conrad's Romanticism*. New Haven: Yale UP, 1974.

Thornton, A. J. P. *The Imperial Idea and Its Enemies*. London: Macmillan, 1985.

Tolstoy, Leo. *"The Death of Ivan Ilych" and Other Stories*. New York: NAL, 1960.

Torgovnick, Marianna. *Gone Primitive: Savage Intellects, Modern Lives*. Chicago: U of Chicago P, 1990.

Tredell, Nicolas, ed. *Joseph Conrad: "Heart of Darkness."* Columbia Critical Guides. New York: Columbia UP, 1998.

Trilling, Lionel. *Beyond Culture*. London: Secker, 1966.

———. *Sincerity and Authenticity*. London: Oxford UP, 1972.

Tutein, David. *Joseph Conrad's Reading*. West Cornwall: Locust Hill, 1990.

United States. Defense Mapping Agency. *Laem Chabang to Mae Nam Chao Phraya: Including Ko Si Chang (Chart No. 93241)*. Washington: DMA, 1996.

Veeser, H. Aram. Introduction. Veeser, *Historicism* x–xvi.

———, ed. *The New Historicism*. New York: Routledge, 1989.

Vergil. *The Aeneid*. Trans. Rolfe Humphries. New York: Scribner, 1951.

Vishwanathan, Gauri. *Masks of Conquest: Literary Study and British Rule in India*. New York: Columbia UP, 1989.

Voltaire. Candide *and Other Tales*. Trans. Tobias Smollett. Rev. J. C. Thornton. London: Campbell, 1937.

Watt, Ian. *Conrad in the Nineteenth Century*. Berkeley: U of California P, 1979.

———. *Essays on Conrad*. Cambridge: Cambridge UP, 2000.

Watts, Cedric. "'A Bloody Racist': About Achebe's View of Conrad." *Yearbook of English Studies* 13 (1983): 196–209.

———. *Conrad's "Heart of Darkness": A Critical and Contextual Discussion*. Milano: Mursia Intl., 1997.

———. "Heart of Darkness." Stape 45–62.

———. *Joseph Conrad: A Literary Life*. New York: St. Martin's, 1989.

———, ed. *Joseph Conrad's Letters to Cunninghame Graham*. Cambridge: Cambridge UP, 1969.

———. "The Mirror Tale: An Ethico-structural Analysis of Conrad's 'The Secret Sharer.'" *Critical Quarterly* 19 (1977): 25–37.

Welles, Orson. "Introductory Sequence to the Unproduced *Heart of Darkness* with a Commentary by Jonathan Rosenbaum." *Film Comment* 8.4 (1972): 24–26.

———, dir. *The Lady from Shanghai*. Columbia, 1948.

———, dir. *Touch of Evil*. Perf: Welles, Charlton Heston. Universal, 1958.

Wexler, Joyce. "Conrad's Dream of a Common Language: Lacan and 'The Secret Sharer.'" *Psychoanalytic Review* 78 (1991): 599–606.

——. *Who Paid for Modernism?* Fayetteville: U of Arkansas P, 1997.

White, Andrea. "Conrad and Imperialism." Stape 179–202.

——. *Joseph Conrad and the Adventure Tradition.* Cambridge: Cambridge UP, 1993.

White, James F. "The Third Theme in 'The Secret Sharer.'" *Conradiana* 21.1 (1989): 37–46.

Wiley, Paul. *Conrad's Measure of Man.* Madison: U of Wisconsin P, 1954.

Wilkie, Brian. *Literature of the Western World.* New York: Macmillan, 1992.

Williams, George Washington. "An Open Letter to His Serene Majesty Leopold II, King of the Belgians and Sovereign of the Independent State of Congo." Conrad, *Heart* [Kimbrough] 103–13.

——. "A Report upon the Congo-State and Country to the President of the Republic of the United States of America." Conrad, *Heart* [Kimbrough] 84–97.

Williams, Jeffrey. "Narrative Calling: *Heart of Darkness* and *Lord Jim.*" *Theory and the Novel: Narrative Reflexivity in the British Tradition.* Cambridge: Cambridge UP, 1998. 146–83.

Williams, Raymond. *The English Novel from Dickens to Lawrence.* New York: Oxford UP, 1970.

——. *Marxism and Literature.* Oxford: Oxford UP, 1977.

Wilson, Robert. *Conrad's Mythology.* Troy: Whitston, 1987.

——. *Joseph Conrad: Sources and Traditions.* Rogers: Weir, 1995.

Wise, Thomas J. *A Bibliography of the Writings of Joseph Conrad.* London: Clay, 1921.

——. *A Conrad Library.* London: n.p., 1928.

Wollaeger, Mark. *Joseph Conrad and the Fictions of Skepticism.* Stanford: Stanford UP, 1990.

Woolf, Virginia. "Modern Fiction." *The Common Reader.* San Diego: Harcourt, 1925. 150–58.

——. "Mr. Bennett and Mrs. Brown." *"The Captain's Death Bed" and Other Essays.* San Diego: Harcourt, 1950. 94–119.

——. *Mrs. Dalloway.* San Diego: Harcourt, 1925.

——. *A Room of One's Own.* San Diego: Harcourt, 1929.

——. *Three Guineas.* San Diego: Harcourt, 1938.

——. *The Voyage Out.* 1915. San Diego: Harcourt, 1948.

Wyatt, Robert D. "Joseph Conrad's 'The Secret Sharer.'" *Conradiana* 5.1 (1973): 12–26.

Zins, Henryk. *Joseph Conrad and Africa.* Nairobi: Kenya Lit. Bureau, 1982.

INDEX

Modern Language Association of America

Approaches to Teaching World Literature

Joseph Gibaldi, series editor

Achebe's Things Fall Apart. Ed. Bernth Lindfors. 1991.

Arthurian Tradition. Ed. Maureen Fries and Jeanie Watson. 1992.

Atwood's The Handmaid's Tale *and Other Works*. Ed. Sharon R. Wilson, Thomas B. Friedman, and Shannon Hengen. 1996.

Austen's Pride and Prejudice. Ed. Marcia McClintock Folsom. 1993.

Balzac's Old Goriot. Ed. Michal Peled Ginsburg. 2000.

Baudelaire's Flowers of Evil. Ed. Laurence M. Porter. 2000.

Beckett's Waiting for Godot. Ed. June Schlueter and Enoch Brater. 1991.

Beowulf. Ed. Jess B. Bessinger, Jr., and Robert F. Yeager. 1984.

Blake's Songs of Innocence and of Experience. Ed. Robert F. Gleckner and Mark L. Greenberg. 1989.

Boccaccio's Decameron. Ed. James H. McGregor. 2000.

British Women Poets of the Romantic Period. Ed. Stephen C. Behrendt and Harriet Kramer Linkin. 1997.

Brontë's Jane Eyre. Ed. Diane Long Hoeveler and Beth Lau. 1993.

Byron's Poetry. Ed. Frederick W. Shilstone. 1991.

Camus's The Plague. Ed. Steven G. Kellman. 1985.

Cather's My Ántonia. Ed. Susan J. Rosowski. 1989.

Cervantes' Don Quixote. Ed. Richard Bjornson. 1984.

Chaucer's Canterbury Tales. Ed. Joseph Gibaldi. 1980.

Chopin's The Awakening. Ed. Bernard Koloski. 1988.

Coleridge's Poetry and Prose. Ed. Richard E. Matlak. 1991.

Conrad's "Heart of Darkness" and "The Secret Sharer." Ed. Hunt Hawkins and Brian W. Shaffer. 2002.

Dante's Divine Comedy. Ed. Carole Slade. 1982.

Dickens' David Copperfield. Ed. Richard J. Dunn. 1984.

Dickinson's Poetry. Ed. Robin Riley Fast and Christine Mack Gordon. 1989.

Narrative of the Life of Frederick Douglass. Ed. James C. Hall. 1999.

Eliot's Middlemarch. Ed. Kathleen Blake. 1990.

Eliot's Poetry and Plays. Ed. Jewel Spears Brooker. 1988.

Shorter Elizabethan Poetry. Ed. Patrick Cheney and Anne Lake Prescott. 2000.

Ellison's Invisible Man. Ed. Susan Resneck Parr and Pancho Savery. 1989.

Dramas of Euripides. Ed. Robin Mitchell-Boyask. 2002.

Faulkner's The Sound and the Fury. Ed. Stephen Hahn and Arthur F. Kinney. 1996.

Flaubert's Madame Bovary. Ed. Laurence M. Porter and Eugene F. Gray. 1995.

García Márquez's One Hundred Years of Solitude. Ed. María Elena de Valdés and Mario J. Valdés. 1990.

Goethe's Faust. Ed. Douglas J. McMillan. 1987.

Hebrew Bible as Literature in Translation. Ed. Barry N. Olshen and Yael S. Feldman. 1989.

Homer's Iliad *and* Odyssey. Ed. Kostas Myrsiades. 1987.

Ibsen's A Doll House. Ed. Yvonne Shafer. 1985.

Works of Samuel Johnson. Ed. David R. Anderson and Gwin J. Kolb. 1993.

Joyce's Ulysses. Ed. Kathleen McCormick and Erwin R. Steinberg. 1993.

Kafka's Short Fiction. Ed. Richard T. Gray. 1995.

Keats's Poetry. Ed. Walter H. Evert and Jack W. Rhodes. 1991.

Kingston's The Woman Warrior. Ed. Shirley Geok-lin Lim. 1991.

Lafayette's The Princess of Clèves. Ed. Faith E. Beasley and Katharine Ann
     Jensen. 1998.

Works of D. H. Lawrence. Ed. M. Elizabeth Sargent and Garry Watson. 2001.

Lessing's The Golden Notebook. Ed. Carey Kaplan and Ellen Cronan Rose. 1989.

Mann's Death in Venice *and Other Short Fiction.* Ed. Jeffrey B. Berlin. 1992.

Medieval English Drama. Ed. Richard K. Emmerson. 1990.

Melville's Moby-Dick. Ed. Martin Bickman. 1985.

Metaphysical Poets. Ed. Sidney Gottlieb. 1990.

Miller's Death of a Salesman. Ed. Matthew C. Roudané. 1995.

Milton's Paradise Lost. Ed. Galbraith M. Crump. 1986.

Molière's Tartuffe *and Other Plays.* Ed. James F. Gaines and
     Michael S. Koppisch. 1995.

Momaday's The Way to Rainy Mountain. Ed. Kenneth M. Roemer. 1988.

Montaigne's Essays. Ed. Patrick Henry. 1994.

Novels of Toni Morrison. Ed. Nellie Y. McKay and Kathryn Earle. 1997.

Murasaki Shikibu's The Tale of Genji. Ed. Edward Kamens. 1993.

Pope's Poetry. Ed. Wallace Jackson and R. Paul Yoder. 1993.

Shakespeare's Hamlet. Ed. Bernice W. Kliman. 2001.

Shakespeare's King Lear. Ed. Robert H. Ray. 1986.

Shakespeare's Romeo and Juliet. Ed. Maurice Hunt. 2000.

Shakespeare's The Tempest *and Other Late Romances.* Ed. Maurice Hunt. 1992.

Shelley's Frankenstein. Ed. Stephen C. Behrendt. 1990.

Shelley's Poetry. Ed. Spencer Hall. 1990.

Sir Gawain and the Green Knight. Ed. Miriam Youngerman Miller and
     Jane Chance. 1986.

Spenser's Faerie Queene. Ed. David Lee Miller and Alexander Dunlop. 1994.

Stendhal's The Red and the Black. Ed. Dean de la Motte and Stirling Haig. 1999.

Sterne's Tristram Shandy. Ed. Melvyn New. 1989.

Stowe's Uncle Tom's Cabin. Ed. Elizabeth Ammons and Susan Belasco. 2000.

Swift's Gulliver's Travels. Ed. Edward J. Rielly. 1988.

Thoreau's Walden *and Other Works.* Ed. Richard J. Schneider. 1996.

Vergil's Aeneid. Ed. William S. Anderson and Lorina N. Quartarone. 2002.

Voltaire's Candide. Ed. Renée Waldinger. 1987.

Whitman's Leaves of Grass. Ed. Donald D. Kummings. 1990.

Woolf's To the Lighthouse. Ed. Beth Rigel Daugherty and Mary Beth Pringle. 2001.

Wordsworth's Poetry. Ed. Spencer Hall, with Jonathan Ramsey. 1986.

Wright's Native Son. Ed. James A. Miller. 1997.